5,10 -847 10-66 (Suewingen)

TRIBES
of the
SAHARA

Ahaggar Tuareg Camel Corps soldier

TRIBES
of the
SAHARA

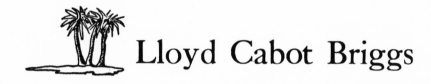 Lloyd Cabot Briggs

HARVARD UNIVERSITY PRESS ~ CAMBRIDGE

1 9 6 0

Distributed in Great Britain by Oxford University Press, London

Publication of this book has been aided by
a grant from the Ford Foundation

Library of Congress Catalog Card Number 60–7988

Printed in the United States of America

TO

CARLTON S. COON

PREFACE

There has been more pure balderdash written and repeated about the tribes of the Sahara than about almost any other peoples in the world. Only three years ago, for instance, I heard a well-known lecturer declare to an unsuspecting audience of honest New England farmers that the warlike nomadic Tuareg are probably descended from a little band of crusaders, who got cut off, centuries ago, in the rock-walled valley of Petra (now in the Kingdom of Jordan), whence they finally escaped and found their way—heavens knows how—across Egypt and Libya to the very heart of the Sahara. And then he added that Tuareg men are about seven feet tall—although he was speaking in a church—whereas the tallest one whose measurements have been recorded stood not quite six feet six inches in his sandal-feet and his fellow countrymen average only about five feet eight, shorter indeed than the average American.

But, because the desert wastes of the Sahara have always been off the beaten track of tourist trade, and because travel there has always been not only expensive and difficult but dangerous as well, it is relatively safe for professional purveyors of mysterious romance to introduce into the Saharan scene pleasing rainbows of illusion at the ends of which they are sure to find pots filled enthusiastically by dazzled audiences with gold. For who among those audiences would ever stumble on the truth? And who would want to? A fairy-tale is such a delightfully cheap and satisfying form of entertainment. The sober truth about the Sahara, however, is more mysterious than anything that has ever been written about it, even by the most irresponsible spinner of fairytales; for the fact is that very little is yet known about the peoples who live there.

The following study is the result of twelve years of field and library work, including a number of trips into the western Sahara as far south as the "Tomb of Tin Hinan" near Abalessa. The library work was easy enough, though laborious, since many of the basic publications are now extremely rare and correspondingly difficult to find, but work in the field was quite another matter. In this connection I must first acknowledge my great debt to Mr. Maurice Reygasse, formerly Director of the Bardo Museum of Algiers and District Commissioner of Tebessa, who gave me the benefit of his inexhaustible fund of miscellaneous information gathered in the course of extensive travels in the Sahara in years gone by. In many long and pleasant evenings together he drew for me pictures of the desert and its inhabitants so clear and vivid that I was reasonably familiar with many parts of the area before ever I set foot in them. I have enjoyed also the invaluable official support and personal encouragement of Mr. Maurice Casset and General Paul Passager, respectively Inspector General and former Chief of the Public Health Service of the Southern Territories of Algeria. Through them every available facility was placed at my disposal, often before I even had time to ask for it.

Benevolent expert consultants have performed for me other onerous and delicate tasks of a kind that all too often go without appropriate recognition. Professors Carleton S. Coon of the University of Pennsylvania and William W. Howells, Douglas L. Oliver, Hallam L. Movius, Jr. of Harvard University and Theodore Monod of Dakar, Mr. E. W. Bovill, formerly of northern Nigeria, and Dr. Raymond Cabannes, who grew up in the Sahara, reviewed those sections dealing with their various specialties. Each of these kind friends and distinguished colleagues has had a hand in making this a better book than it could ever have been without their helpful comments.

So many local military and civilian officials and private individuals, as well as professional colleagues, have helped me at various times and places and in so many ways, that it is a practical impossibility for me to list them all, while to try to single out some for special mention would only put me in the position of seeming to discriminate where no discrimination is intended. And so I will simply take this opportunity to thank them most warmly, one and all.

Lastly I want to express my sincere gratitude to those modest and devoted toilers in the shadows, Miss Margaret Currier, Miss Yvonne Oddon, and Mr. Marcel Koelbert, Librarians respectively of the Peabody Museum, the Musée de l'Homme of Paris, and the University of Algiers; they all found basic source material for me that I would have been hard put to it to lay my hands on otherwise.

L. Cabot Briggs

CONTENTS

ILLUSTRATIONS

Frontispiece Ahaggar Tuareg Camel Corps soldier
(photograph by A. J. Weber)

Illustrations in text

INTRODUCTION

The GEOGRAPHICAL AREA covered in this book is the desert which lies between the western frontier of Egypt and the Atlantic Ocean, and between the northern and southern limits shown in Map 2. Its eastern half is bounded on the north by the more or less hilly and broken coastal strip where classical and modern European cultures have found lodgment, while its western half extends northward only to the fringe of steppe and piedmont country that forms the southern rim of the Atlas mountain complex. Most modern geographers take as the boundary on the south the line which marks the northernmost extension of a prickly weed commonly known as *cram-cram* or *initi,* and the southern limit of *had,* a scrubby thorn bush. The Sahara as thus defined is still by far the biggest desert in the world, stretching some 2,500 miles from east to west along the Tropic of Cancer and varying in breadth between 800 and 1,200 miles from north to south. It has an area of roughly 3,000,000 square miles or a little more, and a native population of probably not quite 2,500,000. It is over twice as big as all of Europe west of the Russian border, including Great Britain and Denmark, an area that has a population of over 385,000,000 altogether. The continental United States is a little smaller than the Sahara but already had a population that numbered 175,000,000 when these words were written and was increasing at the rate of over 2,500,000 a year.

Unfortunately the literature on the tribes of the Sahara is a sorry mess at best. First there is a great body of hearsay information, mixed with mythology, gossip, and wild speculation, and retailed by the geographers and historians of the classical and neoclassical schools from the days of Herodotus down to the eighteenth century. During the Middle Ages Arab historians, geographers, and travelers gave a good deal of attention to the area, but much of the material they collected was hearsay too, and most of it was confined to peoples who were or were thought to be either early emigrant offshoots of ancient peoples of the Near East or remnants of the great invading Arab hordes of Islam. What little the early Moslem authors have to say about peoples who were really strange to them is so incomplete, conflicting, and sometimes simply incredible, that one can learn very little of much use from it, however interesting and often fascinating it may be. In addition Arabs are inclined to look on history as a record of families and tribes, moving freely through time and space alike, whereas we are accustomed to think of it as a record of nations, with their rulers and dynasties or political systems succeeding each other in time but always within a fixed frame of geographical reference. The Arab approach to history is a normal functional byproduct of the basically nomadic tribal culture in which it was developed, while ours, inherited from the urban Greeks and Romans, is a culture trait of ancient city states and, in broad terms, of the basically urban cultures of Europe and America that have grown out of them. The difference between these two underlying concepts is much more profound and far reaching than any mere statement of fact can express, so much so indeed that those brought up under the academic influence of either one automatically find at first that the other yields only very fragmentary and incoherent pictures.

With the dawn of the nineteenth century one begins to find disjointed general impressions, and sometimes remarkably precise detailed observations, scattered through the travel narratives of such famous pioneer explorers as Captain George Francis Lyon of the Royal Navy and Dr. Heinrich Barth; but concise descriptions of communities and tribes as such are still very few and fragmentary. The modern studies published during the last seventy years or so are more coherent, but even they are usually either so generalized as to be woefully superficial, or limited to the population of a relatively small area. No general description of the peoples of the Sahara as a whole, their history, environment, and ways of life, has ever been published in English, or in any other language for that matter. Therefore the main purpose of this book is to make readily available an over-all summary of what is known about the subject. Readers who would like to go into the matter in more technical detail as regards the physical anthropology and pathology of the area will do well to consult my recent monograph, *The Living Races of the Sahara Desert.*

In preparing both my monograph and the present book, I threshed and winnowed all the Saharan literature that I could get my hands on, with special emphasis on firsthand observations made by research workers in the field. Also I myself spent as much time as I could among the desert tribes, so as to gather more direct and more detailed impressions of their ways of life. Although twelve years have been devoted to these tasks, it has not been possible for me to visit more than about a quarter of the entire area, and so I have confined my field research to a few carefully chosen communities which I consider representative of the largest and most important elements of the Saharan population as a whole. The results of this field work are incorporated in my descriptions of the sedentary agriculturalists, artisans, and merchants belonging to various racial, religious, and linguistic stocks, of the Chaamba who are pastoral Arab nomads, and of the Ahaggar Tuareg, who are pastoral nomadic Berbers. My descriptions of other Saharan peoples are based partly on data gathered from the literature, and partly on information supplied by friends of mine who are personally familiar with the communities in question.

The spelling of names of tribes and places in the Sahara presents special problems. Although Saharan Arabic and Berber dialects are easier for English speakers to pronounce than they are for the speakers of most other western European languages, many of their sounds and intonations still seem very strange even to American and English ears. Because of this, and because Arabic has its own written alphabet, which is very different from our own, while Berber (except for the Tuareg dialects) has none at all, precise transliteration is a practical impossibility unless one falls back on some such system as the International Phonetic Alphabet. But such a frightening collection of esoteric symbols would be no more familiar to the average reader and no more easily understood by him than would the Arabic alphabet itself, and it is even more difficult to learn. Most readers will not be interested primarily in precise pronunciation anyway; what they will want most is to be able to locate points on maps with the least possible difficulty. The modern maps and scientific literature of the Sahara are mostly in French, and so I have put place names as a rule in the forms usually employed by modern French cartographers. The names of tribes and other ethnic groups have likewise been presented, as a rule, in their most usual French forms. Unfortunately these are not yet fully standardized by any means; one still finds such extreme variants as *Mouydir = Immidir = Emidir;* and so explanatory notes will be inserted whenever it seems strictly necessary.

TRIBES
of the
SAHARA

Chapter 1

LANDSCAPE AND
NATURAL RESOURCES

THE SAHARA is by no means the unending sea of sand that popular fiction and motion pictures and television have so often led us to suppose; on the contrary it is a vast area of infinitely varied landscapes.[1] Immense gravelly plains and rock-ribbed plateaus cover much of the desert's surface. Dotted here and there are closed depressions of all shapes and sizes which occur singly or in scattered groups or chains. In some regions the relief is very broken but with no more than minor variations in altitude. The valleys of the Mzab and the Metlili, for example, cut through the surface of a plain but only deeply enough so that the tips of the minarets of valley towns do not quite reach up to the main ground level, while the plain itself is not only dissected by these and innumerable other steep walled valleys, disposed in intricate drainage patterns that the Arabs call by analogy a net or *shebka* (French = *chebka*), but is also studded with low buttes of exactly equal height whose perfectly flat tops are all that remains of a still older plain. Here is an excellent example of a landscape illustrating the passage of a series of major erosion cycles and the various transitional phases connecting them, all neatly laid out as though modeled after a diagram in a geology textbook. And there are also regions of extreme relief, notably the volcanic massifs of the Tibesti and the Ahaggar (usually spelt Hoggar) but including also some enormous cliff formations. These cliffs

---

[1] Much of this chapter is based on the latest standard French text, by Capot-Rey, which deals mainly with the geography of the western half of the Sahara. In English, see Meigs' and Bruce Carpenter's excellent though very brief monographs.

may be low and very long like the Hank, in the extreme west, which runs in a nearly straight line for over 300 miles but rarely rises to a height of more than 160 feet, or relatively short but tremendously high like the cliffs which tower over 2,500 feet above Djanet. In the Ahaggar, the modern administrative center, Tamanrasset, lies at an altitude of roughly 4,600 feet, about average for that region (if the term "average" can be used appropriately in describing so uneven an area), while the culminating peak, the Tahat, reaches nearly 9,600 feet above sea level. The volcanic peak of the Emi Koussi, the culminating point of the Tibesti massif, reaches an altitude of about 11,200 feet, the highest in the entire desert and almost exactly the same height as Mount Hood in the Cascade Range of Oregon.

And lastly there are the great sandy wastes or *ergs,* which, however, cover not much more than a fifth of the entire area. Probably about two thirds of their surface consists of rolling sandy plains dotted with occasional minor groups of dunes, while only the remaining third, barely one fifteenth of the whole Sahara, is characterized by the spectacular major dune formations of popular imagination.

Air temperature in the shade is extremely variable, with winter and summer means in the neighborhood of roughly 52° and 98° (Fahrenheit) respectively, while extremes run from about 20° to over 130° in the shade. But the thermometer often falls twenty-five to thirty-five and sometimes over fifty degrees at sunset, such variations being relatively great in the plains and rather less at higher altitudes. Surprisingly enough, the temperature of sand only a foot or so below the surface remains practically constant day and night, at a point slightly lower than the daily average air temperature.

Relative humidity is sometimes higher in the northern desert than at Paris, but in midsummer it often falls as low as 20 per cent and has been known to drop to as little as 2.3 per cent in the Ahaggar. At Ghat, in the central Sahara, the monthly mean ranges roughly from a low of 20 per cent in August to a high of 54 per cent in January, about the same as Phoenix, Arizona, but a little more variable. The total annual evaporation rate varies roughly from 60 to 140 inches, averaging three to four times the annual rates observed along the Mediterranean coast. As one result, not even the most hardened natives of the desert can go safely in summer for more than twenty-four hours without water.

Mean annual rainfall figures for the Sahara are all but meaningless, for several reasons. In the first place the variations from year to year are enormous and there are often long periods of complete or practically complete drought. The desert as a whole (as I have defined it) gets a little less than 2 inches annual rainfall, although parts of the Fezzan get as much as 4 to 6 inches a year. The average annual rainfall at Phoenix in Arizona, the driest state in the United States, is a little over 7 inches. Yearly totals are deceptive also because they include completely ineffectual rainfalls of as little as a single millimeter or even less. In general it can be said that rain which does not penetrate sand or dry soil to a depth of a foot or more is usually carried off by evaporation before it has a chance to affect plant growth to any appreciable extent. At In Salah no effective rain fell between August 1929 and December 1933, while at Tamanrasset there was none from June 1933 to August 1939.

This irregularity of rainfall goes far to explain the startlingly small amount of cultivated land that one finds in the Sahara. Recent surveys have revealed the following ratios of cultivated to uncultivated land: 1 to 270 in the Annex of El Oued, less than 1 to 3,500 in that of El Goléa and less than 1 to 75,000 in the Ahaggar, where a ratio of 1 to 40,000 has been estimated as the best that could be achieved under the most favorable conditions possible. These figures reflect the fact that prolonged droughts in the Sahara increase in duration as one moves from north to south, which makes life exceptionally difficult in the mountain massifs of the Tibesti and the Ahaggar even though their total rainfall over long periods may equal or indeed surpass that in the plains and plateau country farther north.

The most common rate of rainfall (when it does rain) is half an inch or less in twenty-four hours, but truly torrential rains do occur every now and then. At Tamanrasset 1.73 inches fell in three hours in 1950, and 1.42 inches of this came down in only forty minutes. When a downpour of such proportions falls in the desert, powder dry gulleys spring to thundering life as bores of water sometimes several feet high rush down them sweeping away everything in their path. This is one reason why the Tuareg very rarely camp in or even close to the dry bed of a stream. Torrential rains also cause adobe houses to collapse occasionally, sometimes killing the occupants. At Ain Sefra (in the northwestern corner of the desert), for example, twenty-five persons were killed in this way in October 1904, while another twenty-two were buried at Tamanrasset in January 1922, and eight of them were killed outright. Tents too collapse sometimes on top of the people in them, but the results are almost never fatal.

Sandstorms, essentially phenomena of winter and early spring, are more frequent in the Sahara than is rain, and they have only bad and sometimes disastrous effects on crops, domestic animals, and even human life. Often they develop in the following way. A low pressure area over the Atlantic moves toward the African coast and the prevailing winter wind from the northeast swings around to the southeast and then to the south, bringing a slight rise in both temperature and humidity. "Suddenly the wind shifts to the southwest, growing in force from minute to minute; the sun is covered over and a distant wall of sand blots out the horizon. The wind begins to assume the proportions of a gale and streaming wisps of sand like trembling nets race over the ground. This is the moment for action, when shelter must be found as quickly as possible or when, if you must go on, you soon find yourself proceeding blindly and trying only to stay within sight of your

---

Map 1. In the text *Sudan* designates the whole strip of territory that separates the Sahara proper from the tropical rain forest, and extends from the valley of the upper Nile to the Atlantic Ocean; but on this map it indicates only the country formerly known as the Anglo-Egyptian Sudan. The word *Barbary* is used in the text (as well as on Map 2) as an inclusive term covering all but the southern fringes of Morocco, Algeria, and Tunisia. The reader who intends to go beyond the limits of this book and consult other sources should bear in mind that duplication and reduplication of local and regional place names is very characteristic of the Sahara, especially in the west. Names like *Adrar*, *Tadjemout*, and *Taourirt* are found again and again applied to places which may be more than a thousand miles apart or, worse still, fairly close together, and so one must often exercise considerable ingenuity in order to be sure just which place is referred to.

4

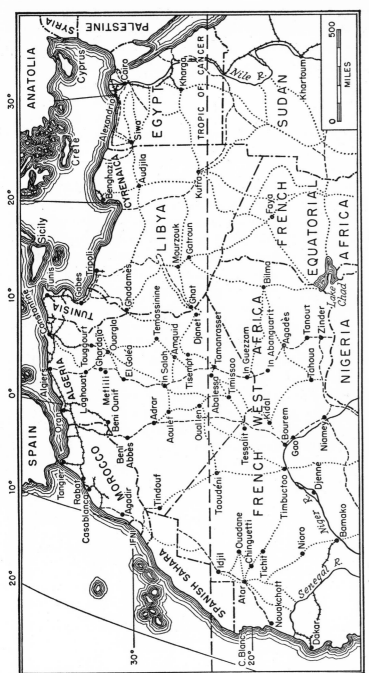

MAP 1 NORTH AFRICA AND THE SAHARA DESERT

POLITICAL BOUNDARIES ——————   AUTOMOBILE ROUTES ——————
RAILROADS ——————   CARAVAN TRAILS ·············

(BASED ON MEIGS, '54)

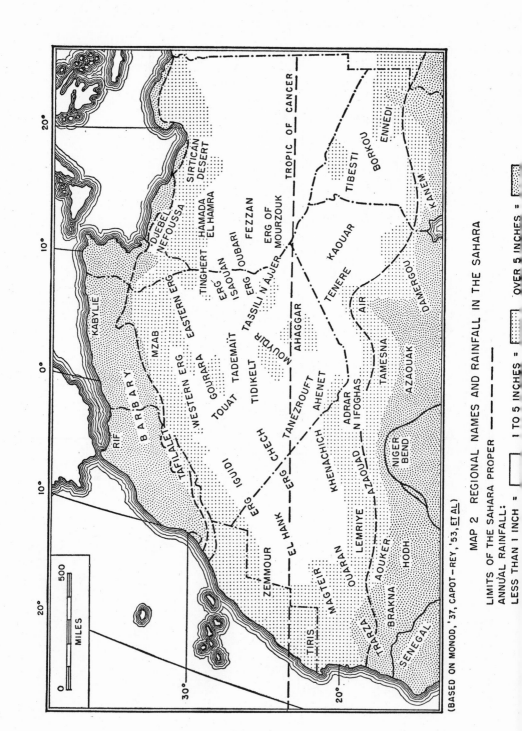

MAP 2 REGIONAL NAMES AND RAINFALL IN THE SAHARA

LIMITS OF THE SAHARA PROPER — — —

ANNUAL RAINFALL:

LESS THAN 1 INCH =   1 TO 5 INCHES =   OVER 5 INCHES =

(BASED ON MONOD, '37, CAPOT—REY, '53, ET AL)

nearest companion." [2] In the first such storm that I experienced, near El Goléa, the air was so full of sand that from the driver's seat of my desert car I couldn't even see the front end of the vehicle. Usually the storm dies down at sunset, but it often begins again next morning and may continue in this way for several days.

Although stories of whole caravans swallowed up and buried by sandstorms doubtless belong to the realm of fable, it is a fact that one such storm did destroy fifteen hundred goats and two thousand sheep near El Goléa in 1947. Occasionally one sees automobiles come up from the desert with body metal shining, all paint gone, and windshields broken out because they had been so ground by flying sand that the drivers could no longer see through them. Recently a workman at an oil drilling site in the northern central Sahara tried to return through a sandstorm to the camp which was only some three hundred yards off: a few hours later his dead body was found five miles away.

In the Sahara, as in deserts generally, cultivation of the soil depends on irrigation, and irrigation there depends mainly on available ground water. Much of this probably arrives by subterranean percolation from the highlands to the north, while most of the rest is derived from the occasional rains which are heavy enough to soak deep into the ground. In the Atlas foothills on the northwestern edge of the desert rainfall usually exceeds 8 inches a year, and it is thought that much of this water eventually seeps downhill into the permeable strata underlying the Sahara. It has even been estimated, rather fancifully perhaps, that a drop of rain falling in the northern piedmont takes over a thousand years to filter southward and so reach the surface in a desert well. There has been much talk too of the possible presence of vast underground reserves of "fossil water," water that accumulated far below the surface during relatively wet periods ages ago and has remained there ever since. Subterranean fossil water does exist undoubtedly here and there in the Sahara, but the reserves are of unknown extent, and, in any case, they are probably all far too deep down to be reached by means of even the best native well digging techniques.

[2] Capot-Rey, 1953, p. 57.

The amount of land that can be cultivated in any given place obviously depends primarily on the quantity of water constantly available within reasonably easy reach, but if repeated overdrafts are made on this supply the water level is lowered appreciably and the rate of flow is reduced, not only by absolute shrinkage of the reserve but also by the additional time required to bring water up to the surface from an increased depth. In well-irrigated palm groves the trees are usually planted about fifty to an acre, and are watered at rates which vary all the way from about 450,000 to as much as 1,800,000 gallons an acre per year, in addition to the rainfall when there is any. When apricots or oranges or other fruits are grown, the trees are planted in between the palms and so get watered at the same time, usually about once every ten days more or less. Winter cereals are watered twice a month while vegetables need water nearly every day, at least in summertime. Gardens, of vegetables or grain, are usually divided by low ridges of earth into roughly square plots, measuring twenty to forty-five feet across, each of which gets anywhere from twelve to twenty gallons at a watering. Thus to water a single acre of garden properly takes about twenty-seven thousand gallons, which require over sixty man-hours to draw from wells.

Although in a few particularly favored spots, such as El Goléa for example, there is enough "head" to produce natural springs and make hand-dug artesian wells possible, water can usually be got only from ordinary wells or from *foggaras* (see Figure 1). The wells vary greatly in depth, from about 20 to 220 feet or more, and are just big enough in diameter as a rule for a well digger to stand inside and swing a short-handled pick. Wells that seem in danger of running dry are sometimes refreshed by digging horizontal galleries outward from the bottom, like the spokes of a wheel. Well water is drawn up to the surface either with rope and pulley or with a sweep and bucket of some sort. The pulley type of well has a pair of uprights, set in the well curbing if there is one, with a pulley mounted on an axle that runs through their upper ends. A rope is passed over the pulley and attached to a folding leather funnel, of about six to seven gallons capacity, by an ingenious system of cords arranged in such a way that when the folded funnel spout is drawn just above ground level it is released automatically and the contents of the funnel pour out into a catch basin or runoff channel. The other end of the rope is attached to an animal, usually a donkey or an old camel (or even both together), that walks back and forth along a narrow ramp which slopes away from the well. The length of the animal's walk is obviously equal to the depth from which water is being drawn, while the full length of the ramp is equal to the full depth of the well, and so a passing traveler can tell at a glance how close a community is to serious drought conditions, provided they use wells of this kind. In the sweep type of well the sweep itself is mounted between two uprights, and is sometimes rigged so that it can be slid back and forth to compensate for changes in water level. A bucket of leather or tightly woven basketry is hung on a rope at the well end of the sweep while a counterweight is tied to the other end: or a small child may ride on the butt end, thus combining business with pleasure. The drawer of water pulls down on the sweep rope until the bucket is submerged and full, and then lets go, allowing the counterweight to raise the load.

Travelers in the open desert have a much more serious water problem, for they must depend on what water they can find beside the trail once the reserve they started out with has been exhausted. There are wells scattered here and there along all the main caravan routes, but it may sometimes be several days' march between them and their water all too often has a high mineral content which makes it very unpleasant to the taste and produces violent intestinal activity. Most desert wells have neither pulley nor sweep, and only now and then a curbing of palm logs across which to draw a rope; and the user must bring his own rope and bucket. Such wells also cave in from time to time, or get choked or even completely obliterated by sandstorms. In the old days nomads used to conceal some of the more important desert wells within their tribal territories by covering the openings with goatskins stretched on wooden frames and spreading sand on top, a system which not only made it more difficult for raiders to ap-

9

proach, but also obliged commercial caravans to employ local guides. Although this practice had the incidental advantage of preventing the hidden wells from getting choked with sand, it added greatly to the dangers of desert travel, and so it was forbidden by the French and has been almost if not entirely eliminated in the western half of the Sahara. When no known well is within reach, the traveler digs for water in a likely looking spot and hopes for the best. On the northern and southern fringes of the desert, and very rarely in between, one finds occasional waterholes of the kind seen in films of big game hunting, but these are usually small and often exceedingly filthy. In the rocky gulleys of the central mountains there are a few permanent or semipermanent springs and pools of delightfully clear, cool water, but they too are often dangerously polluted.

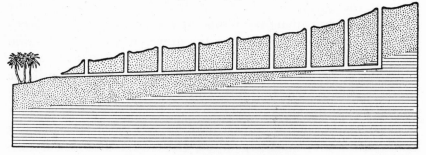

FIG. 1. Cross section of a Foggara.

Earth removed in digging the vertical shafts and the main channel is drawn up through the shafts and dumped around their openings. Horizontal lines in this diagram represent a water-bearing formation, while the dotted portion represents dry earth or sand. The vertical exaggeration is about thirty-six to one.

A foggara is an ingenious device for drawing water off the top of a sloping water table. Water-soaked porous stone, or sand or soil, underlies the earth's surface almost everywhere, although at very different depths in different places, and water tables, that is the uppermost water-bearing layers, tend to follow a contour roughly parallel to the surface of the ground above them. If you bore a hole into a formation of this kind, water will seep into it from all around and you will have a well. The foggara makes use of this principle but with the difference that the accumulated water, instead of being hoisted out through the top of the well shaft, is drawn off from the bottom, as shown in Figure 1. In making a foggara, the first thing to do is to find a point where the water table is at a higher level than the garden to be irrigated. Here a well is driven down into the water-bearing formation and a line of vertical shafts, anywhere from twenty to fifty feet apart, are then dug between the well and the area to be watered. Finally the bottoms of the initial well and the dry shafts are all connected by a gently sloping tunnel, which leads the water off toward the garden while at the same time protecting it to some extent from evaporation along the way. The gradient of the tunnel is rarely more than 1 in 1,000, and sometimes less, while the tunnel itself may be as much as eight miles long or even more. Gravity does the work and so the users of a foggara are spared much physical exertion, but the output is inevitably small. Also the number of those who share the production is always so considerable that there is never enough to allow them all to irrigate whenever they feel like it, and so the water is stored in catch basins from which it is distributed to the various consumers in turn.

Foggara systems are most highly developed in the western central Sahara. The Touat has about nine hundred and fifty miles of such galleries, while even a single small oasis may have over twenty miles. The administrative district of Aoulef, in the western Tidikelt, is served by forty foggaras which together produce a little over seven thousand gallons a minute, or an average of almost a hundred and eighty gallons a minute each. This may seem a tremendous lot of water, and it is, but it has to meet the needs of more than eight thousand human beings scattered over an area of approximately twelve thousand square miles. By the time these people have watered their hundred and seventy-five thousand palm trees, their little fields of grain and their vegetable gardens, there is none too much water left to drink and cook with. It is thought by some that Jews or Judaized Berber refugees from Cyrenaica may have introduced the foggara into the western Sahara nearly two thousand years ago, but in recent times construction and maintenance have been largely in the hands of Negro slave specialists. Since slavery was abolished with the coming of modern European rulers, new foggaras are seldom dug while many old ones have collapsed and been abandoned. They are to be found all the way from southern Morocco southeastward through the Ahaggar and eastward across the Fezzan, but those in the south are only crude miniatures of the elaborate systems of the Touat.[3]

The foggara was known in Persia in the days of Darius, nearly twenty-five hundred years ago, if not before, and it survives to this day, under the name of *quena* or *quanat,* in Oman, Persia, Afghanistan, and even among the Pathans whom Kipling immortalized, the great guerrilla fighters of the Khyber Pass in the old Northwest Frontier Province of India (now Pakistan). The Achaemenian Persian Empire of Cyrus and Darius included Cyrenaica, and the system of government included a corps of special fiscal inspectors ("the Eyes and Ears of the King") who traveled constantly with military escort throughout the provinces. This makes one wonder if the foggara may not have been introduced into the eastern Sahara by the Persians.

Regardless of what mechanical means are used to obtain water for the gardens and palm groves of the desert, merely getting sufficient water out of the ground is not enough alone to insure success, for problems of distribution in relation to land ownership always complicate the issue to some extent. Under Moslem law, only land that is adequately watered can be privately owned. Ownership of the water rights is vested in him who brings the water to the land, and ownership of the land thus cultivated passes to him in consequence. But the title to the land and the title to the water rights often remain distinct legal entities which can be bought and sold separately. Water is usually collected in

[3] There is good reason to suppose that Jews began to settle in Cyrenaica shortly after the destruction of their temple at Jerusalem in 586 B.C., but these Cyrenaican colonies were put to the sword in A.D. 118 by Marcus Turbo, acting under orders from Trajan, and the survivors fled westward. It seems likely that some of these refugees were the first Jewish colonizers of the Touat and its Jewish capital, Tamentit (seven miles south of Adrar), and it may well have been they who introduced the idea of the foggara into the western half of the Sahara.

reservoirs of some sort and thence distributed through an intricate system of channels to the various gardens, at a formally fixed rate of so many minutes' flow to each garden on fixed days and at fixed hours. These water allotments too, and even fractions of them, are often owned as separate entities. To make things even more complicated, trees and crops may be subject to yet a third distinct title, and a single tree can belong to several owners, who may act either as independent individuals or in some agreed form of partnership or association.

Land in general falls into three main legal categories, both within and outside the limits of the oases. In addition to privately owned land, as described above, there is communally owned land, which consists mostly of permanent or perennial pasture, and also unproductive land such as major dune areas and the barren slopes of rocky massifs, which are in actual practice ownerless in the sense in which we understand ownership, although the rights of entry and sojourn are more or less stirctly controlled by the nearest major tribe or confederation. I have gone into the question of the ownership of land and trees and water rights only superficially, but the broad principles must be understood at least in a general way, for they exert a profound influence on the food supply and the distribution of wealth among the sedentary peoples of the desert.

By far the most important cultivated fruit-producing tree of the Sahara is the date palm. Except at altitudes of over 4,500 feet, and in the southern half of the desert and along the Atlantic coast, it furnishes the basic staple food. Indeed the popular saying that "dates are to the peoples of the Sahara what wheat is to the French and rice to the Chinese" is hardly an exaggeration. The importance of the date palm, together with that of oasis towns, decreases progressively however as one moves southward, and dates become increasingly a luxury which fewer and fewer people can afford.

Palm culture, including artificial fecundation and the elimination of all male trees in excess of 2 per cent of the total plantation, seems to be very old in the Sahara, and dates certainly from before the Arab invasions and probably from pre-Roman

13

times. Production is still extremely variable, however, ranging from as little as 40 to over 200 pounds a year per tree, with an average of some 5,300 pounds a year per acre. There are many different kinds of dates, the choicest of which are eaten in their original state, while the more ordinary varieties are stuffed into goatskins to form a kind of stiff marmalade much appreciated by the nomads, or are pressed into huge bricks very roughly two or three feet long by a foot or two square in cross section. Palm trees are also tapped sometimes, much as maple trees are in New England. The sap is usually drunk fresh and then tastes rather like coconut milk, but it is often allowed to ferment, producing a nauseous beverage somewhat similar to Mexican pulque. Sometimes it is distilled, however, and then it has really spectacular effects on the unorthodox who partake of it.

Although a variety of fruits including grapes, citrus fruits, figs, apricots, pomegranates, and even peaches are grown sporadically here and there in the Sahara, none of them ever assumes the proportions of a regular cash crop except occasionally on a very small and strictly local scale. Cereals, on the other hand, are important cash crops wherever they can be grown at all, and they usually bulk large among the standard merchandise of caravan trade. Many kinds of vegetables are also grown in the Sahara, including most of those commonly found in the backyards of residential suburbs in America, but the most popular are onions and tomatoes, as food staples, plus hot peppers for seasoning and mint for use with tea. Tobacco is grown nearly everywhere but always on a small scale, for local consumption and for sale to neighboring nomads, while *kif* (*Cannabis indicus* or "Indian hemp"), although outlawed as a narcotic, is still grown more or less clandestinely in some of the more remote oases. In short the desert as a whole produces a surprisingly rich variety of cultivated plants, but they are very unevenly distributed because of local variations in climate and soil chemistry. Also the rate of yield is almost always low, because of the difficulties of irrigation.

The northern half of the Sahara exports quantities of dates in all directions and thereby covers the cost of imported necessities of life, such as wheat and barley, but the southern half of the area produces no crop that can be exported on anything like a corresponding scale. Salt, however, has long been the chief article of export in the south and still is even now to a considerable extent. During the Middle Ages it was traded to the Sudan, literally for its weight in gold, and the Sudan still absorbs the bulk of Saharan salt production. The oldest known center of extraction seems to have been Idjil, which is mentioned as early as the sixth century A.D., but toward the end of the Middle Ages the deposits of Teghaza (nearly six hundred miles slightly west of north from Timbuctoo), Djado (two hundred and fifty miles or so northeast of the Air), and Mourzouk also began to be exploited. The old mine at Tisempt, about a hundred and fifty miles north of Tamanrasset, is of uncertain date.

The great salt deposits at Taoudéni (roughly five hundred miles north of Timbuctoo) were opened up after the mines at Teghaza had been abandoned following the defeat of their Songhai owners by the Sultan of Morocco in 1585. Here the salt occurs in thick layers which alternate with layers of clay. Production averages roughly 2,500 tons a year. Some two to three hundred theoretically volunteer miners live on the spot the year round, but, as there is no food or wood to be had locally and the nearest pasturage is a full day's journey away, most of them are in fact slaves of the Moorish mine owners for all practical purposes. Twice each year, usually in March and November, a caravan of several thousand camels brings up food and firewood to Taoudéni from Timbuctoo, three weeks' journey away, and returns loaded with salt; but even so the life of the miners is precarious. Fifty-six of them died of starvation in 1910 because a supply caravan was late in arriving, and similar disasters are said to have occurred at Teghaza when the mines there were still in operation.

Natron (carbonate of soda) has long been mined here and there in the Sahara, especially in the Fezzan, the Tibesti, and the Ahaggar. Most of it is used locally in feed for domestic animals, for tanning leather, to curdle milk, and to enhance the taste of chewing tobacco. For the last century and a half natron from the edge of the Erg Oubari, just northwest of Mourzouk, has been shipped out regularly at a rate of between eighty and a hundred tons, or four to five hundred camel loads, a year.

The Sahara is dotted with deposits of varying richness that contain many other kinds of minerals, including iron, oil, and probably commercially profitable concentrations of uranium as well, but all current exploitations of these resources are either very recent or are still in the prospecting or planning stages.

Important though the mineral and vegetable resources of the Sahara are, their natural distributions are so uneven that they could hardly support more than half of the present sedentary population were it not for the fact that they can be transported and so distributed extensively in trade. By this means things that are lacking in one place can usually be got from elsewhere, in exchange for the surplus of some local product which can be produced in excess of local needs. Such a system of trade could never have grown up, however, without a beast of burden capable of carrying heavy loads over long waterless miles of desert trails, in other words the camel. It used to be fashionable in English poetry and elegant prose to refer to camels as "ships of the desert," but this was not such a cleverly original metaphor as it was thought to be; for the nomadic Moors of the western desert speak of a riding camel as a "ship" (Arabic = *markoob*) instead of using the regular Arab word, *mehri*. The term is, however, no less appropriate for all that. Saharan nomads in general distinguish a number of varieties of camel for each of which they have a different word, and they also have a whole series of special words for camels collectively, in small groups or large ones, organized in caravans or running loose at pasture, and so on. These terminological categories are still further complicated by a bewildering series of terms for individuals according to sex, age, size, color, state of health, and various distinctive qualities or defects, and such terms are often special words too. It is evident that all this terminological complexity reflects the vital importance of the camel in desert nomad life, just as the complex Spanish terminology concerning cattle is a

16

reflection of their former importance in the economy of the Spanish people.

Camels in general are usually rather nasty beasts, even in the eyes of those who need them in order to stay alive, for they are stubborn, often frail, and always more or less inclined to be cantankerous. Animals trained by the Tuareg are generally more tractable than those broken by Arabs, for the Tuareg are much more patient and less brutal in their schooling methods. But even so, few who know camels well ever ride one when there is any other way of getting where they want to go. And yet without the camel, very little of this book could have been written, for very few of the nomadic tribes I will discuss could have penetrated the Sahara or survived there until modern times.

There are, in every region of the Sahara, two main types of camel, the mount and the beast of burden (who may also carry passengers occasionally as well as freight). The true riding camel is always a graceful and imposing animal, much taller, higher on the leg, finer boned and freer moving, lighter colored as a rule and less thickly furred, and thus more sensitive and delicate in general than is his servile and less pampered cousin, the camel of the caravans and baggage trains. The riding camel dies suddenly of exhaustion on the march (often in his sleep, shortly before dawn) or, rarely, lingers on, a broken and neglected creature. The baggage camel, on the other hand, works out his last decrepit years pulling on a well rope; although today, if he is exceptionally lucky, he may become an object of undiscriminating admiration and amateur photography in some tourist-ridden oasis, cherished up to a point by his latest owners for his low cost of maintenance and high returns. In this connection it is well to remember that true riding camels, the "racing camels" of popular fiction, are almost never seen in any oasis, regardless of what native guides may say in praise of mounts they offer the unwary tourist.

Good riding camels are capable of long forced marches at relatively high rates of speed, but when the limit of their endurance is reached they are apt to collapse without warning.

Picked animals on a raid have been known to cover nearly four hundred miles in six days and nights, but such performances are most unusual. Baggage camels naturally travel much more slowly, usually between fifteen and twenty miles a day, carrying an average load of four hundred to five hundred and fifty pounds apiece. Caravans of the Berber nomads of the southern desert move customarily in single file or in several roughly parallel files, whereas those of Arab nomads are kept bunched together on the march. The animals are usually allowed to graze during the midday halt, shortly before noon, but are not unloaded until evening as a rule. In defense of the baggage camel it should be said that he literally bears the burden of nomad life in the Sahara. Without him the family and retainers, with all their impedimenta of tents and other equipment, could never move far enough and fast enough to survive. It is he too (aided by his Levantine cousins) who furnishes from his woolly undercoat the luxuriantly soft "hair" that is so prized by connoisseurs of gentlemen's apparel. Desert hunters sometimes use camels for concealment when stalking game on foot. Where pasturage is fairly sparse, grazing camels often wander freely for miles, nibbling here and there as they go, and so become a familiar sight which arouses no suspicion on the part of game animals. The hunter chooses a relatively docile baggage camel, preferably one specially trained for the purpose, and slowly maneuvers it in front of him with the aid of a longish stick and occasional whispered commands. When he has arrived within about fifty yards or so of the animal he is stalking, the hunter slips suddenly to one side and takes his shot.

Camels are sometimes eaten too, but only in sizable towns or on the occasion of a very big and important feast, or when they are so ill or injured so badly that their lives are despaired of. To slaughter a healthy camel in the desert is to destroy a capital investment, but to kill and eat a dying one is to salvage what little there is left. Caravan men in danger of death from thirst have been known to slaughter baggage camels so as to drink their blood and the liquid which can be squeezed from their stomach contents. It was only twenty years ago that a few nomad tribes first began to raise camels expressly for sale to butchers in neighboring commercial centers. Milk is a fairly important byproduct of camel breeding, for camel's milk is a highly prized luxury throughout the desert, but, even under the most favorable conditions, a milk camel gives only some six to ten quarts a day. Personally I find camel's milk unpleasantly heavy and sweet; it is a good deal like what is known commercially as "evaporated milk."

The most important domestic animals numerically in the northern and northern central Sahara are sheep, but as one approaches the more barren regions farther south, where water points are scarce and much of the ground surface consists of stony or sandy wastes, suitable forage becomes increasingly difficult to find and there are fewer sheep in consequence. Although Saharan sheep belong to several distinct varieties (even including fat-tailed strains in some of the more northerly parts of the area) it is sufficient for the present to divide them simply into woolly and usually white, or hairy and usually brown (or piebald), the former type being found mostly in the northern and northern central desert and the latter in the center and the southlands. There has long existed in the western Sahara a spectacular but very little known caravan trade in hairy sheep. The animals, purchased in the western Sudan or the Aïr, are driven northward across the desert from the Adrar-n-Ifoghas region through Timissao to the oases of the Tidikelt, notably Aoulef and In Salah, a distance of some eight hundred to fifteen hundred miles depending on the starting point, while a few flocks are occasionaly driven on to Ouargla,[4] about five hundred miles farther north. Once arrived at their destination they are exchanged for dates, and also for local textiles now and then.

Goats too are important domestic animals in the Sahara and they also can be divided into long and short coated varieties, the first of which seems to be rather more common throughout the desert generally. Saharan goats are small animals by European standards, whose usually long or longish hair is most often black or black more or less marked with white. They are popular

---

[4] On American and English maps this name is usually spelled Wargla or Warqla: the true native pronunciation is Waregla.

throughout the area for their ability to live on all kinds of forage, and so there are still plenty of them in most of the more fertile northern desert, but there they are relatively inconspicuous because sheep are the focus of economic attention. It is sheep that make or break a nomad in the north: his goats are hardly more than accessories, always useful for their milk, hair and skins, but essential only in periods of prolonged drought and dire emergency. Moving southward across the desert one finds that goats increase slowly in numbers while the flocks of sheep dwindle rapidly until, by the time the main east-west line of demarcation between woolly and hairy sheep is reached, goats are already in the majority or very nearly so.

Although cattle were common all over the Sahara in prehistoric times, they are found now only in the southlands. They belong mostly to the humpbacked Sudanese variety, the zebu, and are used chiefly for drawing water in southern agricultural centers, although some have run wild in the central mountain massifs and are occasionally hunted there for meat. Heinrich Barth saw large herds of wild cattle in the mountains southwest of Ghat when he passed that way in 1850, but few if any of them survive today. Where these wild herds came from originally is a mystery, but I am inclined to guess that they were probably descended from domestic cattle which had escaped and returned to the wild state long ago, at a time when it was impossible for any large domestic animal to compete with the camel economically in the increasingly arid environment of the desert. On the other hand, however, it seems likely that cattle were hunted in the Sahara before the introduction there of animal domestication, and so it is barely possible that the herds Barth wrote about may have been the last surviving representatives of a wild strain which had escaped domestication entirely.

Zebus are surprisingly hardy creatures and are capable of long desert marches now and then. Barth tells how, a little over a century ago, a Teda chief is said to have traveled with a caravan of oxen all the way from northern Nigeria to Ghat, and he adds that the animals were watered only every second day during the march. In 1850 he himself saw a caravan from the Sudan passing northward through the Air "with its goods laden almost entirely on pack-oxen." Zebus were already present in Egypt in the sixteenth century before Christ, and perhaps even earlier than that. In the Sahara they seem to have supplanted other and presumably older varieties of cattle, including a type with great lyre-shaped horns which survives to this day on the southern fringes of the central desert and in the Sudan, as well as a more ordinary looking animal with shorter and strongly curved horns, apparently similar to the kind that Barth saw running wild.

Horses were probably never really common in the Sahara, and yet a mass of conflicting and confusing material has been published on the subject of their past importance there, simply because they figure prominently both in prehistoric paintings and in the early semi-mythological accounts of writers like Herodotus. But it is true throughout the world that things which are particularly rare and valuable are usually given a place of prominence in art and literature, a place which is often out of all proportion to their practical value in the life of the community. Probably the importance of horses in Saharan history has been much exaggerated in this way. Two main varieties, the Barb and the Arabian, are found in the desert, together with intermediate hybrid forms as one would naturally expect, and these two basic types have probably been present there for at least two thousand years and possibly a good deal longer. Unfortunately, however, it is not possible as yet to establish the date of their arrival with any greater certainty. Horses have been an increasingly expensive luxury in the Sahara proper ever since the camel came into general use there, and so they have been rapidly disappearing in recent times except along the northern and southern borders of the desert where they are still far less numerous than they were even as recently as a century ago. The Arab nomads around Metlili, Ouargla, and El Goléa, for example, seem to have had nearly three hundred horses in the middle of the last century, but they have none today. Even the noble Tuareg warriors of the central desert, who apparently never had more than a handful of horses at any time and therefore prized them greatly as symbols of prestige, have had none now for over twenty years.

Despite the importance of animals in the Sahara, wheeled vehicles of various kinds have also played an important part in the adaptation of the human population to an increasingly desertic environment. The evidence of rock paintings and engravings suggests that two-wheeled chariots and carts and four-wheeled wagons were the usual means of long distance transportation until they were superseded by the camel, probably about two thousand years ago. Unfortunately, however, pictographic evidence by its very nature cannot serve as a reliable basis for dating, even approximately, because the pictures themselves cannot be dated by any reliable technique. Wheeled vehicles, like horses, were once thought to have been introduced into Egypt by the Hyksos invasion, but it is now known that they did not appear there until a generation or two later, somewhere around B.C. 1,580.

The chariots shown in ancient Saharan art are drawn sometimes by two and sometimes by four animals. Two-horse chariots seem to have appeared in Egypt for the first time early in the Eighteenth Dynasty, around B.C. 1,500, but the question of four-horse chariots is less clear. The ancient Sumerians of Iraq began to hitch four animals abreast to a single vehicle some 5,500 years ago or so, but it now seems certain that none of these animals were horses. According to some authorities, the Sudanese conquerors of ancient Egypt seem to have had four-horse chariots at least as early as the beginning of the sixth century before Christ, and perhaps for as much as two hundred years before that. Herodotus described the mysterious Garamantes of the eastern central desert as using similar chariots in his day, and so implied that this type of vehicle goes back in Saharan chronology to at least as early as the fifth century before Christ. All things considered, it seems probable that the easternmost Saharan tribes knew at least what four-horse chariots looked like no later than 2,500 years ago, and that, conversely, chariots of this type can hardly be much older in the area. And incidentally there seems to be no good reason to suppose offhand that the basic arts of chariot making and driving were introduced from across the seas, as some writers have argued, rather than overland, through Egypt.

The pre-Roman trade routes of the Sahara remain to be worked out, but one seemingly strong hint is to be found in the known distribution across the central and western desert of pictures showing horse-drawn chariots. The distribution is strikingly linear and follows what appear to have been two major trails, one of which seems to have started from the neighborhood of Tripoli and thence proceeded in a general southwesterly direction through Ghadamès and the Tassili-n-Ajjer Mountains to Hirhafok (sometimes spelt Hérafek), Tit, Abalessa, and thence to the Niger somewhere around Gao. The second major trail of chariot pictures starts westward from Timbuctoo, and, skirting around the most inhospitable part of the southwestern desert, continues in a long curve swinging gently northward and then northeastward past the eastern border of the Spanish Sahara and on into Morocco, with various branches presumably connecting its northern extensions with both the Atlantic and Mediterranean coasts. Both trails are used by caravans to this day. Although chariots by their very nature can never be older anywhere than the knowledge of the use of metal, it is interesting to note that the western trail they seem to have followed may already have been a route of northward migration and cultural diffusion in late prehistoric times, while at least the northern half of the central trail may well have come into use at a much earlier date.

Although camels, cattle, horses, sheep, and goats have generally been the most important domestic animals in the Sahara, the desert livestock pool includes a number of more obscure creatures who are useful too in one way or another. Donkeys, for example, are widely used by nearly all Saharan peoples. They carry the rich but frugal merchant of the Mzab to his place of daily business and back home again, they carry the household bric-a-brac and often the women and infants of pastoral nomads on the march, and, in the southern mountains where pitching tents far from springs and wells is a custom that still survives from the days when it was dangerous to do otherwise, they are used to fetch and carry water for the camp.

Dogs too are ever present in the Sahara although relatively rare in most of the south, and they again follow the general rule of being divisible into two main varieties. The northern dog, essentially a camp guard, is a stocky, thick-coated animal of medium size and white or mainly white in color, though often marked with large and irregular patches of pale yellow. His ears are thick and often stiffly erect, and his moderately bushy tail sometimes curls up over his hindquarters. In short he is of the type commonly known in Northwest Africa as "the Kabyle dog," probably a survivor of the very ancient generalized form from which the Asiatic Spitz and Chow, the Norwegian Elkhound, and the Husky of the Eskimo were derived. The southern dog, the famous *sloughi* (pronounced sloōgui), is a kind of greyhound, somewhat smaller than those of Europe and America and with a slightly thicker head. His coat is smooth and short, and ranges in color all the way from pure white (with dark eyes, nose and nails) to a dark reddish fawn with a very dark gray or black mask. The sloughi is a relatively rare luxury animal, used primarily for hunting, bred and fed with care, and sometimes even endowed with a social personality and status superior to that of the lower classes of the human community in which he lives. The rare southwestern variety found among the vanishing Nemadi and the southern Moors is relatively coarse in all respects, and is probably a residual of stabilized hybrid form. He does double duty as both camp guard and sight hound,[5] and enjoys no special privileges.

Dogs other than sloughis are eaten occasionally in the northern and central Sahara, and more rarely in the south, but this practice seems always to have some ritual significance, either purely magical or magico-medicinal. In a few cases its adepts have claimed that they ate dog meat only because they liked the taste, but the reports make it clear nevertheless that what they

---

[5] "Sight hounds" follow game with their eyes, and depend on their superior speed to run it down, whereas "scent hounds" follow a trail by using their sense of smell, and often hardly look where they are going.

were really up to was making a demonstration in ritual defiance of traditional dietary taboos by joining in semi-overt orgies that involved the consumption of dog meat along with immoderate quantities of alcoholic beverages. Sedentary Berbers of the desert, and particularly the Mzabites, are notoriously fond of dog meat, and it is barely possible that some of them may eat it simply because they like it and for no other reason; but I still doubt it.

Cats are to be found in almost all Saharan settlements, but they are very rare in the south and never very numerous anywhere. They are valued mainly for their enthusiasm and skill in killing scorpions and poisonous snakes, but they are rarely given any special care. The males are occasionally eaten ritually, particularly on two or three specified days at the end of March or early in April, and they are sometimes bred and fattened expressly for this purpose. Sedentary women eat cat meat as a medicinal specific, or to promote general well-being or fertility, and the charm is thought to work best if the pieces of cut up meat are swallowed whole without being chewed. Each spring the women of Bou Noura, in the Mzab, are led by the chief woman of the town up out of the valley to the plateau above, and there they have a general jollification and ritual picnic with cat as the main course. Throughout North Africa cats seem to inspire some sort of magico-religious awe, but apparently this question has never been investigated systematically.

Small, scrawny, nondescript chickens are to be found wandering about in practically all Saharan oases and in many camps, although there seem to be no attempts made at systematic breeding or feeding. The birds usually nest where they can, and scavenge as best they may on the garbage dumps of towns and in camp refuse. They are seldom eaten, but are kept mainly as producers of eggs and killers of scorpions. Little hedgehogs too are often kept as scorpion killers in the houses of sedentary desert oasis dwellers; and they are also eaten occasionally, just as they were apparently in prehistoric times judging by the bones one finds in the garbage dumps of ancient habitation sites.

Still other, and less useful creatures used to be kept for sport. The nomadic Arab aristocrats of the Sahara have always been inordinately fond of hunting in the grand manner of medieval lords, and, even in recent years, when the desert had still been touched only very lightly by European influence, some of them maintained surprisingly elaborate hunting establishments. Cheetahs, for example, were caught, trained, and used for coursing game, a practice which must have been very difficult and also very expensive. But today there are no hunting cheetahs left in the Sahara that I know of, and no wild ones either except possibly a very few in the Tripolitanian desert of northwestern Libya. Falconry too used to be practiced widely throughout the northern desert, and in fact came to an end in the northwest only four or five years ago, as a result of the unrest caused by the Algerian rebellion. Incidentally, it is interesting to note that the hoods used for Saharan falcons were practically identical, both in construction and decoration, with those in vogue in Europe since the Middle Ages and those used by the nomads of Arabia today.

Various closely related varieties of gazelles are and have long been among the main game animals of the Sahara. Now they are pretty nearly the only game left, and are fast disappearing in their turn under the motorized pressure of military and oil company personnel looking for fresh meat free of charge and a tacitly accepted excuse to fire off their guns. Occasional antelopes and mouflon were to be found in the region of the Mzab as recently as seventy years ago, but the former have since disappeared from all but a few remote corners of the northern central Sahara and the extreme southern edge of the desert, while the latter, reduced in numbers to hardly more than a few scattered families, have sought refuge mainly in the central mountain massifs.

Ostriches were once numerous and used to be hunted extensively as far north as Laghouat, but the last of the great western flocks were exterminated some ninety years ago by a series of organized hunts in which General Jean Margueritte of Mexican fame was the leading figure. In the northern and eastern central desert, the chief agents of destruction were Tuareg bands of commercial hunters in search of feathers, but here the work of extermination was not completed until the early years of the present century. Hares, fennecs, bustards, and a few rare quail and partridge have always been and still are hunted occasionally. Various kinds of small rodents, lizards, and skinks are eaten at times, usually when on the trail far from any settlement. Locusts too are eaten in season, raw or fried, and are also preserved in salt or oil occasionally.[6]

Near Mourzouk, in the Fezzan, small "water worms" (actually *Artemia salina,* a primitive kind of miniature shrimp) are collected and pounded together with a little salt until the mixture becomes a black paste, which is then rolled into balls about the size of a big orange and set out in the sun to dry. The finished product is eaten preferably mixed with a greasy sauce used on millet or barley bread. Captain George Lyon, writing in 1821, said of these "worms" that "They resemble very bad caviar in taste, and the smell is extremely offensive; but habit and necessity overcome all prejudices in this country, and I soon became very partial to them."

Natural resources, vegetable, mineral, and animal, are all vital factors in the adjustment of human beings to desert life, but most important of all are those internal factors which govern the physiological adaptation of the individual to a very dry and often very hot environment that is characterized also by sudden and extreme changes in temperature. The combination of extreme dryness and heat makes it absolutely necessary for animals and human beings alike to develop special mechanisms of adaptation in order to survive. The hairy desert sheep are excellent illustrations of thermal adaptation. They are tall, long and lean in body, with long stringy ears, neck, legs, and tail, and instead of a woolly fleece they have a coarse coat of short and more or less wavy hair with only a very sparse undercoat of fine, woolly fibers. Camels in particular show a gradual change in thermoadaptive characters as one proceeds from north to south and from highlands down to lower altitudes. Moving southward and

---

[6] Small fresh-water fish are found almost wherever there are permanent accumulations of surface water, even in artificial irrigation channels, but they are never important either in communal economy or in local diet. Among many tribes they are taboo as food.

27

downhill one sees their bodies become slighter, their extremities more elongated and refined, and their coats progressively lighter in texture and usually in color also. Selective breeding for a preconceived ideal, a fast and graceful mount that moves smoothly, has doubtless played some part in this occasionally, especially among the Tuareg, but it is certainly not the prime factor involved. As for water requirements, camels can go indefinitely without drinking in winter when a minimum of good lush pasturage is available, but they must have water or green forage every third or fourth day in summer in order to continue in reasonably good condition. Sheep must be watered at least every fourth day in winter and every day if possible in summertime, while goats and particularly donkeys seem to be somewhat more resistant to thirst. Cattle should be watered every second day or so and horses every day, regardless of the season.

Since Roman times it has been believed generally that the camel has a special system of reservoirs which he can fill up when water is available and which make it possible for him to survive long waterless periods, but recent investigations have completely demolished this time honored theory. No such special equipment exists. The camel's secret of success lies mainly in the following facts. His rate of water elimination is remarkably low in all respects and under all conditions, less than a third in fact of the average figure for mammals in general, including man, and the water that he does lose is drawn mostly from interstitial and intercellular sources rather than from plasma as is the case with us. Thus a camel can lose in liquid over a quarter of his total weight without serious results, and, conversely, when he does get a chance to drink his fill, he can comfortably absorb the equivalent of this loss at a single watering; for, in spite of such extremes of water loss and intake, his blood volume remains practically constant under all conditions. And finally, the camel's "normal" body temperature can vary by as much as 12 degrees Fahrenheit in a few hours without doing him any harm, and this eliminates the need for thermostatic regulation by sweating unless the temperature of the surrounding air rises above 105°.

Dehydration is the greatest single danger to human and animal life alike in a hot desert, and it sometimes causes truly terrible disasters, as happened in the case of one caravan of two thousand men and eighteen hundred camels, all of whom died of thirst while crossing the southwestern Sahara a hundred and fifty years ago. As human beings grow up, they all establish automatically an habitual ratio between water intake and elimination, between the quantity of liquid that they drink during the day and the quantity they lose, by sweating and in other ways. Therefore, when an individual sweats substantially more than he is accustomed to, he must increase his rate of water intake in proportion, or dehydration will soon strike him down. In spite of popular theories to the contrary, there is no evidence that human beings can adjust to a rate of water intake very much below their normal rate in relation to loss of water by sweating, nor is there any convincing evidence that any particular race can do so better than any other, even over periods of several generations. The maximum possible rate of sweat loss in Europeans seems to be about a quart an hour, but such a heavy drain cannot be maintained for more than five or six consecutive hours at the most. Some authors have claimed that Negroes secrete nearly twice as much sweat as do whites under similar conditions, which would enable them to stand up better under extreme heat, but this seems more than doubtful in view of recent experiments by Paul Baker and others, working with volunteer American white and Negro soldiers. Probably the sweat loss rates of both races are very nearly the same.

When sweating rises above the normal daily level, water intake must be increased accordingly if normal levels of efficiency and health are to be maintained: it is for this reason that the daily water ration of desert road gangs in the French Sahara is over two gallons a day per man, for drinking and cooking only. On a caravan march one can get along on as little as a single gallon a day, but it is considered dangerous to drop below this minimum allowance even in winter. Alonzo Pond has stated, as a very general rule, that an ordinary American or European can live for about two days in a mean temperature of 100° to 120° Fahrenheit without any water at all, after which three quarts or less a day will not be enough to save him although a gallon a day will enable him to survive indefinitely if he remains quiet in the shade. It has been estimated too that an average white man walking only at night in a hot desert can cover about twenty miles on a gallon of water every twenty-four hours. Camel Corps detachments sometimes cover as much as seven hundred miles or even more in two weeks using only the water they had with them at the start, roughly fifteen gallons or so for each rider and his camel, but such performances are most exceptional. Once more it appears that the ratio of a gallon of water a day per man is the minimum safe allowance. Substitutes like salty or polluted water, or urine, are worse than nothing, for they only hasten collapse by increasing the load on the kidneys. Blood, however, and especially liquid squeezed from the stomach contents of camels and game animals, have proved to be reasonably satisfactory substitutes for water.

When extreme conditions of heat and dryness are encountered, auxiliary mechanisms of protection and radiation must be employed. Under extreme dry heat, desert mammals are protected from excessive heat absorption by coats of fur that shade the skin and still are sparse enough to allow full radiation by the evaporation of sweat at skin level. Man can achieve a similar result by wearing voluminous but loosely fitting garments. Man and specialized desert mammals alike can and often do extend their adaptive potential even farther by observing rules of conduct according to which they avoid conditions that impose excessive heat absorption, and seek, whenever they can, places where relatively economical radiation is possible. Many nomads of hot deserts, the Tuareg for example, move on foot with an easy and deliberate grace that has usually been written off as due to their feeling of inborn superiority, their aristocratic pride of race. Their slow, imposing gait together with the flowing robes and impressive veils that swathe their bodies, heads, and faces, gives them an air of such extremely supercilious pretentiousness that it never seems to have occurred to anyone that if they habitually dressed or acted otherwise they would die.

Salt in the human body tends to reduce the loss of water, but the water that is eliminated always takes some salt with it, in sweat or otherwise. Thus, in spite of the human body's remarkable though individually variable powers of adjusting its rate of salt elimination, some increase in salt intake becomes vitally necessary when sweating and the consequent flow of water through the body rise substantially above their habitual levels. It has been found that an initial lack of sufficient salt is counterbalanced up to a point, at least in persons whose habitual consumption of salt is fairly low, by a marked automatic physiological reduction of salt elimination. So, among Europeans freshly exposed to desert heat the salt content of sweat diminishes progressively until a state of equilibrium between salt intake and salt elimination has been reached; and this economy is effected first by the kidneys, followed after a few days by the sweat glands themselves.

In spite of the fact that evaporating perspiration is an important cooling factor, it is not the only one, for bodily proportions are important too. The radiation potential of a cylinder increases in inverse proportion to the square of its diameter, and this simple fact is probably responsible to a great extent for the lean and lanky build of most of the inhabitants of hot deserts and subdesertic regions. Also the radiation of a sweating human body is greatly increased by free air circulation and dryness which promote evaporation, and is decreased by still air and high humidity; and so an attenuated body build with slender extremities is a great advantage in adjusting to hot desert or breezy savannah environments where a high evaporation rate raises the cooling effect of sweat to its maximum. In the still, humid air of tropical rain forests sweat does not evaporate freely but merely trickles down the skin without cooling it to any appreciable extent; so in such places a fairly stocky build is no disadvantage in the struggle for adjustment to heat. Russell Newman has pointed out also that there is in general a definite negative correlation in man between the relative fatness of the individual and the heat of his habitual environment, while Baker found that fat or very muscular men suffer greater physiological strain under hot desert conditions than do thin ones. Apparently a layer of fat underneath the skin prevents internal heat from reaching the surface where it can be radiated freely.

Much has been written about the supposed advantage to human beings of a black skin in resisting desert sunlight, but not enough is yet known about the subject to justify any definite conclusions one way or the other. There is some evidence that black skin does block much radiation which might otherwise damage or even destroy the sweat glands, major agents of adaptation to dry heat, but heavily tanned white skin does so too, perhaps even more efficiently. Extreme tanning is found among all white people who move freely about in hot deserts, and so one is inclined to suppose that this form of adaptation must be of value for survival. The untanned skin of a white man, on the other hand, is said to reflect about three times as much incident solar radiation as does that of a Negro, and so the latter is clearly at a disadvantage in this respect.

Individuals, even of a single community, vary a good deal in size and shape and color, and all such variations are more or less advantageous or disadvantageous in a hot desert environment. Over a period of many generations, the forces of natural selection in the Sahara have undoubtedly eliminated the least adaptable human types until there now remain only those whose representatives can live long enough to perpetuate their kind. Thus, the original genetic compositions of Saharan populations have probably been modified gradually until the maximum potentials of adaptation were fully realized or at least closely approached, until those traits which were fatal or seriously disadvantageous in a hot desert were reduced to an insignificant proportion of the total or disappeared entirely.

The supposed inability of European families to adapt themselves successfully to extreme tropical desert environments, like that of the Sahara, is almost certainly due in the main to their unwillingness or inability to change their psychological and material habits, and especially their diet, rather than to the many supposedly inherent and unalterable limitations, psychological, neurological, or physiological, which so many people talk and write about so much but for which no one has yet found any demonstrable evidence whatever. As Weiner [7] wrote a few years ago: "The fact is that rules of living have to be acquired for desert life as for other parts of the world and that this can be done efficiently is obvious from the successful survival of the great variety of desert peoples."

[7] Weiner, 1954, p. 199.

Chapter 2 ~

THE BACKGROUND
OF THE PAST

Long, long ago, during the prehistoric ages before the dawn of written history, the Sahara was very different from what it is today, for much of it was fertile and relatively thickly populated. Stone implements of all shapes and sizes are scattered nearly all over the desert, in a profusion which proves beyond all doubt that the land once supported a very substantial human population, thanks to a climate far more salubrious than that it now enjoys. Fishhooks and barbed harpoon points made of bone have been found as far north as the center of the western Sahara, and so there must have been good fishing there once upon a time. Indeed recent excavations have shown that, up until perhaps as recently as three or four thousand years ago, much of what is now desert was relatively fertile and well watered country, dotted with shallow lakes and swamps, and even clumps of trees, shrubs and ferns belonging to species which are no longer found south of the Atlas Mountains. Unfortunately, however, the remains of almost no human beings who were surely prehistoric have been found so far within the limits of the desert proper, and so we can only guess what the prehistoric peoples of the Sahara were like physically. But, since it is evident that they must have come from somewhere else to start with, some reasonably safe guessing can be done on the basis of what is known about the prehistoric populations of surrounding regions.

Early in geologically recent times, probably about twelve thousand years ago, there arrived in the northwestern coastal zone of Africa a people who were modern although somewhat coarse and primitive in type, and who belonged undoubtedly to the same basic racial stock as the earliest known inhabitants of the Near East and the Greek peninsula. They seem to have come from the Near East into North Africa, and to have gone on westward following the shore line at least as far as the Atlantic coast of Morocco; but at present there is no good reason to suppose that they ever entered the Sahara. A few thousand years later, apparently, there arrived another kind of people, belonging this time to a relatively big and rugged variety of the modern Mediterranean type. Skeletons of similar people have been found in prehistoric village sites in Palestine and Greece, and also Egypt, and so it looks as though the members of the second invasion also came from the Near East. But they appear to have come by a different route from that followed by their predecessors, or perhaps by more than one. Some of them probably traveled southwestward through Egypt, then westward through the Sudan, and finally northward and northwestward across the central desert and so into southern Tunisia and Algeria; but another wave of them may well have followed the Mediterranean coastline. Once settled along the southern frontier of the early invaders who barred them from the sea, some of them seem to have turned their eyes southward again and set out to explore and exploit the northern and central portions of the Sahara.

All the peoples I have mentioned so far in this chapter were in what prehistorians call a mesolithic (middle stone) phase of culture. This is simply an abbreviated way of saying that they had developed considerable skill in making small and efficient tools, such as knife blades and needles, out of flint flakes, bone, and wood, and that their way of life was based on hunting and the gathering of wild plants for food. Although some chose to live in caves, most of them preferred semi-permanent camps out in the open, located often in a commanding position overlooking the junction of two valleys. They must have been very dirty people, for they simply threw their refuse out the door where it piled up gradually into huge mounds, often as much as ten or twelve feet deep and a hundred yards across. Bodies of the dead too were thrown out, along with the garbage, or were buried right at home underneath the kitchen hearth.

The prehistoric Northwest Africans seem to have gone on living in this casual and messy way until perhaps some five thousand years ago, when they finally began to receive the first elements of what prehistorians call a neolithic (new stone) phase of culture. Neolithic culture is characterized by the invention or importation of the arts of animal domestication and agriculture, accompanied or followed shortly by the introduction of pottery, of finely chipped stone arrowheads, and of heavier stone implements, such as axes, gouges, and pestles, that are blocked out by chipping and then finished by grinding or pecking and polishing. Judging by what little evidence is available, it looks as though this new way of life was not imported bodily into Barbary by a new wave of immigrants, but rather filtered in bit by bit, through trans-Saharan trade; for the resulting changes in technology were not accompanied by any marked change in the physical characteristics of the local population as a whole. A few distinctly negroid individuals do begin to appear occasionally among the skeletons dating from this period, but they are so few in number and so widely scattered geographically that they can hardly have been members of even a small migrational wave. Probably they were traveling traders for the most part, although some may possibly have been imported slaves. In any case, both they and the neolithic way of life seem to have come simultaneously into Barbary from the south, and so that is the next direction in which to look.

Along the southern edge of the western Sahara there lie a series of great piles of neolithic refuse, characterized particularly by barbed harpoon points and fishhooks of bone, fishbone needles, and grooved clubs or hammers made of stone shaped by grinding. Finely chipped stone arrowheads with concave bases and polished stone axes were found also, and it seems likely that they belong to a slightly later period although the circumstances under which the collecting was done make it impossible to tell, from the reports, whether this is really so or not. Bones of at least sixteen human beings were found in one refuse heap, but unfortunately they were so fragmentary that not even a single complete brain case could be recovered. They did include, however, recognizable remains of a Negro type which is still found today among the natives of the French Sudan and Senegal.

Bone harpoon points and fishhooks, and other typical southern neolithic implements, have been found also in ancient habitation sites as far north as the center of the desert, together with animal remains including bones of cattle, fish, and various kinds of game. A spindle whorl too was found in one such site, which suggests that the people of the central Sahara may already have known how to make cloth in neolithic times. All things considered it seems highly probable that neolithic culture was introduced into the southern and central Sahara by Negroes who came there from the Sudan, probably about five thousand years ago. Although hunting and fishing on the one hand, and cattle raising on the other, seem to have been their two principal means of livelihood, it is not yet possible to say whether these two ways of life were practised by two more or less different kinds of people, or were merely different local manifestations of the great adaptability of an otherwise essentially uniform population.

Putting the evidence from the north and south together, it looks as though neolithic negroid groups from the Sudan began to spread northward some five thousand years ago through the entire length of the then relatively fertile Sahara. It seems practically certain too that the more advanced parties met and mingled to some extent with bands of adventurers from the north who had settled in the desert at some earlier date, and who were basically white Mediterranean in type. As century after century rolled by, the Sahara became progressively drier and drier, and yet these marginal elements of the northern and southern neolithic populations apparently did not retreat to their respective homelands. Instead they broke up into increasingly small and isolated groups, concentrated in the steadily shrinking fertile areas which were destined to become the oases and agricultural centers of today. And here their sedentary negroid descendants still live and till the soil.

A number of human skeletons dating supposedly from late

neolithic and classical times have been dug up in various parts of the Sahara, and reports on some of them have been published. On the basis of these remains it has been argued that the rugged Mediterranean physical type is the oldest of which traces have been preserved among the living peoples of the desert, and that it survives to this day, practically unchanged, among the Tuareg aristocracy. Unfortunately, however, it is obvious that the material on which this argument was based was wholly inadequate in quantity: it was too small a sample to justify any definite conclusions whatever in the field of racial analysis.

But stones and bones were not all that the ancient peoples of the Sahara left behind them; for the surfaces of boulders and the sheltered faces of overhanging walls of rock are often decorated, and sometimes literally covered, with engravings and paintings, many of which are aesthetically arresting while some are of really striking beauty. The things shown in these pictures range all the way from unquestionably prehistoric subjects, like extinct species of buffalo and war chariots, through modern fauna no longer known in the Sahara but common in the lands adjacent to the south, to frankly modern themes like men in European clothes, with firearms, and traveling in automobiles or even airplanes. Although this whole corpus of native art has been the object of many costly expeditions and the subject of as many painfully detailed analyses, as well as expensively elaborate though sometimes highly profitable publications, three main obstacles have thus far blocked inexorably every attempt to extract from it information of decisive archaeological value.

The most formidable of these obstacles is the fact that it is almost always impossible to date such pictures even approximately, not only in absolute terms of years or centuries, but even in relation to the relative chronologies of geological formations or archaeological deposits. It can only be by some very unusual coincidence that a definite chronological relation to either kind of evidence, or to material datable by laboratory analysis, can ever be established. Another major difficulty is the question of whether or not the prehistoric artist depicted things that he saw around him every day of his life, or other things, unknown in his homeland, which he had seen on some trading or raiding expedition far away. Did he usually draw only what was constantly before the eyes of the whole community, or did he present to his admiring family and friends pictures of things that were strange and wonderful to them, just as do returning tourists and commercial travelers and soldiers, and even the Saharan nomads of today? And then there is also the question of copies. One picture that was found recently in the central Sahara is obviously a copy of an Egyptian tomb painting, made apparently by someone who had seen such a thing but did not remember all of the details: or it may only be a copy of someone else's copy of the Egyptian original. Unfortunately there is no way of knowing how many desert pictographs are relatively late copies of undeniably prehistoric ones, or which are copies and which are true originals.

Weathering and superposition have both been used as bases for dating pictographs in relation to each other, so as to establish developmental sequences, but neither is at all reliable. Although differences in the patina of lines engraved on rock sometimes furnish reliable clues as to relative age, patina can vary considerably even on one face of a single boulder. Long hypothetical sequences of styles have been constructed on the basis of superpositions, cases where a rock painting done in one style overlaps one done in another; but even though two such paintings may have been done at different times by different artists, one is left wondering how great was the time interval that separated them? Was it a century or a thousand years? Or was it only a few days, or perhaps a month or two? At present there is no way of knowing.

In spite of these difficulties, however, there is still something to be learned from ancient Saharan art. It is quite certain, for example, that prehistoric man was contemporaneous in the Sahara with animals which are extinct today, although that fact was established long ago on the basis of archaeological excavations. It is clear that he sometimes rode on cattle, and in horse-drawn chariots and carts and also in wagons and chariots drawn by cattle; and that he sometimes had herds of cattle which were

39

domesticated; and that he was in touch with ancient Egypt in some way. But that is about all that the ancient native art of the Sahara has to tell, aside from purely aesthetic considerations. Although many authors who write about the Sahara seem to delight in romantic speculations the plain truth is usually fascinating enough in itself, if only one stops to think just what it really means.

Over the more than twenty centuries that have passed since the first flickering rays of the light of history began to dissipate the shadows of prehistoric times, the peoples of the Sahara have been in practically constant touch commercially with southern Europe and the East, both Near and Far; [1] and yet this very important fact has been overlooked by nearly everyone. Even though the commercial relations were usually indirect, because of intervening middlemen, they resulted in a steadily increasing flow of foreign trade goods and ideas into and across the desert, and so must have exerted a continuous and increasingly profound influence on Saharan ways of life. And, in addition to the kind of influence produced by trade, special political situations gave rise every now and then to cultural relations which, although less close in general and less far-reaching geographically in most cases, must have left some mark on the Saharan tribes, especially those of the northern desert. For example, the Roman administration in the north maintained a chain of outposts along the northern boundary of the Sahara, in direct contact with the nomad tribal territories immediately to the south. The settlement of Ghirza (a hundred and seventy-five miles southeast of Tripoli), made up of a group of large fortified farms and two elaborate cemeteries with imposing monuments, may be taken as indicating the general nature of such installations from the third to the sixth centuries. The farm owners of Ghirza were retired veterans of the Roman Army, Europeans at first and later Berbers, who acted both as vanguards of Roman civilization and as militia to keep desert raiders at a distance. Most of their farm laborers, however, must have been recruited locally, and so must have been active in spreading Roman culture. One

[1] Bovill (1933 and 1958) is the chief authority in this field.

or two Roman military expeditions are known to have crossed the Sahara to the Sudan about two thousand years ago, but unfortunately almost no information has survived concerning what they saw or what they did along the way, nor do they seem to have left behind them any lasting traces of their passage.

Unfortunately too the extent of Roman trans-Saharan trade and its importance for the tribes inhabiting the interior remain unknown. Negro slaves, gold, and ivory were probably brought up across the western desert, but it seems likely that these operations were almost entirely in the hands of native nomads. Nevertheless the impact of Roman material culture made itself felt to some degree far to the south; for the rich grave furniture from the "Tomb of Tin Hinan," at Abalessa, included at least three impressions of coins of Constantine the Great as well as jewelry and other objects of eastern Roman style which date probably from between the fourth and sixth centuries. Surprising as it may seem, Roman coins were still in circulation less than sixty years ago in some of the commercial centers of the northern central desert. Indeed the common North African word for small change, *floos,* is merely a corruption of the Latin *follis.*

The Arab invasions of the seventh and eleventh centuries must have displaced many tribes and even whole confederations of pre-Islamic Saharan nomads, and at the same time overrun and engulfed to some extent the sedentary communities of negroid agriculturists, Jewish artisans, and Berber refugees in and around many oases and trading centers of the northern desert. As early as the second quarter of the eighth century Arab expeditions from Morocco were already marching southward to seek gold in "the land of the Negroes." In the tenth and eleventh centuries, the nomadic Berber peoples of the western half of the Sahara seem to have expanded with a suddenness and force that carried them northward through Morocco and into Spain, as the Almoravides, and southward, under the name of Zaghawa, into the Sudan. The fact that the word Almoravide is a Spanish corruption of the Arabic *mrabteen,* meaning holy men of Islam, suggests that it was the massive shock of Arab invasion and the resulting turmoil of conflicting cultures which set off this explosion. But in spite of such dramatic shiftings of populations, the Saharan peoples in general seem to have been but little affected in their ways of life except by the gradual and usually very superficial spread of Arabic language and Moslem religious doctrine.

During the Middle Ages as a whole, trans-Saharan trade seems to have become increasingly lively. Sugar, cloth, brassware, coral, books, horses, and many other things were shipped southward in exchange not only for slaves and gold dust, but also ivory and ostrich feathers, "Morocco" leather, civet, and even occasional live civet cats. The channels of this trade passed through the various Saharan oases and commercial centers, and these in turn exported their own local products such as dates, ostrich feathers, and a few manufactured articles of gold. Indeed, as early as the eleventh century merchants from Barbary and the Mzab were frequenting the slave market of Kumbi, the capital of the original Ghana, which lay between the Niger and the headwaters of the Senegal.

Striking evidence of the ease with which merchants moved in all directions at this time is to be found in the diary of a famous Moroccan traveler, Abou Abdallah Mohammed ibn Battuta, of Tangier, who set out in 1352 to visit the Sudan. Before venturing into the desert wilderness, he stopped off for a few days at a town on the northwestern edge of the Sahara, where he stayed with a learned man whose traveling merchant brother he had known some years before in China, possibly at Foochow on the coast opposite Formosa. Continuing southward he then crossed the western desert to Teghaza, which he found to be "an unattractive village, with the curious feature that its houses and mosques are built of blocks of salt, roofed with camel skins," and he added, "There are no trees there, nothing but sand. We passed ten days of discomfort there, because the water is brackish and the place is plagued with flies." From Teghaza, Ibn Battuta went on to Timbuctoo and Gao, through country which was then all under Tuareg control. In 1353 he left Gao with a caravan that included a singularly disagreeable commercial traveler from Barbary, several merchants recently arrived from Ghadamès, and six hundred Negro slave women. The exact route followed has been much disputed, but it seems to have led south-eastward and then eastward along the northern border of Nigeria to a place called Tagadda (the modern Tegguidda, or Tedjidda, a hundred miles northwest of Agadès), and from there northward through the Air to In Azaoua (three hundred odd miles north of Agadès). Here the trail divided, one branch leading eastward into Egypt and the other northward through the Ahaggar, and then northwestward through the Mouydir and Tidikelt to Bouda (twelve miles west of Adrar) in the Touat, and finally to Morocco.

The first European who is known to have crossed the Sahara in post-Roman times was a Frenchman from Toulouse, named Anselm d'Isalguiers (or Ysalguiers), who left home in 1402 and traveled to the Niger Bend by unknown means. There he married a Songhai princess of Gao, and returned northward with her right across the desert, accompanied by their infant daughter and six Negro slaves. In 1413 the whole party at last reached Toulouse, where one of the slaves, a eunuch named Aben Ali according to the story, established himself in medical practice using West African "witch doctor" methods. A few years later when the French Dauphin, Charles, who was destined to be crowned as Charles VII by Joan of Arc, fell seriously ill while visiting Toulouse, the doctor-slave cured him and was richly rewarded in consequence.

In 1447 a Genoese traveling merchant, named Antonio Malfante, sent home a report from the Touat stating that he had landed at a seaport on the coast of western Algeria, and had gone on from there southward across the desert with a grain caravan as far as Tamentit. He reported that the population of the Touat was largely negroid, but that trade was mainly in the hands of the Jews while nomadic Tuareg tribes controlled the open country. Dates were the staple food, meat of any kind was a great luxury, and grain had to be brought in by caravan. Copper was imported from Alexandria to be traded to the south for salt and Sudanese gold. There was also an active local trade in camels and cattle; but since the cattle seem not to have been eaten ordinarily, presumably they were kept for milk. The merchants of Tamentit must have constituted a highly privileged class, for the normal profit margin in transactions of all kinds was at least a hundred per cent. Malfante wrote that he was the first Christian ever seen in the Touat; but where he went from there or what finally became of him remains a mystery.

During the first half of the fifteenth century the Portuguese, under the leadership of Prince Henry the Navigator, established a series of commercial outposts in what is now the Spanish Sahara, and began to extend their trading operations southward along the coast beyond. By 1448 they had built up a flourishing slave trade all along the Atlantic coast of West Africa, from Rio de Oro to the mouth of the Senegal River. About this time they also established regular commercial relations with the western desert trading center of Ouadane, where the Tuareg supplied them with slaves in exchange for horses, silk and "other merchandise." Weapons doubtless figured prominently among the "other merchandise," for many Tuareg swords that are preserved in collections, as well as a few still in use among the modern Tuareg, bear the marks of sixteenth- and seventeenth-century German bladesmiths of Solingen and Passau, as well as those of the royal swordsmiths of Spain which were so freely copied in both Germany and northern Italy, and even in the Sudan.[2] Apparently the Tuareg still trade for European sword blades now and then, for in 1955 I saw one, bearing a late nineteenth-century dated mark of the Spanish Royal Arsenal of Toledo, in the workshop of the smiths at Tamanrasset in the Ahaggar. Cheap copies, often with forged European marks, have long been made and still are made occasionally by Saharan and particularly Sudanese smiths, both for the Tuareg and for the tourist trade.

Foreigners other than the Portuguese were also active during the fifteenth century in developing commercial relations with

[2] A Tuareg sword in my own collection bears on its blade the inscription: VIVA EL REY DE PORTUGAL. Sir James G. Mann, Keeper of the Armouries of Her Majesty's Tower of London, agrees with me that the style of the lettering and the form and quality of the blade alike suggest that it was made at Solingen in the seventeenth century.

the peoples of the southwestern Sahara and the western Sudan. A commercial agent of the great Florentine merchant house of the Portinari, a man named Benedetto Dei, is the first European known to have reached Timbuctoo, where he arrived in 1470 and set up shop as a dealer in cloth imported from Lombardy. And at that time there was already a system of regular and direct caravan connections between Timbuctoo and Fez in Morocco, Tunis, and even Cairo. El Hassan ibn Mohammed (better known as "Leo Africanus"),[3] wrote in the early sixteenth century that commercial agents from Algiers and Bougie, on the Mediterranean coast, were in the habit of meeting and trading in the Mzab with merchants from Timbuctoo.

Intellectual exchange across the desert naturally increased along with the development of commercial intercourse. From the early Middle Ages onward, traveling Moslem scholars of the north kept their Saharan colleagues in touch fairly regularly with the rest of the Moslem world and even with countries far beyond its boundaries. Men like El Bekri, Ibn Battuta, Ibn Khaldoun, and many others, wandered about freely for years over tremendous distances. The surprising ease with which they traveled was made possible by the fact that they could read and write, whereas most of the populations that they visited could not. Because the Koran is written in Arabic, pious Moslems look on Arabic writing as more or less sacred, while some of them go so far as to think it a grievous sin to tear up or even crumple up a piece of paper which has been written upon—in Arabic of course. This reverence for writing is automatically extended to the writer, so that even a mediocre Arabic scholar is looked on as a holy man of sorts. Every door is open to him, and there is a place for him at every table and in every caravan. In addition, scholars

[3] Leo Africanus was an Arab, originally named El Hassan ibn Mohammed el Wezzan (but also known as "El Fasi," meaning "the man from Fez"), who was born at Granada about 1490, and a few years later accompanied his parents into exile in Morocco. When about twenty-five years old he was captured at sea by a Christian pirate from Sicily, Pietro Bovadiglia, who gave him as a present to Pope Leo X, a son of Lorenzo the Magnificent. Two years later the Pope freed him, converted him to Christianity, baptized him Giovanni Leone (the Pope's own name), and put him on a pension because of his remarkable knowledge of African geography.

who achieved even minor reputations were usually adopted by patrons, just as European scholars were in the days of Rome's greatness and in the Middle Ages and the Renaissance; such patrons often paid for travel in the interests of pure scholarship as well as for the gathering of political and commercial intelligence. Another factor which facilitated travel in those days, and which has generally escaped notice, is the degree to which banking facilities were developed throughout the Moslem world. Ibn Battuta, for example, was able, in the middle of the fourteenth century, to have a sum of money sent all the way from India to Meknès in Morocco.

While Barbary continued to influence the Sahara intellectually more and more, from at least as early as the twelfth century onward, European commercial influence also became increasingly important during the fifteenth and sixteenth centuries. During the closing years of the sixteenth century, however, the economic situation began to change again, chiefly because of two new factors which came into being at that time. In the first place, the discovery of the Americas, whose undreamed of riches apparently were available within easy reach of even the humblest adventurer, quickly turned the attention of European speculators away from the comparatively negligible profits of Saharan trade. For the same reason, trans-Saharan trade with the Sudan fell off sharply, as Sudanese gold quickly lost much of its previously almost unique charm, and as slave traders discovered that it was often more profitable to deliver their merchandise to New World buyers on the Guinea Coast than it had been to ship it northward into and across the desert. And, in the second place, while all this was going on, Morocco entered a period of rapid economic growth.

Under the Moroccan Sultan Moulay Ahmed el Mansour, the pressure generated by new-found prosperity led in turn to the organizing of a series of expeditions designed first to capture the commerce and particularly the salt trade of the southwestern Sahara, and then to establish Moroccan control over the great commercial centers of the Niger Bend. In 1590 a huge army was assembled under the command of Judar Pasha, a blue-eyed

Spanish eunuch [4] from Andalusia, who had been captured in infancy and brought up in the royal palace at Marrakech. Judar's forces, made up mostly of Moslems but including also a few Christian renegades, are said to have numbered two thousand cavalry, a camel corps of a thousand mounted men, two thousand infantry, six hundred engineers, and a baggage train of a thousand horses and eight thousand camels. Artillery support was included in the shape of six large cannon and "various smaller pieces" which, together with the ammunition for them, had been obtained from England in exchange for sugar and saltpeter. The gunners were mostly British sailors. Water for the expedition was carried on camelback in bullock skins.

Judar crossed the Sahara, losing perhaps as much as two thirds of his army along the way, and finally reached the Niger on February 28, 1591. After destroying a Sudanese army, which greatly outnumbered his own forces, he entered Gao unopposed and found there, among many other odds and ends, some Portuguese cannon, a crucifix, and a statue of the Virgin. He then turned west to Timbuctoo, where again his entry was unopposed.

As a result of Judar's victorious campaign, trade between the western Sudan and Barbary remained under effective Moroccan control until 1610, when the last of the Moroccan military governors was driven out by a revolt of his own officers. The bulk of the Moroccan troops, however, stayed on in the Sudan after this uprising, and proceeded to elect their own local pashas in an attempt to establish themselves as independent rulers of the area. But soon they became more and more mixed with the local population, and thereby lost not only their tight military organization but also the prestige of glamour and fear of the unknown that had clothed the original Moroccan conquerors from across

---

[4] In our natural horror at the medieval Moslem custom of making eunuchs of exceptionally promising slave boys we should not forget that the same practice was long tolerated in Europe. Bovill (1933) has pointed out that "During the Middle Ages large establishments, mostly under the direction of Jews, were maintained in France, notably at Verdun, for the supply of eunuchs to Muslim Spain," and he adds that "The *Soprani* of the Sistine Chapel, 'the musical glory and moral shame' of the papal choir, were not abolished until late in the nineteenth century, but the gelding of boys continued in Italy for some time after that."

the desert. Out of this new hybrid population there arose a distinct ethnic group, the Arma, who survive to this day.

The western Sudan and the adjoining regions of the southwestern desert were characterized during most of the seventeenth century by a varying state of political chaos, with the Arma, based on Djenné, Timbuctoo, and Gao, exercising a fluctuating and more or less limited control over these commercial centers and the waterways connecting them, and paying tribute now to the Sultan of Morocco, now to the pagan Negro king of the Bambara. But, in spite of this confused state of affairs, trans-Saharan trade between Barbary and the western Sudan flourished unabated, and many merchant houses of Barbary, and Italy as well, continued to maintain resident representatives in Timbuctoo and Gao.

Almost no definite information has survived concerning the relations between the eastern half of the Sahara and the outside world during the thousand years or so that followed the abandonment of the last Roman establishments along the coast of Cyrenaica and Tripolitania, the modern Kingdom of Libya. And yet this very lack of information suggests that the situation there must have been quite different from that which characterized the western desert during the same period. Indeed, it seems that after the final collapse of Roman power in Africa, the eastern desert was cut off almost entirely from outside influence and trade, excepting on the small and strictly limited scale made possible by more or less regular caravan connections with northern Egypt. Although there is no way of knowing how long this state of affairs lasted, it seems likely that more generalized interregional and intercontinental commerce did not begin to assume significant proportions until the seventeenth or early eighteenth century, and that it continued to expand slowly after that.

The trans-Saharan trade of the eastern desert, as it was during the first quarter of the nineteenth century, has been described in some detail by an early British explorer, Captain George Lyon of the Royal Navy. He tells us that the assortment of goods passing southward through the Fezzan, from Tripoli, Cyrenaica, and Egypt to the central Sudan, included cloth, rugs, and garments, sheet tin and tinplated copper vessels, iron and steel tools, needles, swords, and firearms, gunpowder and shot, green leather, and horses. There were many luxury articles too, such as silks, silver and gold thread, embroidered cloth, gold and silver jewelry and cheap trinkets, glass arm bracelets from Venice, beads of china and glass, mirrors, sugar, and perfumes of various kinds, sacred books, and even "handsome girls from Abyssinia, educated in Mecca or Egypt." Northward across the Fezzan there moved slaves ("chiefly female") and ivory, gold, and cotton cloth and garments, leather goods of various kinds including ostrich skins with the feathers still in place, mortars and bowls of wood, civet, pepper, honey, kola nuts, and even live parrots. Lion skins had once been imported, but they were no longer to be had in 1820, "owing," says Lyon, "to the Sultan of Bornou buying them all up for his negresses to sleep on, to prevent their bearing children, as he has already a large family. It is implicitly believed," the author added, "that a woman who sleeps on a lion's skin never can become pregnant." Toward the end of August 1819, Lyon saw a mixed caravan of Arabs and Teda, northward bound from the Sudan, arrive at Mourzouk with "1,400 slaves of both sexes and of all ages, the greater part being females." This seems to have been a perfectly ordinary occurrence. Local exports from the Fezzan itself are said to have been mainly dates, soda (natron), and hairy sheep.

However great the volume and the value of Saharan commerce may have been at various times in different parts of the desert, commercial activity on an important scale was always at the mercy of those warlike tribes through whose territories the main trade routes passed. Although it is not known just when the various nomad confederations of the Sahara first established systematic control over its three main channels of north-south caravan traffic, it is clear that by the sixteenth century the Ajjer [5] Tuareg controlled the eastern route through the Fezzan from Ghat northward, while the Tuareg of the Air controlled its southern extension. The central route, from the

[5] Pronounced Azguer or Azjer, according to the district.

neighborhood of In Salah southward, was in the hands of the Ahaggar Tuareg confederation, while its northern part was under Arab control. The western route too seems to have been under Tuareg control at times, although to exactly what extent it is difficult to say. Eventually it fell into the hands of the Tadjakant and finally the Moors, but for a long time thereafter it still remained more or less subject to Tuareg raids designed to force payment of tribute or to obtain plunder when payment was not forthcoming. And the Niger Bend country, the southern terminus of the great western trans-Saharan caravans, suffered so regularly from raids of the southwestern Tuareg, who were being driven farther and farther southward by the expansion of their Arab nomad neighbors, that it was under almost constant Tuareg domination for all practical purposes from the early seventeenth century until the early twentieth.

During the seventeenth and eighteenth centuries life in the Sahara seems to have flowed along monotonously and with very little change, aside from the local territorial reshufflings and minor shifts of power which always go on unendingly between nomadic tribes. But the dawn of the nineteenth century marked the beginning of a completely new phase of Saharan history, the era of modern European penetration. In September 1798, a young German named Frederick Horneman left Cairo, with orders from the British "African Association" [6] to cross the desert to the Niger River. Traveling westward along the pilgrim road with a commercial caravan, he arrived in November at Mourzouk, in the Fezzan (westward Libya). Both he and his interpreter promptly came down with malaria, however, and the interpreter died. Horneman stayed on for several months, recovering his strength and gathering information, and then went north to Tripoli to send off a preliminary report. He returned to Mourzouk in January 1800, and, in April, dispatched a letter saying that he was about to leave with a caravan for the Sudan. Nothing more was ever heard from him, however, and he was given up for dead. It was not until nineteen years later

[6] The official name of this organization, founded in 1788, was The Society Instituted for Exploring the Interior of Africa.

that Captain Lyon met in Mourzouk a native merchant who had been a friend of Horneman, and who told of how they had gone south together with a caravan and had indeed reached the Niger; but Horneman had died there before he could send back news of his success.

In 1818 the British Government sent an expedition southward from Tripoli under the command of a civilian named Ritchie, who was accompanied by Captain Lyon and by John Belford, a ship's carpenter from the British naval base at Malta. Shortly after the expedition reached Mourzouk all three came down with dysentery and fever (probably malaria); Ritchie died, and Lyon took over the command. But repeated illness and lack of funds unfortunately made it impossible for the survivors to go more than about two hundred miles beyond Mourzouk, and so finally they were obliged to return to Tripoli in the spring of 1820. Even though this expedition turned out to be something of a fiasco, Lyon's report remains one of the very best sources of miscellaneous information concerning life in western Libya as it was then.

A second British Government expedition, headed by an Army officer, Major Dixon Denham, and including Lieutenant Hugh Clapperton, Dr. Walter Oudney, and a shipwright named William Hillman, all of the Royal Navy, arrived at Mourzouk from Tripoli in the fall of 1822. This expedition was stronger in numbers and also much better equipped than the previous ones had been, and it soon added to its strength a considerable retinue, including two highly picturesque persons who today would be called "service specialists." The first of these was "Columbus," the interpreter and majordomo, "who spoke three European languages and perfect Arabic." His real name was Adolphus Sympkins, and he had run away in boyhood from his island home in the West Indies to see the world. The second quaint recruit was "Jacob, a Gilbraltar Jew, who was a sort of store-keeper." As the expedition drew near Mourzouk, Jacob, who was riding some distance ahead on his white mule, reached the city gates before the rest of the party came in sight, and "was received with great respect by the inhabitants." In Major Denham's words, "He very sensibly received all their attentions in silence, and drank the cool water and milk which was handed to him; and we always had the laugh against them afterwards for having shown so much civility to an Israelite—a race they heartily despise. 'We thought the English,' said they, 'were better looking than the Jews—Death to their race! but then God made us all, though not all handsome like Mussulmans are, so who could tell?' "

Denham describes Mourzouk as a hotbed of disease, where "amongst the inhabitants themselves, anything like a healthy looking person was a rarity." Apparently endemic malaria was still the principal complaint. In any case, all the British members of the party promptly came down with dysentery, and all, excepting Denham himself, were soon delirious with fever too. Late in November, when they were again strong enough to travel, the expedition got under way at last and, on February 4, 1823, came in sight of "the great lake Tchad, glowing in the golden rays of the sun in its strength." A base camp was soon established on the southwestern shore of the Lake, in a little town called Kouka or, more correctly, Kukawa (pronounced Kōokawa). Here the party was joined in December by Ensign Toole of the British Army, and in April 1824, by a Mr. Tyrwhitt, each of whom had come all the way across the desert from Tripoli alone.

From Kukawa the various members of the expedition made a series of adventurous and valuable reconnaissance excursions in several directions, the most notable being Clapperton's journey westward through Kano to Sokoto; but the cost was high. Everyone, except the apparently indestructible Major Denham, fell ill repeatedly, and Oudney and Toole died. In August 1824, Denham, Clapperton, and Hillman finally decided to return to Tripoli, leaving Tyrwhitt behind in the role of British Consul to look after the interests of the eager English merchants who, it was hoped, would soon begin to swarm into the Sudan. But Tyrwhitt died barely two months after the departure of his companions; and no English merchants came to Kukawa after all.

The Denham-Clapperton expedition seems to have found the eastern central Sahara in a state of unusal political stability, for not only did the main party cross the desert almost without incident, except for illness, but Toole and Tyrwhitt, each traveling alone, apparently met with even fewer difficulties. The relatively ample funds with which this expedition was provided probably did much to smooth the way. And it is obvious that the hostility of some of the more powerful local chieftains, notably the Sultan of Mourzouk, was overcome thanks to the great personal influence of that legendary figure, Colonel Hanmer Warrington, who was British Consul General at Tripoli from 1814 to 1846. But one gets the distinct impression that the relative safety of the eastern Sahara at that time was due primarily to increased prosperity, resulting from the growth of trans-Saharan trade between the Mediterranean and the Sudan.

The next European explorer to attempt to cross the Sahara was a Scottish officer in the British Army, Major Alexander Gordon Laing, who left Tripoli in 1825 to reach the Niger by a more westerly route. Traveling with one caravan after another he passed through Ghadamès, In Salah, and the Touat, and had almost reached his goal when his party was attacked in their sleep by a band of raiders. The presence of a Christian European in the caravan so enraged these bandits that they beat him to death, or so they thought, before departing with their booty. Laing's companions finally revived him, however, tied him on the back of his riding camel, and took him on with them to Timbuctoo. Here he recovered gradually, thanks to his great physical strength and also, in great part, to the attentive care of a resident merchant from Tripoli in whose house he stayed.

After exploring and mapping the city and some of the surrounding countryside, Laing finally left Timbuctoo with a northbound caravan, but after only three days' march he fell into the hands of a band of Arab nomads. The nomad chief, a fiercely fanatical old man, tried to force Laing to accept Islam and acknowledge his conversion by repeating the ritual formula: "There is no other god than God, and Mohammed is God's Messenger." Over and over again Laing repeated: "There is no other god than God," but he would go no further. And so at last the old chief, in desperation, had two Negro slaves strangle him with a

53

turban cloth. Such is the story of Major Laing as it was told at Timbuctoo in later years by natives who had seen him there; but extracts from his own letters, published in 1828 and 1829 in the *Quarterly Review* of London, gave a version which is slightly different though no less gruesomely romantic.[7]

In the spring of 1827 a young Frenchman, named René Caillié (often misspelled Caillé), set off for Timbuctoo from the Rio Nuñez, on the Atlantic coast of what is now French Guinea. Although he was only twenty-seven years old, Caillié had already spent more than ten years wandering about in the coastal regions of West Africa, and he was also thoroughly familiar with the adventures and misfortunes of previous explorers in West Africa in general and in the Sahara too. He fully understood the dangers that awaited him, and so his courage was more than usually admirable. Caillié was not foolhardy, however, nor did he run unnecessary risks; and so he took the very sensible precaution of inventing an ingenious and convincing excuse for his journey. Claiming to be an Arab and a descendant of the Prophet, he spread the word that he was born in Egypt, but that Napoleon's army had gathered him up in infancy and carried him off to slavery in France. Recently, he explained, his French master had taken him along on a trading trip to the Senegal, and there had set him free as a reward for faithful service. Now, according to his story, his dearest wish was to go back to his Egyptian home; and the most natural way to get there was, of course, by way of Timbuctoo and the pilgrim road across the eastern desert. This false autobiography worked literally "like a charm," for it made it possible

---

[7] The whole truth will probably be known only after someone has been able to decipher and digest two enormous bundles of Laing's letters and other related documents which E. W. Bovill has just discovered in the Public Records Office, London (catalogue numbers C.O. 2/15 and 2/20 and F.O. 76/22), where they seem to have lain practically unnoticed for the last hundred and thirty years! There is also a rumor that a detailed report of Laing's adventures and murder, made verbally by his native servant to the French Consul at Mogador (on the Atlantic coast of Morocco), has been preserved in French Government archives, but its exact whereabouts have not yet been discovered. And other pertinent archives are presently in the process of being transferred from Tripoli to the Public Records Office.

for Caillié to pose successfully as a poor but devout and moderately learned Moslem, even though he spoke very little Arabic. Unquestionably it saved his life on a number of occasions.

Caillié, together with a little party of native porters and servants, traveled inland by a roundabout southern route to Djenné on the Niger, where he arrived in March 1828. Here he left his retinue and took to the river, in a huge dugout canoe full of slaves which brought him to Timbuctoo at last toward the end of April. Thanks to his false identity, and to his naturally alert and cautious nature, he was able to wander about the city freely and examine even the interiors of the mosques without arousing any dangerous suspicions.

Although the commercial importance of Timbuctoo had fallen off badly since the days of Moroccan domination, apparently it was still considerable; for Caillié noted the presence of numerous merchants who continued to receive their stock regularly by caravan from Morocco, Algiers, Tunis, and Tripoli, as well as from such intermediate trading centers as Adrar and Ghadamès. He remarked too that "diverse merchandise" were imported in quantity from Europe, and that double-barreled guns from France were particularly prized. This flow of imports from the north was balanced by the export of Sudanese products, the most important of which continued to be slaves and gold.

After two weeks at Timbuctoo, Caillié started homeward across the desert, with a caravan of Moors who proceeded to make his life miserable. "They are the most barbarous men I know," he wrote, "and the most insufferable beggars in the world." Fortunately, however, he was soon able to leave them and join another party. And in this way he continued northward, changing caravans from time to time, until he reached the northwestern edge of the desert in late July. Early in September Caillié arrived in Tangier, where the French Consul hid him until he could be smuggled aboard a schooner of the French Navy which took him to Toulon. After visiting Paris, where he received a most enthusiastic welcome together with all the honors and rewards he so richly deserved, Caillié returned at last to his home town in western France, and was elected mayor. But fever he had caught in Africa never left him; and he died ten years later, at the age of thirty-eight.

Of all the heroic pioneer explorers of the Sahara and the neighboring Sudan, Heinrich Barth, a young German, was certainly the most important; for not only did he travel far more widely than had any of his predecessors, but he kept a minutely detailed journal and a sketchbook the whole time, and he managed to get out alive with them. Barth had already spent three years exploring the lands that lie along the southern and eastern shores of the Mediterranean, and had only just settled down to the peaceful life of a young professor at Berlin University when he received an invitation to join the latest trans-Saharan expedition to be sponsored by the British Government. He accepted with alacrity. The civilian leader of the expedition, James Richardson, had been to Ghat and so was already a hardened desert traveler too, but the third member of the party, a young German geologist named Adolph Overweg, was a happy-go-lucky, often thoughtless tenderfoot. As Barth rather bitterly remarked: "Having never risked his life on a dangerous expedition, he never for a moment doubted that it might not be his good fortune to return home in safety."

The party set out from Tripoli in March 1850, with great quantities of baggage and equipment including, of all things, a large wooden boat which had been cut in two to make it less difficult to carry. Barth wrote in his journal that, "After a great deal of trouble, we at length succeeded in making a start," which was a masterpiece of both brevity and understatement. The sad truth of the matter is that the party was split from the beginning into two uncongenial groups which had as little contact with each other as possible. During the daytime Barth and Overweg rode ahead, followed at a considerable distance by Richardson and a sailor who had been sent along to handle the boat. At night the two groups settled down in separate camps.

Proceeding in this painfully formal and inconvenient manner the expedition arrived at Mourzouk in May, and was welcomed by a Mr. Gagliuffi who is identified in Barth's journal only as

"H.M.'s agent and our host." [8] Although Gagliuffi had formal orders to assist in every way possible, he seems to have been so devious and so greedy that he only complicated still further the pattern of unnecessary delays, tedious dickering, and general frustration that had already been established. And the sailor, who had been an unpleasant traveling companion from the start, became so completely unbearable that Richardson had to send him back to Tripoli.

After five exasperating weeks at Mourzouk the expedition set off once more, this time along the pilgrim road used by pious natives of the western desert on their way to and from Mecca. Word had been sent ahead that they were coming, and so they were soon met and warmly greeted by an old and famous chief of the Ajjer Tuareg, Hatita, who had been helpful to both the Ritchie-Lyon and Denham-Clapperton expeditions many years before. Hatita escorted them as far as Ghat (where they arrived in the middle of July), and gave them much valuable information and advice as they sat around their evening camp fires along the way. After a few days of dickering at Ghat, Barth and his companions managed to make arrangements to continue southward with a small Tuareg caravan which accompanied them into the Air. There the expedition separated, Richardson heading directly for Lake Chad while the two Germans set off together and then separated in their turn, to explore more westerly approaches to the Lake. Barth finally reached Kukawa from Kano early in April 1851, and learned that Richardson had died the previous month only a few miles from their appointed meeting place. In May Overweg arrived, from Zinder, and proceeded to explore the Lake in the boat which he had kept with him ever since leaving Mourzouk. But he too died, in September 1852, at the age of twenty-nine.

After several extended reconnaissance trips into the country farther south, Barth left Kukawa late in November and returned

---

[8] James Richardson, who had come to know Gagliuffi well in the course of an earlier expedition, wrote that he was an Austrian, born in Trieste, and was for many years British Vice-Consul at Mourzouk. On this earlier occasion Richardson had found him most kindly and obliging.

to Kano. From there he followed Clapperton's route westward to Sokoto, crossed the Niger, and, turning northward, came at last to Timbuctoo in September 1853. Even though he was suffering much of the time from fever and dysentery, Barth managed to explore the city and its surroundings with all his customary thoroughness. His position was made dangerously difficult, however, by the attitude of the inhabitants, most of whom found the presence of a Christian so offensive that he had to move out and camp in the open country several miles away on a number of occasions, often for several days or even weeks. In fact he would surely have been killed had it not been known that he was well equipped with modern firearms and ammunition. One day Barth and a semi-religious chief, who had become his local patron and protector, found themselves surrounded by a crowd of inquisitive and sullen townsfolk, whereupon the chief persuaded Barth to fire off all six chambers of his revolver into the air. According to the journal, this startling display of force "caused extraordinary excitement and astonishment among the people, and exercised a great influence upon my future safety, as it made them believe that I had arms all over my person, and could fire as many times as I liked."

Barth found Timbuctoo somewhat more prosperous than it was at the time of Caillié's visit, although still by no means the great emporium that it had been in the sixteenth century and before. Gold continued to be exported on a substantial scale, but the tremendous slave trading operations of former days had shrunk to relatively insignificant proportion. European cloth, Moroccan tobacco, and Saharan dates were still imported in considerable quantities, however; and the journal suggests, surprisingly enough, that German sword blades were still being imported. In short it is evident that Timbuctoo did not lose its somewhat unstable but always dominant position as the main southern terminus of trans-Saharan trade until less than a century ago.

Barth left Timbuctoo at last in March 1854, and began working his way back by easy stages toward Lake Chad. On the last day of November he had reached a point some ninety miles be-

yond Kano when suddenly there appeared out of the jungle a
blond stranger riding in the opposite direction. By this time any
European face would have been a heart-warming sight, and
Barth was naturally overjoyed to find that this one belonged to
a fellow-countryman, the young and energetic Dr. Vogel. To
quote once more from the journal, they "rushed forward, and,
taken by surprise as both of us were, we gave each other a hearty
reception from horseback." Then, "In the midst of this inhospitable forest, we dismounted and sat down together on the
ground; and my camels having arrived, I took out my small bag
of provisions, and had some coffee boiled, so that we were quite
at home." Vogel explained that he had been sent out from Tripoli
to replace Barth, whom everyone had now given up as dead, and
to make contact if possible with an expedition which was attempting to reach Lake Chad from the Gulf of Guinea. After a brief
discussion of what was to be done now, since Barth was not dead
after all, it was decided that he would go on to Kukawa and
wait there, while Vogel would continue as far as Zinder and
then return to join him.

On arriving at Kukawa, Barth found two young combat engineers of the British Army, Corporal Church and Private Maguire, who had come south from Tripoli with Vogel. And once
again the painful problem of conflicting personalities arose, for
it turned out that Vogel and Maguire didn't get along any too
well, while Church was on very bad terms with both of them.
Vogel returned from Zinder two days after Christmas, and, a
month later, set off alone to explore the lower Niger. He was
never seen again.

In May 1855, Barth left Kukawa for the last time, taking
Church with him and leaving Maguire behind to wait for Vogel.
After an uneventful homeward journey, via Mourzouk and Tripoli, Barth arrived at last in London on September 6. Incredible
as it may seem his return was not even mentioned in the news-
papers! The unfortunate Maguire waited patiently at Kukawa
for nearly a year, until he received news of Vogel's death, and
then he too set off for home. But he had gone only a little over
a hundred miles when a band of desert raiders met and murdered

him, beside the desert well of Bedwaram. So ended the most remarkable expedition in the history of European exploration in the Sahara and the Sudan, an expedition whose success was due almost entirely to the courage and extraordinary single-mindedness of one man, Heinrich Barth. Acting largely on his own initiative, in the face of innumerable difficulties and every imaginable sort of danger, he carried through to a successful conclusion a program far exceeding that which had been assigned to him. No other explorer working in the same area, either before or since, ever managed to do so much so well.

The foregoing brief summary of Saharan history, though very far from complete, brings out the following important points. The Sahara as a whole has never really been the land of impenetrable mystery, the vast, unknown, and culturally stagnant wilderness that so many seem to have believed. From prehistoric times it has continuously harbored settlements of sedentary gardeners and artisans as well as countless tribes of nomadic hunters and herdsmen, and it has for ages been crisscrossed by a constant flow of commercial traffic between the lands adjacent on the north and south, and, to an only slightly less extent, between the east and west. If there are no very full descriptions dating from much more than a century ago, it is doubtless only because commerce and commerce alone was of interest to the Europeans who visited the area before then. It is indeed surprising that there is so much early source material available, enough in fact to make it possible to see the Sahara as a living scene, a stage on which one can observe the constant activity and interplay of the various human populations which, with the dawn of the fifteenth century, begin to emerge from the mists of antiquity and to assume the features of their modern descendants.

Another important point to remember is that foreign domination is not an exclusively modern phenomenon in the Sahara. Foreign control over the eastern desert has seldom if ever been as extensive or effective as it seems to have been in the days of the Persians and the Romans. Even the great Arab invasions of the eleventh century appear to have left only relatively superficial and essentially formal religious traces among the native peoples of that area. Turkish rule was loosely established over much of the eastern Sahara during most of the nineteenth century, but came to an end with the Italian conquest of Tripolitania in 1913. During the second half of the nineteenth century the French gradually extended their sphere of influence farther and farther southward across the western desert until, in 1905, they at last brought the warlike Tuareg nomads of the Ahaggar under full control. In 1916, however, Turkish and German agents persuaded the Senoussi to lead the nomads of the central Sahara generally in a revolt against the Italians and the French. From then on sporadic fighting continued throughout the central desert until the end of the First World War, after which the prewar situation was gradually restored and so continued, very little changed except for slowly increasing stability, until the Second World War, when the Italians were thrown out of Africa by the British drive westward from Egypt and the northward drive of Free French forces from the central Sudan.

The extension of European influence and the maintenance of European administrative authority have been enormously facilitated, of course, by the increasingly rapid introduction and expansion of modern transportation. The first railroad connection between the Mediterranean coast and the Sahara proper was established in 1906, when a line from Oran was pushed down to Colomb-Béchar in the extreme northwest. In 1922 a second and more central connection was opened up with the extension of the Constantine-Biskra line southward to Touggourt. Regular scheduled trans-Saharan transportation by motor vehicle dates only from 1927, while the first regular civilian airplane service to connect the central desert with the outside world was not established until late in 1952.

Once more I would like to emphasize the fact that the peoples of the Sahara as a whole have never, since pre-Roman times, found themselves completely cut off from their neighbors or from the outside world, but rather have continued to live essentially as they live today, as links in a network of chains of communication, some strictly local, some regional or interregional, and others reaching far beyond the continent of Africa. But the old Saharan social, political, and economic systems are fast breaking down under the combined pressure of mechanized transportation and economic expansion. Frontier boom towns are springing up around the oil wells of the northern central desert, and desert tribesmen are flocking to them, to sleep in air-conditioned huts with running water and eat European food, prepared under the direction of professional dietitians. Teams of prospectors in fleets of jeeps and special desert trucks (equipped with refrigerators and deep-freeze units that use bottle gas) are now combing whole areas where no vehicle of any kind has been seen since the days of chariots. And only a year ago an aristocratic young desert warrior of the Ahaggar Tuareg was observed boarding a northbound plane at Tamanrasset, dressed in a soft felt hat, a jacket of black leather, and blue jeans!

Chapter 3 ~

THE SEDENTARY
POPULATIONS

IT IS AN AXIOM of social science that cities are often centers of power, and this is as true in most of the Sahara as it is anywhere. Minor oases and agricultural centers too are minor foci of power in that they serve as trading centers and supply depots for the nomad tribes of the surrounding country. As Henri Duveyrier pointed out nearly a century ago, such towns are "essential organs of the internal life and external relations of the tribes." Nomads depend on them not only for the procurement of manufactured goods, but also for such things as vegetables and grain, fruit, salt, sugar, tea, and tobacco. Therefore the sedentary peoples of the Sahara should be considered first, for without their help the great Saharan nomad tribes could never operate as such.

Most of the urban and near-urban communities must have sprung originally from simple agricultural centers, such as those which can still be found in the Sahara wherever there is cultivable land and a reliable supply of water sufficient to irrigate it regularly. Hunters and food gatherers, who were of a rough and rugged Mediterranean physical type, probably penetrated the northern half of the western central desert some eight thousand years ago or thereabouts, when conditions were certainly less arid than they now are, although just how much less it is difficult to say. If any of these people had acquired (or invented locally) the primitive beginnings of agriculture, no traces of the fact have been reported, but the possibility of such developments should be borne in mind pending more thorough investigation. Two or three thousand years later, neolithic negroid folk from the Sudan began to spread northward along and perhaps around the southern and southwestern limits of the territory occupied by the earlier mesolithic invaders. Whatever else these neolithic people may have done, they were certainly great hunters and fishermen, for the refuse dumps they left behind are rich in arrowheads and fishhooks and harpoons, in animal bones, and sometimes even in the fragile bones of fish as well. At some stage in their history, some of them at least took to raising cattle as their main means of livelihood, but it is not yet clear whether this development occurred before or after they moved northward from the Sudan into what is now the desert.

The Sahara of early neolithic times was studded with marshes and even shallow marshy lakes of considerable size, often surrounded by Mediterranean varieties of trees and shrubs and inhabited by crocodiles and hippopotami. This climatic optimum slowly degenerated however, as increasingly severe aridity began to spread between and around the ever shrinking areas where surface moisture and readily available ground water remained. The effect on all of the Saharan peoples was apparently rather like that of a creeping flood, for they retired little by little before the advancing and encircling forces of destruction, and sought refuge in the slowly dwindling islands of permanent vegetation. And many of these islands too must have been wiped out, leaving at last only the widely scattered oases and isolated watering points which still survive. It was probably during the closing years of growing attrition, when movement from one fertile refuge area to another had become really difficult and dangerous at last, that fast wheeled vehicles became a virtual necessity of

---

Map 3. The many Berber dialects of the Sahara fall into two main groups—Zenatan in the scattered oases of the northern and central desert and extending sporadically eastward as far as Siwa, and Senhadjan in the Tuareg country. Teda speech is also broken up into numerous dialects, but their relations to each other and their distributions are not yet clearly established.

It is said that Hausa, a member of Greenberg's Afroasiatic (formerly Hamito-Semitic) family of languages, is still spoken generally in Ghadamès, and this doubtless reflects the extremely close ties that many merchant families of that city have maintained for centuries with the Sudan.

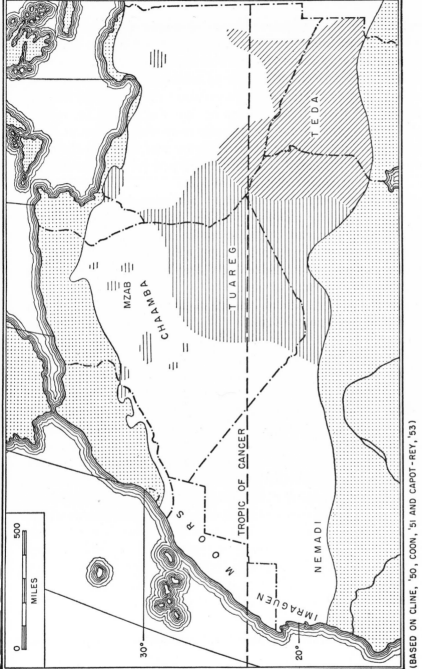

(BASED ON CLINE, '50, COON, '51 AND CAPOT-REY, '53)

MAP 3 THE APPROXIMATE DISTRIBUTION OF LINGUISTIC STOCKS IN THE SAHARA

ARABIC = [ ]   BERBER = [ ]   TEDA = [ ]

REGIONS OUTSIDE THE LIMITS OF THE AREA = [ ]

travel and so were widely adopted. Possibly the domesticated camel first came into general use at the same time, although that remains a moot question for lack of material evidence. But in any case I doubt if either camels or wheeled vehicles were ever used to any great extent by self-sufficient sedentary gardeners, who probably cared little or nothing for what might lie beyond the horizon as they stood gazing out from the security of their little settlements over the barren wastes that hemmed them in. The survivors of the Saharan Stone Age peoples in general seem rather to have achieved a new and stable way of life, based on practically complete immobility and systematic gardening of slowly increasing complexity. They learned in short to relax in the procrustean bed into which climatic circumstances forced them three or four thousand years ago, and in which their children and their children's children have lain in reasonable though frugal comfort ever since.

Most of the agricultural centers of the southern half of the Sahara are still peopled mainly by negroid folk, known as Chouchan,[1] Fezzanese, or Dauada in the eastern and central desert, and in the west as Haratin,[2] a more general term which I will use to encompass them all. Although the neolithic nucleus of this population seems to have been a mixture of slender negroid Sudanese and sturdy white Mediterraneans, varying widely in proportions in various parts of the area, that ancient base has been modified continuously across the ages by increments of many kinds—Berber refugees from the north, bush Negro slaves from south of the Sudan, Sudanese negroid prisoners brought home by desert nomad raiders, and even occasional social or economic outcasts from the Saharan nomad tribes themselves. This is doubtless one reason why the Haratin rarely have a language of their own, but usually speak that of the white group with which they are in most regular and frequent contact.

Physically the Haratin are distinctly negroid, as one would naturally expect, but although they almost always have very dark

[1] Pronounced shooshahn.
[2] Plural, pronounced Harateen. Masculine singular Hartani; feminine singular, Hartania.

skin and very curly or kinky hair, their faces and noses are extremely variable in form. As a rule they are about two inches shorter than the average American, but their arms tend to be relatively long. Most of them are strongly built and yet they often have a worn-out look which makes them appear a good deal older than they really are, probably because of chronic dietary deficiencies. Curiously enough their ABO blood group pattern [3] is quite different from that of any other people of the Sahara or even the Sudan, but resembles rather that of the Pygmies of the western Congo rain forest.

The word Haratin, as commonly used in the desert, carries a connotation of class even more than of race, for these are landless and peaceful Blacks and Browns who work as sharecroppers in the plantation of landlords who are nearly always white and are often warlike nomads. The Haratin gardener's share is theoretically a fifth of the crop, for which reason he is often known in Arabic as a *khamès* or "fifther," but in actual practice it varies greatly according to the region and the kind of crop involved. Land, water, seed, fertilizer, and tools are furnished by the landlord who, however, can seldom keep close track of the variable yearly yield so that the gardener usually gets rather more than he is supposed to. By and large the gardener's actual share runs to somewhere between a third and a half of the total crop; and he seems to be treated rather more generously perhaps among the Berber-speaking tribes than he is among speakers of Arabic.

[3] When blood transfusion first began to be practiced it sometimes had the opposite result from that intended. Sometimes the patient died abruptly and for no apparent reason. Investigation of this phenomenon led to the discovery that the blood of different human beings is not all uniformly the same, and that the blood of one person may contain some element which will cause the blood of another to coagulate. Dozens of different elements have now been identified, and it has been observed that they occur in different percentages among different populations. "Serologists," as students of blood are called, classify related elements together in what they call a "series" (for example, the ABO series and the Rh series, to mention only two), and they describe blood of the B type, for example, as belonging to the "B blood group." The percentages in which various elements occur in a given human population constitute what is known as a "blood group pattern." When two populations are characterized by similar patterns, it suggests the possibility that they may be related.

In theory a Hartani can rise in station, he may even cultivate a plot of previously untilled communal land and so become a landlord himself, but in practice this is rarely possible. In the Arabic-speaking parts of the Sahara, white men of outstanding religious or temporal importance usually seize any land thus brought under cultivation, and the Hartani who made it productive has no effective recourse because of his debased social and economic status. Haratin do, occasionally, manage to rent several separate garden plots at once, and in such cases they may sometimes employ secondary sharecroppers of their own kind, but this is about the limit of material prosperity and socio-economic importance that they can reasonably hope ever to attain.

The more prosperous Haratin live in one-story adobe houses with two or three windowless rooms and a small courtyard that has an open hearth in one corner and a dry latrine in another, sheltered by a screen of long grass, reeds or palm fronds. For the sake of economy these houses are usually built in blocks, of ten or fifteen units in the larger centers. They may belong either to nomads who rent them out, or to successful Haratin who occupy the space they need themselves and rent the rest to less fortunate members of their own class. In the smaller and more remote centers, and especially in summertime, the Haratin often live in *zeribas*,[4] which are cubical or sometimes cylindrical huts made of grass or palm fronds attached to a framework of sticks. Semi-dugouts roofed with branches, brush, and mud, are used occasionally in the central Sahara, while a few of the poorer Haratin sometimes live in miserable little patched up tents pitched on the outskirts of a settlement.

Agricultural centers of the southern desert often have a few tiny shops that offer cloth, salt, sugar, tea, and tobacco, and sometimes simple hardware, cheap perfume, and manufactured leather goods from the Sudan as well. There is always a baker or two, and maybe a tailor somewhere about, and a couple of butchers who ply their trade in the open market place. Any or all of these tradesmen may be local Haratin, but the shopkeepers are more often semi-sedentarized Arabs from the north, while

[4] Pronounced zereebas.

the tailor may be either an Arab or an immigrant Negro from the Sudan.

The Dauada, who live in the eastern central Sahara, seem to differ markedly from the Haratin in general in that they are not servile sharecroppers but apparently independent though sedentary food gatherers, who also practice palm culture and gardening—and livestock breeding on a very modest scale. All of them have been converted to Islam, recently perhaps but thoroughly. Physically they are heavily negroid, and all are said to show painfully striking marks of serious and chronic undernourishment. Nevertheless they are extremely tough, and cover tremendous distances on foot at a quick running-walk, moving through deep sand on tiptoe with their knees slightly bent. The Dauada number only some four hundred souls in all, who, together with a handful of assimilated refugees from neighboring nomadic tribes, are settled in tiny clusters of zeribas on the shores of three small and very salty lakes in the Erg Oubari, sixty odd miles northwest of Mourzouk. It is said that some of them were nomads once upon a time, and even fairly recently they were notorious as robbers of passing caravans. Socially they are organized in clans based on descent from common ancestors, but these kinship units, and the various regional groupings too, despise and avoid each other. Indeed the Dauada seem to have no feeling of over-all solidarity, nor, apparently, any kind of clear-cut socio-political organization above the level of the clan. It is at least possible that they may have some kind of tribal system, grouping together perhaps clans that live in a single village, or in adjoining villages, but not enough is known about the situation to be sure. The preferred form of marriage is between the children of brothers, a custom which fosters fragmentation of the community as a whole.

The Dauada still have a few camels and sheep, together with small though more substantial numbers of goats, donkeys, and chickens. But by far their most important economic resource, both for local consumption and external trade, is a primitive kind of proto-shrimp (*Artemia salina*), about an eighth of an inch long, which flourishes so abundantly in their little lakes that the water actually looks pink at times. Known locally as *dood,* an Arabic word for "worms," these tiny creatures have given their name to the Dauada, a name which means literally "wormers" or "wormermen" (as one would say "fishers" or "fishermen"). Shrimp are gathered the year around by women, or sometimes men, working usually in groups; but no woman who is menstruating is allowed to take part in this activity. The fishers wade along knee-deep in the water, parallel to the shore, with sleeve-shaped nets made of cheap European cloth which they swing in front of them, much as a farmer swings a scythe when cutting hay. Shrimping, gardening, and the weaving of reed mats appear to be primarily women's work while the men look after the livestock and also weave floppy baskets. Neither pottery nor cloth is manufactured locally. In general the Dauada seem to be a basically Haratin people who have become highly specialized occupationally in response to a very special kind of local opportunity, a practically inexhaustible supply of shrimp. And that is about all that can be said about the Dauada; for they are one of those humble, colorless, and rather unattractive little groups which pass almost unnoticed in the presence of relatively spectacular and interesting neighbors, in this case warlike pastoral nomads and rich merchants of the caravan trade.

Most southern agricultural communities of the Sahara include two or three families of smiths, settled in hovels or in some abandoned building beyond the outskirts of the village, a mile or two away from the market place. They are known as *Maalmin* to speakers of Arabic, as *Duti* to the Teda of the Tibesti, as *Enaden* among the Tuareg, and, in the Spanish Sahara, as *Majarreros.* Groups of gypsy-like people of much the same kind are found scattered clear across the Moslem world, from the Atlantic Ocean to Baluchistan; such are the Sulaba (or Sleyb) and the Sunna of Arabia, and the Doms of the Baluchi country just west of the lower Indus Valley. Some are found even among the Berber mountaineers of the Moroccan Rif. Throughout all this vast area their economic function and social position remain essentially the same, and they are always more or less negroid or at least are said to be, but unfortunately no good physical description or series of photographs of them has been published. Their history too is uniformly obscure, although one does find occasional hints that some of them may have enjoyed an unexpected degree of importance in the past. Kano, in northern Nigeria, for instance, is said to have been founded in the tenth century, or thereabouts, by a tribe of smiths who were known as the Abagazawa.

The smiths have a monopoly of the local production of iron, copper, and brass ware, and of the manufacture and decoration of articles of wood. They are also the jewelers, tinkers, tanners, and makers of sandals, and their womenfolk do fancy leatherwork. As is often the case with smiths and tinkers throughout the world, there is something faintly yet frighteningly supernatural about them; for they are makers of amulets and charms, brewers of insidious concoctions, and casters of powerful spells. They are also professional hunters in the southeastern desert. Despised, and at the same time feared, they live apart from the community, but come and go as they please. They fight rarely if ever, and no one dares molest them. Usually they speak the language of the group with which they are in most frequent contact.

As one moves northward into the central zone of the Sahara, the agricultural situation changes. There are fewer and fewer agricultural centers proper as the oasis gardens become increasingly accessory elements in the primarily commercial economy of desert trading centers. The landlords in such places are usually Arabs, many of them sedentary oasis dwellers whose primary functions are those of merchants and investors of accumulated capital. Roughly a half to two thirds of the gardening population in most places is made up of negroid Haratin, but one also finds sedentarized white or faintly negroid Zenatan Berbers owning and tilling the soil together with their Haratin *khamès* helpers. This intimacy in work naturally breeds social intimacy, and so there is always much interbreeding wherever two such groups find themselves in daily contact.

Only a very few Zenata have ever been examined physically and so not much can be said about their racial characteristics.

7 I

They seem most often to be of medium height and rather slender in build, with small heads and faces, and narrow shoulders and hips. Their hair is almost always very dark brown or black and their eyes usually are too, but in most other respects they are extremely variable. Their ABO blood group pattern suggests that they may be related to both the northern Berbers and the Negroes of the western Sudan. Thus what little physical evidence is available seems to support the generally accepted theory that the Zenata of today are descended from a mixture of early immigrants from Barbary, Haratin survivors of the neolithic population of the Sahara, and Negro slaves or freedmen of Sudanese extraction. Socially and economically they occupy an intermediate position between the lowly Haratin and the lowest level of the sedentary Arab landlord class.

The function of gardeners in the central Sahara is no longer as simple and essentially local in character as it is farther south, but has been expanded to include that branch of agricultural economy which in America is called truck gardening, though on a very small scale. Here the gardeners furnish food not only for both sedentary and nomadic landlords and, of course, themselves, but also for sedentary merchant middlemen, both great and small, who trade in the local market where goods and foodstuffs from outside are exchanged against each other as well as for local produce. Once more, however, the gardener is at an economic disadvantage, for the landlord, especially if he is not a nomad, interposes himself in effect if not in theory as an inexorable intermediary between the actual producer and the trader in the market place.

As one moves still farther northward, garden agriculture decreases in importance, and again becomes primarily a matter of supplying local needs, while palm culture assumes ever increasing proportions and dates become the major article of commercial production. With this change in agricultural emphasis the labor situation changes too, for the Haratin fade progressively out of the picture the farther north one goes, until they finally disappear almost entirely.

Just as agriculture is the basic activity of sedentary communities in the southern desert, so commerce forms the economic basis of sedentary communities in the central and northern zones. Cities and towns [5] of the Sahara in general fall into three main categories when classified according to their economic functions. A small minority of little desert towns, like Teghaza and Taoudéni, exist solely for the exploitation and export of locally concentrated natural resources. Most of the larger urban centers lie fairly near the northern and southern boundaries of the desert, and these are primarily transfer points as is shown by their location on the main caravan routes and at the crossroads of desert trade. In the north there is a chain of them running from east to west along the southern edge of the intermediate zone of transition that separates two major ecological areas, the Sahara proper on the one hand, and, on the other, the relatively fertile steppe and piedmont regions that form the southern fringe of Barbary and the coastal zone of Cyrenaica. The main southern urban centers, like Timbuctoo and Agadès, lie outside the area with which we are primarily concerned.

The five little walled cities of the Mzab, with Ghardaia as their capital, are fairly typical of the northern group of urban commercial centers. Their collective function, now concentrated almost entirely in Ghardaia itself, is to provide a market place where merchants from the north and south can meet and exchange goods, and so to act in a sense as a pumping station on a pipeline of trade, to stimulate the flow of commercial and, incidentally, of cultural currents across and beyond the limits of the desert. The same basic pattern is also readily discernible in many other Saharan centers of this kind, such as Kufra. It should be noted, however, that the fragmentary nature of such clusters of several neighboring but separate settlements is rarely if ever the result of the political drawing together of a group of what were once wholly independent communities. On the contrary, it is

[5] The cities and towns of the Sahara form such an evenly graded series, when considered from the point of view of either function or absolute size, that one is often at a loss as to which term should be employed in referring to a particular settlement. I have made no attempt to draw sharp lines of distinction where none exist in fact, and so the reader must not be shocked at finding both terms used rather loosely and sometimes even alternatively.

caused by centrifugal forces resulting from the fact that the land is too barren and the water supply spread too thin to allow a population of more than a strictly limited size to assemble and live permanently together within a single city.

Urban centers of yet another and relatively variable type are found in the heart of the Sahara proper. These include cross-road stations like In Salah and Mourzouk, which act as pumping points for both main and lateral branch lines of commercial and cultural flow, and also way stations like Adrar, El Goléa, and Gatroun, which often began as only stages on long and difficult trails but have since come to serve also as trading centers linking the nomadic tribes of the surrounding country with the outside world. Early descriptions, dating from the middle of the fifteenth century to the middle of the nineteenth, show that centers of this kind have long occupied much the same place in the life of the Saharan population: they are not recent "civilized" developments by any means.

Naturally these various urban categories are not always as clear-cut and mutually exclusive as my brief preliminary description may have made them seem, for there is much overlapping. Many centers, like Ouargla and Tamanrasset, are intermediate in character, while still others, like Metlili of the Chaamba, are, or were until very recently, primarily the headquarters and operational bases of pastoral nomads, caravan men, and raiders. Local trade in places like Metlili was limited as a rule to camels, sheep and goats, milk and butter, while almost nothing was exported except dates. Merchandise received from outside the area included tea, sugar and spices, guns, powder and shot, knives, cotton cloth, manufactured leather goods, trinkets, perfume, and, more recently, cheap hardware. In spite of their seeming variety, however, the true urban centers of the Sahara are fundamentally alike in that all depend primarily, in one way or another, on interregional as opposed to purely local trade. And their sedentary business communities are typically divided into two main commercial classes, made up of shopkeepers on the one hand and freight forwarders and brokers on the other.

The character of Saharan towns also varies according to the

physical relation between house and garden, although here again there are many intermediate cases. In some centers, like Laghouat (more correctly written El Aghouat) and El Goléa, the houses of nearly all but the poor are set in walled gardens so that the settlement as a whole presents the appearance of a collection of gigantic roofless rooms, with trees and vegetables growing on their floors and box-like dwellings set in corners here and there. The fortified business and semi-residential center, with its houses, shops, and market place, is located in the middle or at one end of the primarily residential garden area, and the whole is surrounded by a broad belt of palm groves and more extensive gardens, many of them unwalled. This is the typical "oasis town" pattern of the northern half of the Sahara; and yet one wonders to what extent it may not be largely a function of the peaceful conditions recently imposed by European occupation. Even the now proverbially peaceful towns of the Mzab were almost constantly at war with one another even after they first began to come under French control a century ago.

In the other main type of town plan, as at Metlili and in the Mzab, the dwellings are jammed together on a rocky outcrop while their gardens and palm groves lie on the bottom land, anywhere from a few hundred yards to as much as five miles or more away. This second and older pattern is typical of the Saharan *ksar* or fortress type of town. Often the detached gardens and groves have among them houses to which the well-to-do can move in summertime, sometimes followed, notably in the Mzab, by a few of the lesser tradesmen who cater to them on the spot.

It should be noted that the commercial and semi-residential core of the oasis type of town is also referred to frequently as "the ksar," especially if it is raised above the general level of the oasis as is usually the case when possible. The main difference then between the two town types lies in the fact that the ksar proper is a fortified town in the true medieval sense, surrounded by exposed slopes which make it impossible for an enemy to approach under cover, while the ksar of an oasis town is embedded in the midst of the plantations so that its military value as a fortress is seriously impaired. Ghardaia is exceptional in that it shares something of the character of both types, for the development of its oasis of walled gardens and groves, five miles west of the city-fortress, has almost reached the point where the whole could be described as two towns, one of each kind, but with a single over-all socio-economic structure and a single population, much of which moves from one to the other and back again according to the seasons.

There seems to have been a growing tendency in recent centuries for sedentary townsfolk to move down from their old hill forts and closer to the plantations. El Goléa, for example, used to be a settlement of the ksar type, but Taourirt, the old fortified town perched on a rocky outcrop, was finally abandoned when the inhabitants moved down to the bottom land for good and established a new town in the midst of their plantations. Hilltop ruins suggest that many other Saharan towns have moved downhill too, not very recently perhaps but often not so very long ago. Ghardaia (founded in 1053) is dominated by the ruins of a perhaps older town, Arrem Baba Saad, which is perched on the rim of the escarpment that hems in the valley of the Mzab; Bou Noura, not quite two miles down the valley to the east, lies just below the ruins of an older town that was once heavily fortified.

Town houses naturally vary in design in different parts of the Sahara and among different categories of the population, but the essential features and general over-all character remain fairly constant throughout the entire area. The average town house is cubical and measures some thirty to forty feet on a side. It may sometimes be a two- or even three-story affair, but in any case it has a flat, walled-in roof terrace and perhaps a cellar as well. The walls are very thick, made of stone or adobe bricks usually covered with a finishing coat of clay. There is only one outside door, and if there are any outside windows they are in an upper story. Figure 2 shows a common arrangement of the rooms in such a house. A right-angled turn in the entrance corridor prevents anyone outside from seeing into the living quarters even when the door is opened wide. In some places however, as at Ghadamès, the house is entered through a tunnel. The central court on each floor is partially roofed over so as to leave an open-

76

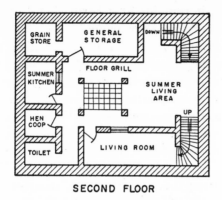

SECOND FLOOR

GROUND FLOOR

Fig. 2. Plan of a Saharan house. (This is a generalization rather than any particular house.)

ing in the middle, from four to eight feet square, which is protected by a heavy iron grill. Rooms on the ground floor are about eight to ten feet high, while those above are a foot or two lower. Bedrooms are usually windowless. The heavy housework, weaving, grinding of grain, cooking, and the like, is done in the downstairs court, which is also the everyday dining room, while the upstairs court serves as a family sitting room, and here honored guests are sometimes entertained. Rugs, bedding, and laundry are put out to air and dry on the roof terrace, along with the dog if there is one and maybe a young goat too, and here the women sit and sun themselves and the small children play about, weather permitting. The cellar is used chiefly as a refuge from the heat in

77

summertime, for it remains at a surprisingly uniform and comfortable temperature the year around.

A striking feature of the political organization of Saharan urban centers is the almost universal division of the community into two parties, commonly though loosely referred to as *sofs*. These are seldom if ever associations designed primarily for mutual aid in the material sense, as are the sofs of Barbary from which the term was originally taken. Rather they are essentially political factions, groupings usually of the more conservative citizens on the one hand and the progressive partisans of change on the other; although the dividing line sometimes falls between different ethnic groups in the population or between the supporters and the opponents of some specific program of basic internal or external policy. Such a dichotomy extends, of course, throughout the economic and social organizations of the entire community, either by allegiance or alliance. Although the openly avowed reason for its existence is almost always said to be a matter of theological disagreement, it seems more likely that the true basis is essentially economic in most cases, and that the reasons of sectarian difference so often invoked are in fact put forward primarily to screen some less selfless motive. Carleton Coon has pointed out that "pairs of sof-like parties" are common among Moslem communities in many lands. They are found, for example, among the townsfolk and the nomads of southern Arabia, and arose during Ottoman times in Anatolia, Syria and Egypt. Wherever they occur, they usually have much in common with our own dual political division into Democrats and Republicans, much more indeed than is apparent at first glance.

This division of urban communities into two parties is influenced by various local factors and so manifests itself in various ways in different places. At Laghouat, on the extreme northern edge of the western desert, the two major parties have always occupied respectively the northwestern and southeastern halves of the oasis, which is cut in two by a high ridge of bare rock, and so, in this case, the political division was strengthened by the nature of the terrain. At El Atteuf (properly pronounced El Atf), the oldest surviving town of the Mzab which was founded in

1011 or thereabouts, the traditional dichotomy finds concrete expression in the presence of two mosques belonging respectively to the Cheraga (easterners) and Gharba (westerners) who quarreled originally, or so the story goes, over a point of religious doctrine, the burning question of the conjugal fidelity of Aisha, the young and reputedly frivolous wife of the prophet Mohammed. At El Oued, some seventy miles east of Touggourt, the main dividing line between the two parties is basically that of ethnic origin, with the Arabs on one side and the Berbers on the other; and a similar situation has been observed among the Hassaouna of the Fezzan.

But such formalized subdivisions within a community do not always furnish adequate outlets for the emotional heat generated by the frictions which arise periodically between various segments of any urban population. Prosperity, for example, often causes cities and towns to grow, thereby producing increased crowding and general discontent, and this in turn may build up pressure, more or less gradually, until the internal stress becomes so great that a fraction of the original mass flies off at a tangent and settles somewhere else. The new settlement thus formed is usually far enough away from the parent center for safety and to avoid the danger of producing another disintegrating explosion, but still near enough to keep in touch, to keep a finger in the political pie of the community as a whole. Twice dissident minorities broke away from Ghardaia in this manner and founded new settlements, at Guerrara in 1631 and in 1679 at Berrian, but these new centers still remain integral parts of the Mzabite confederation although they lie some sixty and thirty miles respectively outside of the Mzab proper.

The system of dual political parties seems to be a very ancient institution among the Berber mountaineers of Barbary, whence it probably spread to the Sahara. Its main function seems to be to divide the community into two factions of usually almost equal strength and so prevent a basically republican form of government from turning into a dictatorship, either by the disproportionate weakening of one party or by the breaking up of both into splinter parties so small and numerous as to be functionally inefficient in the absence of a strong and autocratic central authority. Membership in such parties is not necessarily hereditary, however, for members can and sometimes do change sides with bewildering suddenness. In the Sahara the dual-party system seems to be most highly developed in the commercial centers of the northern desert, and apparently fades out gradually toward the south as the commercial function of sedentary centers in general becomes more and more attenuated.

Another characteristic feature of the Saharan dual-party system is that socially debased groups take no part. It is essentially a mechanism of the temporal ruling classes in the broad sense, a dichotomy centered around strong party leaders as well as established traditions. Some minority groups do, however, reproduce the pattern in miniature within their internal political structures. The Jews of Ghardaia, for instance, though numbering only about twelve hundred souls in all, are split into two bitterly opposed factions which disagree violently on nearly all questions of general policy. Whatever the real underlying reason for their rivalry may be, they stand shoulder to shoulder against the Moslems, and often in their dealings with Christians too, but have as little as possible to do with each other in any other way, social or economic, even though their members often live in adjoining houses.

The majority of the population in each sedentary center of the Sahara is fairly homogeneous as a rule, and speaks a more or less distinctive dialect of one of the principal languages of the area, Berber, Arabic, and Teda, whose distributions are shown on Map 3. In the midst of these majorities, however, one almost always finds minorities whose members appear to be more or less markedly different physically, and sometimes linguistically as well, and often specialize in certain specific occupations. These minorities belong to alien stocks, foreign or more ancient locally, which the now dominant elements of the modern population encountered and either subjugated or absorbed at various times during the past. They are living evidence of cultural diffusion and change, the best and almost the only evidence there is concerning the shifts of population and of power that have taken place in the Sahara during the period of the last two thousand years or so.

Long ago, both before and after the first Moslem invasions of North Africa, Berber clans from the northern mountains were driven southward from time to time by the pressure of a growing population or the political and economic turmoil resulting from invasions. Singly and in groups they fled into the northern desert and took up pastoral nomadism as their way of life; but when Arab invaders in their turn began to spread across the desert, competition became unbearable for most of these displaced Berber nomads, and so they were obliged to settle down to the relatively safe though socially degraded life of gardeners in oases. Tradition has it that Taourirt, the ruined hilltop ksar that overlooks the oasis town of El Goléa, was founded by just such a refugee tribe which is said to have settled there roughly a thousand years ago. The modern descendants of these Berber immigrants are the Zenata, who, although they can be found today in many sedentary centers of the northern half of the desert, and especially in the northwestern quarter, are rarely numerous enough anywhere to constitute a majority of the local population. And, although they have been Islamized quite thoroughly, their women still go unveiled as a general rule, and also have a distinctly higher social standing within the family than Arab women do. Zenata men tend to have a number of wives in succession, but rarely more than one at a time.

Another people, apparently of the same general kind, the Tadjakant,[6] are to be found scattered all along the western edge of the desert, from southern Morocco southward through the Spanish and western French Sahara. They seem to be the debris, so to speak, of an old and powerful Berber confederation that was converted to Islam, perhaps as early as the ninth century, and then rapidly extended its activities southward to the Senegal River and northward through Morocco and even into Spain, thus playing an active part in the formation of the Almoravide Empire. For a time the Tadjakant controlled the salt trade between the western Sahara and the Sudan, and they continued as nomadic

---

[6] Masculine singular, Jakani.

81

caravan men and slave traders until around the end of the eighteenth century. Their power reached its peak shortly before 1760, in which year they roundly defeated the Rguibat Moors, but from then on their fortunes declined slowly in the face of increasing competition until, in 1896, the Rguibat won a decisive and final victory. The sedentarization of the Tadjakant was a gradual process which followed the decline of their fortunes in war. Today most of them are gardeners or small tradesmen, although a few still live the life of impoverished camel nomads.

Tadjakant are to be found scattered in small communities here and there all the way from southern Morocco to the western Sudan, and as far east as the neighborhood of Aoulef. They speak an Arabic dialect which is characterized by survivals of Berber vocabulary and syntax, while socially and economically they seem to occupy a position almost exactly like that of the Zenata. Although a Tadjakant father is absolute master in his own household, he never makes a serious decision without consulting his wife, provided she has given him a male child. Women veil their faces and stay at home, and yet when they are married they retain title to the property they brought with them as brides. Monogamy is the rule, and girls can marry at any time after they reach the age of twelve. In fact the position of women in Tadjakant society seems to be based essentially on pre-Islamic Berber concepts thinly veiled by Islamic practices of Arab origin.

No good physical description or series of photographs of the Tadjakant is available, but at least it can be said that they seem to look much like the Zenata in that their usual appearance varies from moderately to very heavily negroid. On the other hand, they share a number of material culture traits with the Berber-speaking Tuareg, chiefly in matters of clothing and in the manner in which the women arrange and ornament their hair. Many of their tools and utensils also are very similar to or exactly like those of the Tuareg; but the stylistic similarities of such articles may well reflect the ethnic unity of their makers, the Saharan smiths, rather than an undeniably possible blood relation between the different groups of users, while the similarities in clothing may be due to nothing more than a common dependence on the same Sudanese sources of cotton cloth. As yet one cannot be sure one way or the other, even though the northern Tuareg of a century ago are said to have believed that they and the Tadja-kant sprang from a common ancestral stock.

Presumably comparable peoples of Berber origin, at least lin-guistically, are to be found in many other parts of the northern and central desert, but very little is known about any of them. In the eastern half of the Sahara, people of mixed Berber and Arab ancestry are said to make up about a quarter of the non-Arab population, while the remainder consists mainly of the Teda. Most of these hybrid groups have invented fanciful Mos-lem Arab genealogies, and in general have done everything they could think of to acquire full Arab social status. But even so, they have not been able to rise above a position intermediate be-tween their Berber cousins, whom they look down on and who in turn despise them, and the Arabs who accept them grudgingly on a sort of probationary basis.

The most curious and picturesque sedentary Berbers of the Sahara live in Ghardaia and its satellite towns in the Mzab, whence they are known as Mzabites (or Mozabites). The Mzabites are Berber-speaking folk, although they often use Arabic for business purposes. They belong to a puritanical and fundamentalist schismatic Moslem sect, known as Ibadites or Abadites, which split off from the main body of Islam and was obliged to go underground late in the seventh century. One group from Basra, at the head of the Persian Gulf, fled to North Africa under the leadership of a young Persian nobleman named Abder-rahman ibn Rustem, or so the story goes. This tiny band of refu-gee missionaries arrived at a singularly favorable moment, for the country was in a state of violent religious turmoil, and so they were able to recruit Berber converts in large numbers. In the words of Alport: "The Berbers, who had been Christian sectarians and rebels under Byzantine rule, became Muslim sec-tarians and rebels under the Caliphs," or, as Bernard said: "Is-lamic Calvinism found in North Africa its Scotland." After var-ious triumphs and vicissitudes, the members of this new religious community finally settled, about 760, in the neighborhood of

Tiaret (a hundred and sixty miles by road southeast of Oran), but they were driven out a century and a half later by orthodox Moslem fanatics. They then fled southeastward and settled down near Ouargla, but there they suffered further persecution and so, late in the tenth century, they made their final move to the valley of the Mzab. The first permanent Mzabite settlement, a trading post named Arrem-n-Tlazedit, was abandoned long ago and now lies in ruins. The oldest of the five surviving towns, El Atteuf, was founded about 1011, and the fifth and latest, Ghardaia, in 1053. It is possible, however, that the first Ibadite Moslems to arrive in the Mzab may have found orthodox Islamized Zenata already settled in the region, and that this earlier population was converted, submerged and eventually absorbed by the newcomers.

The Mzabites of today are extremely variable physically. They are short as a rule, averaging about five feet four inches in height, although individuals range all the way from well under five feet to a little over six. They are set apart from all other Saharan peoples by the fact that their arms are remarkably long although their legs are relatively short. They have narrow shoulders but rather broad hips, and they often become paunchy in early middle age. Heads vary greatly in breadth, while faces are usually oval, medium in size and rather flattish. Noses are narrow, and either straight or slightly convex in profile. Beards are often dense, eyebrows often meet above the nose, and lips are usually fairly thick. The skin is naturally very white but tans heavily, while hair is almost always very dark as are eyes. The Mzabites speak a dialect of Zenatan Berber as their "mother tongue," but practically all of them speak Arabic and French as well, while some, who have worked in and around Oran, are reasonably fluent in Spanish also.

The typical costume of Mzabite men consists of a striped European cotton shirt without a collar, very baggy trousers made of dark blue cotton or European woollen cloth, and a waistcoat of European style which is usually left unbuttoned. Over all this is worn a *gandoura,* a voluminous flowing garment like an out sized nightshirt but with neither sleeves nor collar, made of lightweight cotton or woollen cloth. Most gandouras are white, but pastel shades of pale blue, yellow, and even pink are coming into fashion. In wintertime men wear a heavy woollen outer garment known as a *djellaba,* or *kshabia,* which is merely a loose and baggy short-sleeved overcoat, sewed up the front and provided with a big pointed hood that is left hanging down behind except in rainy weather or at night. The djellaba is of European origin, but it was introduced into North Africa by the Romans and soon became a typically Berber article of clothing. The customary headgear of Mzabite men is a tightly wound turban of white cotton cloth, arranged with a loop passing underneath the chin. Mzabite shoes, made either of rawhide or red and yellow goatskin, are cut low on the sides and have no laces; and their soles are usually made from old tires nowadays.

Mzabite women in their homes wear baggy belted dresses of cheap and garishly printed cotton cloth. When they go out, however, they shroud themselves in an all-concealing sheet (*haik,* pronounced ha-eek) of white or dark blue cotton, which is about the shape and size of an ordinary bed sheet. The sheet is draped over the head and shoulders so that the middle of one side rests on the head with its edge hanging down over the forehead to the level of the eyebrows. Next the ends of the sheet are crossed in front of the body forming a double thickness, the middle of which is tucked into the belt. The two folds that are left hanging down on either side of the head are then seized from within and crossed in front, thus covering the chest and face completely except for a tiny triangular hole barely big enough for one eye to peek out through. Indoors the head is covered with a shawl, which is covered in turn by the haik when a woman leaves her house.

Since many of the Mzabite social, political, and economic practices have been described earlier, I will discuss them only briefly here. The Mzabite form of government is a theocratic autocracy, for each community is ruled with a rod of iron by two councils of elders who are chosen mainly on the basis of age and religious learning. The supreme power, including the legislative and judicial functions, is vested in a theocratic council known as the *halga,* while executive functions are performed by a lay council, the

8 5

djemaa (a word borrowed from Arabic). The power of these councils is so absolute, and the fear which they inspire such, that Mzabites are said to have been tried secretly, condemned to death, and even executed in the City of Algiers without the knowledge of the French authorities. And even if the Algiers police should learn of such a case, they could never find a single witness who would testify, so rigid is the internal discipline of the Mzabite community.

The preferred form of marriage among Mzabites is between children of brothers, but marriages outside the home community and even with Arab women of other Moslem sects are beginning to occur. Boys usually marry when they are seventeen or eighteen years old and girls when they are twelve to fourteen, but ten-year-old mothers are by no means unknown. And, although a recent French law forbids the marriage of native girls under fourteen years of age, the Mzabites are expressly exempted from its provisions. Mzabite men often take several wives in succession, but rarely have more than one at any given time. When a man dies, his widow customarily marries one of his brothers, and her children, if she has any, then refer to her new husband as "father."

Many Mzabite men have set up grocery shops in the cities of northern Algeria, and they often go to work in these for two or three years at a time leaving their womenfolk at home. This practice has given rise to the Mzabite legal theory that a child is legitimate if born not more than two years after his supposed father's last departure from the Mzab. Also a departing father customarily hangs up a pair of his trousers in the conjugal bedroom, behind the door, where they remain until he comes home again; but it is not altogether clear whether these trousers are thought of as his proxy, endowed with the power of magical procreation, or only as a concrete symbol of his spiritual presence. In any case, people of the Mzab sometimes use the sarcastic term "children of the trousers" when referring to persons who were born after their mothers' husbands had been away from home for more than nine months.

Much has been made of the supposedly strict communal

endogamy of the Mzabites. It has been said even that none but Mzabites used to be allowed to settle in any of the towns of the Mzab except Ghardaia and Melika, and that to this day only a Mzabite can pass the night in the holy city of Beni Isguen.[7] And yet the census of 1926 showed that sedentary Arab families were established in all of the five towns of the Mzab, and Negro slaves have lived in all of them for centuries. In the Mzab there is also a special class of half-breeds known as *Hamria* ("red ones"), so called because they are visibly negroid in color. These folk are usually the offspring of male Negro or negroid servants and Mzabite women whose husbands are away, although a few are probably children of Mzabite men and female Negro servants. Several whom I know are children of Mzabite boys whose wealthy parents provided them with Negro concubines, both to keep them out of trouble and to give them sexual training prior to marriage. Hamria are generally accepted and treated as legitimate children of the Mzabite families into whose households they were born, and yet they seem nevertheless to have some vague sort of separate special status in the community. They are tacitly regarded as "not quite like other people"; and they also have a strong feeling of group solidarity among themselves. For example, closely related Hamria men often band together in small orchestras which play at weddings and other festive gatherings; and they do this obviously more for fun than gain, for they appear to enjoy themselves tremendously although they are paid only by very small voluntary contributions from the audience. Their feeling of group solidarity is expressed far more dramatically once or twice a year, when the Hamria men all meet at night in the northeast corner of the market place of Ghardaia. Here, in the light of a blazing bonfire, they form up in two long lines which shuffle rhythmically forward toward each other and then slowly drift apart, over and over again, chanting as they go. Every little while a man will break away in an ecstatic

[7] Most authors seem to have overlooked the fact that the status of "holy city of the Mzab" was acquired by Beni Isguen only quite recently. When Trumelet passed that way in January 1854, Melika was still the "holy city" as well as the principal slave market of the region.

seizure, circle around and around the dancing lines in great leap-
ing bounds, and finally fling himself headlong into the fire. He is
rescued instantly, however, by a pair of burly guards, who lay
him out on the ground to one side and cover him with a *burnous*
(a hooded cloak made of wool or a mixture of wool and camel's
hair). After ten or fifteen minutes he will drag himself slowly to
his feet and slowly walk away into the night. While all this is
going on, the two long dancing lines continue swaying rhythmically back and forth, mumbling their chant and apparently obliv-
ious of all around them. Performances of this kind may last for
only an hour, or they may go on for two or three, but there is no
general climax even at the end. Finally the dancing lines simply
dissolve spontaneously and the dancers wander off, singly and in
little groups, to their respective homes.

A few Arab nomad groups have settled occasionally, by invitation, in Berber-speaking urban communities in the Sahara.
Thus, some three centuries ago, the Mdabih tribe from the
steppe country northwest of Laghouat came to camp under the
walls of the Mzabite city of Ghardaia, invited by one of the two
main political factions there in order to secure the whip hand
over its rival. Finally, when the need for the services of the
Mdabih had passed, they were absorbed into the urban communal structure by a kind of mass adoption, but they still remained
in a residential quarter of their own outside the old city wall,
and they remain today in a status which is difficult to describe
precisely but can best be summed up perhaps in the term "socially
poor relations." Even so, they sometimes can and occasionally do
control the balance of political power by maintaining or switching
their party allegiance. Like Negroes in America, they are but a
small minority of the total population, and yet, as is the case
with the American Negroes, neither major political party can
well afford to offend them if it wishes to win political control of
the community or to keep it.

After the absorption of the Mdabih there came to Ghardaia
the Beni Merzoug, part of a minor sedentary clan of the
Chaamba nomad confederation, who were brought in as mercenaries for the defence of the city against attacks by their maraud-

ing nomadic relatives. In recent years, however, they have never numbered more than a handful of families, and so their political influence has been negligible. Today they are still socially unacceptable to the Mzabites because of differences in religious doctrine, and they are looked at askance also as quarrelsome and uncooperative guests by their now reluctant hosts.

Another group of sedentary Arabs, the Makhadma,[8] are also settled in Ghardaia where they seem to have arrived relatively recently. They are intermediate in numbers between the Beni Merzoug and the Mdabih, but, since they are socially debased manual laborers for the most part, they are practically insignificant politically. The Mdabih and the Beni Merzoug are also economically specialized, for the former are largely agricultural land owners and tillers of the soil, while the latter are noted for their skill in tailoring and particularly embroidery. Various sedentary Berber communities elsewhere in the Sahara doubtless include similar Arab minorities, but almost nothing seems to be known about any of them.

In the northern half of the desert metalworking and woodworking too are almost entirely in the hands of Jews. They are the smiths and jewelers, and the makers of furniture and of cards for the combing of wool. They also engage in moneylending and in the collection of taxes and fees in the market place, as well as in the sale of alcoholic beverages, all occupations which are either expressly forbidden by the Koran or are looked on as degrading by devout Moslems. In the old days, desert commerce was at times largely in their hands, and today they still constitute a large majority of the cloth merchants and tailors. A few pastoral nomadic Jewish groups used to roam the northern central desert, but the last of them settled down some sixty years ago, excepting a handful of isolated families who were converted to Islam and absorbed into neighboring nomadic Arab tribes.

The first Jews to arrive in North Africa may have come to the Mediterranean coast with the Phoenicians as early as the eighth century before Christ, but if so they must have been very

---

[8] From the Arabic root *khadama*, meaning "to labor."

few in number and can hardly have exerted any appreciable influence on the native population of Barbary, let alone the Sahara.
The first true wave of Jewish immigrants to North Africa seems
to have arrived late in the sixth century before Christ, in Cyrenaica, but it was probably soon thoroughly submerged racially in
a sea of local Berber converts to Judaism. Massacres early in the
second century A.D. caused the Cyrenaican Jews to flee westward, and a new Jewish capital was then established at Tamentit,
near Adrar in the Touat. In 1492 there were more massacres,
Tamentit was utterly destroyed, and most of the survivors fled
northeastward through the Gourara to the Mzab. And so Ghardaia became the new Jewish capital of the Sahara, even though
Jews never formed more than a very small minority of its population. Only a little over a century ago the Jews of Ghardaia
still used to end the opening prayer of their spring fast with the
words "and may we return next year to Tamentit" instead of saying "to Jerusalem," which is the universal Jewish formula elsewhere.

Physically the Jews of the Mzab look very much like eastern
Berbers, and much like most of the other peoples that are found
living near the shores all around the central and western Mediterranean. Careful examination only strengthens this visual impression. The most distinctive physical characteristics of these
Jews are the prevalence of remarkably long and narrow heads
and of dark brown eyes which have a reddish tinge when seen
in a strong light. Curiously enough these distinctive traits are
not shared, so far as I know, by any other group in the Sahara
or even in Barbary. They were probably developed locally by a
process known as "random genetic drift," a phenomenon which
is fairly common in small communities that inbreed over periods
of many generations. Isolated Jewish physical characteristics
do crop up now and then in Jews of the Mzab, but they seem
to occur singly rather than in the usual combinations. In other
words, very few Saharan Jews look noticeably Jewish. Although
the nature of their blood has not been investigated so far, studies
carried out among the Jews of southeastern Morocco suggest
that they may have distinctive ABO and Rh blood group pat-

terns, markedly different from those of the Arabic-speaking Moslem peoples of Barbary, but less unlike those of the southern Haratin and the montane Berber tribes of both Barbary and the central desert.

The preferred form of marriage among Saharan Jews, as among Mzabites, is between children of brothers, but it sometimes happens that a man marries his brother's daughter or even a sister of his father. In spite of the resultant intense inbreeding, mental defects are certainly no more frequent here than in the United States, while physical defects, even of known hereditary types, are not unusually common either. Marriage outside the home community used to be very rare, although now it is rapidly becoming less so. A widow normally goes to live in the household of a brother of her deceased husband, who marries her if she is childless but not otherwise. Well-to-do Jewish men often take Arab mistresses, but the offspring of these unions are usually absorbed by the Arab community, for they are generally thought to be the children of their mother's husbands.

Arabic is the language usually spoken in Saharan Jewish family circles, even by those who live in Berber-speaking Moslem communities, but men and boys from the age of about fifteen onward all speak Hebrew as well. Thus, Hebrew is not merely a ritual language but a true living tongue; and it also assumes the character of a secret language resorted to by men when they don't want their womenfolk to know what they are saying.

The Jews of the Sahara have never been seriously persecuted as a matter of established policy, although they have suffered occasional wholesale massacres of rare violence and thoroughness like that in the Touat, in 1492, which was actually no more than a furious and hysterically fanatical reaction to the Christian expulsion of the infidels from Spain. Their place in the Saharan scheme of things has always been generally recognized by their Moslem neighbors, and so their presence has been tolerated, though often grudgingly. At Ghardaia they live and have their shops in a special quarter of the city, now extramural only in the symbolic sense, but formerly so in fact as well. Before the arrival of the French they were forbidden to own land or to live in any town of the Mzab other than Ghardaia, and were also obliged to wear distinctive clothing, a black turban and black outer garments, as in Morocco. Today they wear voluntarily a different but equally distinctive costume consisting of a soft fez of red felt, worn on the back of the head like a skullcap, and a gandoura of white cotton worn as an outer garment. In spite of all handicaps, however, the trans-Saharan trade of the Mzab was largely in the hands of two or three Jewish families a century ago, and Jews are still in the front rank of sedentary Saharan merchants.

Although northern Saharan Jews practically never marry women of other faiths, even today, Jewish groups farther south, like the Mehadjeria [9] of Timimoun (roughly a hundred and fifteen miles north-northeast of Adrar), have for the most part become converted to Islam and customarily marry sedentary Arab neighbors. Even here, however, there remains a small core of diehards who cling tenaciously to their original religion and marry only among themselves.

One of the most important minorities in the Saharan population, indeed numerically the most important in many places, is that made up of the descendants of Negro slaves imported from the Sudan. Slaves seem always to have been among the most important goods and often the principal merchandise of the great trans-Saharan caravans. In 1884 a French explorer, Camille Douls, saw five hundred and twenty Bambara slaves in a single caravan as it passed northward through Tindouf, and these were doubtless only the survivors of a substantially greater number. But the European nations that have taken over effective control of the western and at times much of the eastern desert during the last fifty years or so, have outlawed slavery progressively as they extended their power farther and farther southward. The measures taken to enforce this prohibition have been successful in suppressing the old slave trade throughout most of the Sahara, but slavery still survives to all intents and purposes, and in various forms, among many of the peoples of

[9] Which means "ostracized."

92

the area. Negroes from the region of Lake Chad, brought northward through Libya, were still being sold publicly in the market places of Yugoslavia at the beginning of the First World War; and it has been said that slave caravans continued to pass northward through Mourzouk until at least as recently as 1929. Negro slaves from the Sudan were still smuggled regularly into Morocco, and occasionally into some of the northern oases of the Algerian Sahara too, only twenty-five years ago; and perhaps a very few are still being brought in even today; but this late development has never been more than a clandestine luxury trade in which none but a few of the very rich and politically powerful could afford to play the role of customers, and then only on a very small and elaborately discreet scale.

Slaves and their descendants (all now at least theoretically free) occupy a position at the very bottom of the social ladder, for even freedmen and their children are considered inferior to the lowly Haratin. Although legally freed or freeborn, they and their descendants are still practically bound to the community in most cases, or sometimes to a single individual, simply because their debased socio-economic status prevents them from accumulating the resources necessary to achieve personal independence. Although theoretically free to seek out new paths, they usually cannot. Thus their function is almost always that of the most menial kind of manual labor, and occasionally that of household servants, a class which forms the upper crust of this lowest socio-economic stratum. The traditional ties that now tenuously bind a member of the slave class can be greatly strengthened by debt, and so the financial element of the Latin American peonage system is often the chief mechanism for keeping slaves and also freedmen in their traditional place. This is usually the case with miners in salt centers like Taoudéni, and often in the agricultural centers and oasis gardens too, where freed slaves and their descendants work as sharecroppers beside but second to the Haratin. The slave class in most Saharan centers retains a considerable degree of internal cohesion which is formalized in a seemingly simple and loosely knit kind of brotherhood. The solidarity of such groups is demonstrated ceremonially by annual animal sacrifices, and, more frequently, by ostensibly social reunions in which Sudanese music and dance patterns constitute the ritual framework.

It should not be forgotten that a slave, and especially a household slave, whatever his social, political, and economic handicaps may be, is usually better off on the whole in sedentary Moslem communities than are destitute members of his master's race. Although Saharan slaves have very seldom risen to such giddy heights of favor and personal power as slaves sometimes attain in Arabia, they still enjoy an established and relatively secure status in the social organization of the community. According to the doctrine of Islam, the lame, the halt, and the blind, the sick, aged, feeble-minded, and insane must all be cared for, and this principle is universally respected as the will of God. Since the principle is applied directly through the mechanism of the family, immediate or extended according to its group potential, fallen relatives of the rich are better cared for as a rule than poor relations of the relatively poor can be. Slaves are considered a family responsibility for the purpose of this system of social security, and so, since only the relatively well-to-do can afford to own them, they are relatively well cared for when disaster strikes and in their economically useless old age, even though they are seldom clothed otherwise than in rags at any time.

The household slaves of major religious chiefs seem to occupy an exceptional position, however, for they are often treated badly and sometimes very brutally indeed. They are seldom adequately fed, and, when aged or infirm, they are commonly turned out to fend for themselves. Nor is it unusual for them to be flogged in public by their saintly master in person, for what we would consider only petty crimes. Less than half a dozen years ago one of the greatest religious leaders of the Sahara is said to have cut off the breasts of a young Negress who had offended him, and who died as a result. Although it is simply inconceivable that European administrative authorities can remain uniformly unaware of happenings of this kind, and although the local native population as well as minor European civil servants on the spot are only too keenly aware of them, effective counter-measures are seldom if ever taken. Such is the power and consequent immunity of major "holy men" in the Sahara even to this day, for they are still "above the law" of Islam and Christianity alike.

Yet another interesting though numerically tiny minority is represented by the well diggers of Ouargla, survivors of a class that may once have been relatively widespread in the northern third of the Sahara. They are known as Ghattasin (commonly spelled Rhetasin) which means "divers," and they well deserve the name, for they dive down to depths of eighty feet and more to clear wells that are becoming choked with silt and refuse. In the old days, before mechanical well digging came into vogue, the Ghattasin were true well diggers; and they were often killed by the sudden geyser-like eruptions which occurred when they broke through into a water-bearing formation. Their only special equipment for their perilous and painful work consists of tallow plugs placed in the ears and nostrils, and they are said to die almost invariably of pulmonary disturbances. Practically nothing else seems to be known about these people, but it is said that they are descendants of prisoners to whom the Turkish provincial governors in the north granted the choice between undergoing capital punishment on the spot or going to dig wells in the oases of the desert. Aside from their work, two things only can be said about them with some assurance: they are a socially debased and a racially hybrid group. In their superficial appearance they look not unlike some of the less negroid Haratin but they seem to have an even lower social status in spite of their relatively important function. Within the last few years, however, the Ghattasin have nearly all abandoned their age-old profession and gone to work in neighboring oil fields, at far less risk and infinitely higher wages than they ever dreamed of.

A special social category among the sedentary Saharan population consists of the religious and semi-religious aristocratic classes commonly known collectively as Marabouts. In broad terms it can be said that there are two main classes of this kind, the Shorfa (singular: Shereef), who are supposed to be lineal descendants of Mohammed and to derive their power directly from him, and the Mrabteen (singular: Mrabet) or Marabouts proper, men who have acquired holiness themselves or, more often, lineal descendants of such men. The Mrabteen are theoretically inferior in rank to the Shorfa, but in actual practice the reverse can also be true, for when Shorfa are relatively poor in worldly goods their religious prestige may be largely outweighed by the great wealth of some major Mrabet. Thus, "holy men" may be reduced at times to a primarily commercial status. Minor Shorfa merchants from Metlili, for example, used to accompany nomad Chaamba raiders and cater to them in the field, just as Jewish peddlers a century ago accompanied and shared the dangers of the first waves of pioneers moving into our own Far West. Little by little they set up small shops and trading posts farther and farther away from their home bases, so that Shorfa shopkeepers are to be found today scattered all over the western desert, from the Mzab to the Sudan.

With rare exceptions the early histories of the major religious families of the Sahara are shrouded in such clumsily complicated mythology that no clear factual background can be seen through the seven times sevenfold veils of tradition, much of it obviously spun out of thin air, but one curious fact does stand out; such leading families are often more or less visibly negroid, and some of the most powerful religious chiefs are practically indistinguishable from full-blooded Negroes.

A major Marabout is usually the current representative of a long family line of "living saints" who have possessed for many generations a quality known as *baraka,* which is the mana of anthropological parlance though in a primarily prophylactic form. Baraka can mean supernatural power in almost any sense, but the term is used mainly in connection with the power to ward off or circumvent supernatural forces of evil. Although all major holy men are automatically placed in the first rank of Moslem society, as the most favored of God, the ritual practices of their followers show that their basic appeal is often essentially magical rather than religious in the true sense. As Hans Kissling has said, "The common man praying to a saint in his need or turning to a saintly man . . . hardly reflects upon whether the saint is an intermediary between him and God or is an independent power. The latter is even more probable."

Minor Marabouts exist, of course, throughout the Sahara, and they are of many kinds. Some are solitary saints, while others have more or less numerous followings whose members are often organized into relatively local minor orders. Some of them are gentle, pious men, mystics who pass their time in contemplation and prayer; others are hysterical or insane and achieve prestige by magic and witchcraft; and there are many intermediate types between these extremes.

The underlying function of the Marabouts seems to be to bring members of their flocks into communion with the supranatural, in simple terms which a local layman can readily understand and so find emotionally satisfying. Thus, they relieve pent-up stresses of serious social maladjustment by channeling the explosive force into mystic ceremonial outlets through mechanisms of self-hypnotic group ritual that are emotionally exhausting and often physically strenuous as well. This function is extended in a passive way through the mechanism of the *zaouia,* a monastic kind of establishment to which the maladjusted faithful of both sexes can retire to be sheltered for the rest of their lives in return for the gift of all their worldly goods to the presiding Marabout. Such establishments are concentrated near the northern and southwestern edges of the desert. In all this there are some curious parallels to certain Christian practices, for not only are the essential elements of lay brotherhood and the retreat present, but women who retire to a zaouia do so apparently in a spirit of mystic union with God, as represented by the presiding master. Instruction too is an important function of some zaouias which maintain Koranic schools for little children, and to which older students also come to learn the finer points of Moslem theology and legal theory. Although practically all zaouias are fixed sedentary establishments, it has been reported that a few small wandering zaouia-schools are to be found among some of the nomadic tribes of the central Sahara.

The Marabout, big or little as he may be, acts again as a

97

stabilizing social influence in that his following, or "order," represents at least a partial cross section of the community or series of communities in which its members live; for it cuts across the secular lines of social, economic, and even racial division, and thereby tends to weaken the kinds of stress to which they naturally give rise. The Maraboutic type of order or brotherhood seems to have had its roots in the medieval religious turmoil of the Near East, when systematically induced ecstasy as a means of attaining "the vision of the light of God's glory" began to be formalized in rituals of both Moslem and Christian religious communities. All through the Islamic East one finds religious brotherhoods, organized to this same end and employing much the same methods to attain it. And it is interesting to note that their members are generally known collectively as Sufi (pronounced soofee), from the Arabic word *suf* which means "wool," for this is striking evidence of the overwhelming importance of sheep and their wool in the Arabian pastoral nomadic state of mind out of which Islam arose. Most of the Maraboutic congregations of the Sahara are independent or semi-independent manifestations of this very widespread concept, which finds expression throughout the Moslem world in organizations that cut across lines of political, racial, and linguistic division, but extend only in a few cases beyond the limits of a single geographical area.

A major Marabout is something in the nature of a modern Moslem counterpart of the prelate of medieval Europe except that he has no hierarchical superior, for he is the absolute autocrat of a theocracy made up of his followers. "In his sensation of union with the world soul," says Kissling, he "does not feel bound to a definite religion and thus undermines his own orthodoxy; he refuses to be bound by laws, and so becomes an anarchist; he denies being subject to the moral laws, and thus becomes an absolute nihilist." His followers accept his holiness as an article of faith that transcends all reason and so excuse automatically even the most unorthodox conduct on his part. In theory and to some extent in fact he acts as a counterpoise to the roughshod warlike bandit on the one hand and the merciless merchant on the other, but he not infrequently partakes of the characters of both. In theory he is a man of peace but he can fight fiercely in defense of his prestige and his material belongings. Although he normally attacks only at the magico-religious and financial levels, he is an awe-inspiring enemy all the more for that. It is no more than natural that such magico-religious preëminence should be reflected in the field of justice, and it often is; for among many of the Moslem tribes of the Sahara Marabouts are the judges, either by simple hereditary right or by virtue of authority vested in them by the tribal council as the case may be.

It is impossible to estimate, even approximately, either the personal or official fortunes of major Marabouts, for the bulk of their income takes the form of gifts from faithful followers. They cultivate their human flocks assiduously by visiting all the far-flung centers of their cults, or by sending agents out to them, at least once every two years or so, and these attentions are always very richly rewarded. The vast wealth thus accumulated enables them to maintain efficient administrative control and communication channels throughout the network of their widely scattered groups of devotees, and thus strengthens and preserves the continuity of their socio-political influence over enormous areas.

The youngest and at the same time the most powerful of the major religious orders in the Sahara is that of the Senoussi, whose present leader is the King of Libya by the Grace of God and the United Nations. This order was founded a little over a century ago by Mohammed ben Ali es Senoussi, a native of Mostaganem on the Mediterranean coast (some twenty-five miles east of Oran), who first studied in the famous religious school of the Tidjani order at Fez in Morocco and then went on a pilgrimage to the East.

Mohammed ben Ali pursued his religious studies in Mecca and the Yemen, and finally again in Mecca where he took to preaching puritanical religious reform. He was unable, however, to stand off the orthodox authorities and so was obliged to return to North Africa, where he first set up headquarters near Cyrene, on the coast of Cyrenaica, and then in 1856 at Jaghabub, just west of the Oasis of Siwa. His son, also named Mohammed, transferred the headquarters of the order to Kufra in 1896. While all this was going on, Senoussi missionaries lost no time in spreading the doctrine of their cult far and wide across the face of the eastern and central desert. Though merely a detail, it is none the less significant that, within the memory of men who are still alive, it was customary for animals and also slaves belonging to the order to be branded with the name of God; for this is symptomatic of the overbearingly autocratic authority that major religious leaders exercise in Moslem countries, though usually in a less blatant manner.[10] This aspect of Moslem character is very old, however, for Rameses III of Egypt, is known to have had prisoners of war branded with his name long before the coming of Islam, at a time when the Egyptians looked on their ruler as a living god.

The first explosive expansion of Senoussi power extended westward through Ghadamès and Touggourt to Ouargla and Metlili and even, briefly, to Laghouat, but this thrust into the western desert had little lasting effect except to bring the nomadic Chaamba into the Senoussi fold, where some of them still remain. The tremendous expansion in all directions of Senoussi influence was speeded by the blessing of the Sultan of Turkey, in accordance with the then traditional Turkish policy of supporting the cults of "living saints" for political purposes. Thus the Senoussi gained effective political and commercial control of the whole eastern half of the Sahara, and their power eventually became so great that during the First World War, again with Turkish and also German support, they raised the tribes in their territory against the Allies and were even able to persuade most of the Tuareg of the western central desert to revolt against the French. Even after the First World War had ended, and a new treaty of peace between the Senoussi and the Italian Government had been signed, it was still impossible to travel freely in the eastern half of the Sahara without the express permission of the paramount chief of the order. And today theirs is the Kingdom of Libya if not of Heaven.

[10] For further details regarding the Senoussi see Evans-Pritchard (1949) and Coon (1958, pp. 134–135).

The Senoussi, whose iron hand clothed in the velvet glove of religion and old-fashioned diplomacy has thus ruled most of the eastern half of the Sahara so effectively for a hundred years, are merely another manifestation of the profound affinity of Moslems for government by dictatorship, preferably though not always based on magico-religious prestige, which is rooted in a power concept, the cult of The Strong Man. And this affinity springs quite simply from the psychological compulsion of a tradition, the stony imprint left in the cement of Moslem thought by the ancient nomadic tribal organization that gave birth to Islamic doctrine.

In the western half of the Sahara, as well as in the Sudan, the Tidjani brotherhood has been for centuries almost if not quite as influential as the Senoussi in the east. And yet, although I have been a guest of the head of the Tidjani and his brothers in their great fortress-home at Ain Madhi, some fifty miles west of Laghouat, neither I nor anyone else has been able to learn anything to speak of about the inner workings of the organization. Unfortunately it is impossible, at least for the time being, to discover the true nature and extent of the undoubtedly great power of the Tidjani, for their methods have always been most secretive. Unlike the Senoussi, they have never tried to implement their policies by open warfare, and so have never had to show more than a very few of the many cards they hold.

In addition to the racial, linguistic, and theocratic minorities which are found in various sedentary centers of the Sahara, there is always present everywhere a floating population of wandering entertainers, itinerant musicians, magicians, and storytellers who are constantly traveling about, singly or in small groups, from oasis to oasis all over the area. Members of the first category are usually Negroes or heavily negroid, but the others are most often Arabs. Almost nothing is known about any of these people, however, and in any case they are so very few in number and so widely scattered that they can hardly have played any important part in the formation or transformation of Saharan social, political, or economic systems.

The various racial and social segments of the sedentary population of the desert naturally are not entirely shut off from each other biologically, as my rather brief descriptions of them may have seemed to suggest. On the contrary, more or less sporadic and usually clandestine interbreeding has been going on between them for centuries, regardless of theoretical prohibitions which are respected more or less strictly as the case may be. Marriage below the social rank into which one was born is unthinkable for almost every self-respecting native of the Sahara, and even within these limits it is very rare for anyone to marry outside his own tribe or at the most his confederation. In spite of this, however, continuing race mixture is widespread among the sedentary peoples of the area and presumably always has been. By way of an example I will describe the situation in the oasis towns of the Saoura region, in the northwest corner of the desert. Here white landowners, be they Arab or Zenatan Berber, single or married to women of their own kind, always take one or more Haratin mistresses and usually start with the wife of one of their share-croppers. The injured gardener-husband, however, is by no means irremediably frustrated by such proceedings; for, as a socially negligible person, he can come and go in his landlord-master's house pretty much as he pleases, while the landlord's wife, traditionally kept at home shut off from all outside contact except for rare and carefully chaperoned visits back and forth with female friends of her own class, is often only too glad to kill two birds with one stone by actively consoling the poor gardener and herself at the same time for the infidelity of their respective spouses. It is not at all surprising then that many sedentary Arabs and well-to-do Zenata of the Saoura are easily mistaken for Haratin and vice versa.

Situations of this kind are irregular enough in Saharan social theory, but in practice they are undoubtedly the tacitly accepted rule far more often than the exception among sedentary peoples of the desert in general and particularly in the northern half of the area, where sedentary communities are more complex both racially and socially than is the case farther south. Even among the notoriously puritanical inhabitants of the Mzab, where marriage between the children of brothers is the preferred form in both the Moslem and Jewish communities, one sometimes sees the face of a handsome Negro woman peering from the parapet of a housetop terrace down into the street. She is probably a children's nurse or some other kind of household servant, and a slave or a descendant of slaves, but she and others like her have occasionally left the mark of their race clearly stamped on the features of both Moslems and Jews of the Mzab who firmly maintain, often enough no doubt in full sincerity, that they surely have no negroid, far less Negro ancestors. Here the result is probably accomplished in two stages rather than directly. Apparently the usual process is for a Negro serving woman to bear a male child whose father is her white master, after which the half-breed son grows up around the house and one day has secret relations with his master's wife who, in due course, produces a hybrid child which all the family assume to be the master's. This kind of race mixture has resulted in a rather unusual distribution of hybrids within the populations of commercial centers; for it is only members of the economic aristocracy (of which the religious aristocracy automatically forms a part) who are in a position to have sharecroppers or household servants, slave or free, and so it is often the blood of the most aristocratic families that may be the least "blue" when all is said and done. In other words Negro blood tends to seep into the veins of white Saharan peoples through the top as well as through the bottom of the socio-economic range, so that the least Negroid families in white communities are often found among those who are in an intermediate position.

Nothing of importance remains to be said about the sedentary peoples of the agricultural centers in the southern half of the Sahara, but my remarks concerning the broad outlines of the social and economic organization of sedentary communities in the more commercial centers farther north still need pulling together. By way of summarizing the socio-economic structure of such communities one can hardly do better than review briefly the situation in the Gourara area. In many ways this region is intermediate in character, as it is geographically too, between the truly urban centers of the northern desert and the more agricultural though still primarily commercial settlements that characterize much of the central zone, and so it is about as typical of the predominantly commercial sedentary centers of the northern half of the Sahara as any single region I could choose.

The upper layer of Gouraran society consists of Arabs, supposedly descended from invaders who came into the area in the twelfth century. This upper layer is divided into an upper middle class made up of sedentary landlords and tradesmen and of pastoral nomads, all known simply as Arab, and a semi-religious capitalistic aristocracy which, in turn, is subdivided into Shorfa and Mrabteen, both of whom derive their incomes mainly from rents, from trade on a relatively large scale, and from the generosity of their devotees. The nomadic Arabs of the region (who are Chaamba) often own gardens in an oasis to which they return for a few months each autumn, arriving just in time for the date harvest.

The upper crust of the lower layer of Gouraran society consists of the Zenata, a very few of whom are still nomads although most have long since settled down, and among these latter one finds again a fairly numerous elite of semi-religious families. The socio-economic status of the Zenata varies all the way from that of a moderately prosperous middle class of small landowners and tradesmen through that of tenant gardeners to that of common laborers. And, although the few Zenata who are still nomadic often show almost no signs of Negro admixture, traces of such mixture become increasingly apparent as one descends the socioeconomic scale to the level of the very poor, many of whom appear to be physically indistinguishable from heavily negroid Haratin.

Next in the social scale of Gouraran towns come the originally Jewish Mehadjeria, who have embraced Islam for the most part and who usually marry women of the sedentary Arab population when possible, thus crossing over the line of socio-religious demarcation to an intermediate position on the lower fringe of the upper middle class. These folk are craftsmen, they are the jewelers, smiths and woodworkers of the oasis towns. The few Mehadjeria who have retained their Jewish faith follow the same trades, but they keep strictly to themselves, socially aloof from the rest of the community. Below the Jews in social and economic rank come the Haratin, and finally the slaves. And of course there is always a small floating population of Arab storytellers and magicians, wandering Negro minstrels, and passing caravan men.

Both Arabic and Berber dialects are spoken extensively throughout the Gourara, but they have been much corrupted by close and prolonged contact between their speakers. Although both languages are spoken in nearly every population center, as well as by most individuals, there are indications that the preferential use of one or the other follows a patchwork distribution, socially and also topographically. Slaves and their descendants used to speak a variety of mongrel Sudanese dialects which together constituted a kind of lingua franca, commonly known as Kouriya, but this third language (if it can properly be so called) has been all but completely forgotten within the last fifty years, probably because of the suppression of the slave trade.

Chapter 4

HUNTERS, FOOD GATHERERS, AND NOMADS GENERALLY

Nomadic tribes are to be found all over the Sahara, but they are not all alike or even closely similar by any means. Some of them are very small, and so primitive that they seem to have practically no social or political organization beyond the simple framework of single isolated family bands of wandering hunters. They sleep in the open, dress in skins or rags, and are desperately poor, owning no property except the barest necessities of life. Other tribes, numbering as many as several thousand persons each and subdivided into clans, are organized in confederations and have elaborate political, social, and economic systems. Their tents are strongly made and comfortable, their clothing and equipment are elaborate and at times luxurious, and they are often rich in livestock and in slaves. In between these two extremes are still other kinds of tribes whose status is more or less intermediate in various respects.

Angus Buchanan has given a tantalizing thumbnail sketch of a group of three men, two women, and five small children that he stumbled on in 1920 while exploring in the Aïr, some two hundred miles or so north of Agadès. The men were dressed in ragged sleeveless leather shirts and short trousers, and their heads and faces were veiled (with white cloth) in the Tuareg manner. Each carried a spear of medium length with a wooden shaft connecting a long iron point and a long, flat blade-like iron butt with flaring end, a cheap but reasonably effective substitute

1. The extreme northern Sahara

2. The Great Eastern Erg

3. The extreme southern Sahara

4. The western central Sahara

5. The Oued Mzab, normal and in flood

6. A typical Saharan pulley well

7. Foggaras near Ouargla

8. Waterhole in the Ahaggar

9. In a Teda village

10. Bey-ag-Akhamouk, Amenokal of the Ahaggar

11. Baggage camels

12. Market day at Ghardaia

13. Tent of a Chaamba nomad family of Ouargla

14. A noble woman of the Ahaggar Tuareg

15. Young Tuareg nobles of the Ahaggar, out on the town

16. Ahaggar Tuareg **Camel** Corps soldiers

17. The Ajjer Camel Corps Company on parade

18. Ghardaia, capital of the Mzab

19. The main square of Metlili

20. A street in Ghardaia

21. Yahia Ballalou, former paramount chief of Ghardaia

22. Wandering entertainers

23. Haratin mother and child

24. A tent of the Ahaggar Tuareg

25. A zeriba of the Ajjer Tuareg

26. Wife of the chief of the smiths of Tamanrasset, in the Ahaggar

27. A Jewish girl of Ghardaia

28. A Chaamba nomad

29. A Moorish Camel Corps soldier

30. A Mzabite shopkeeper

31. A Mzabite woman of Ghardaia

32. On the trail in the central western Sahara, thirty-five years ago

33. Camp in the Ahaggar

for the slender one-piece iron spear of the Tuareg. These people had no animals at all with them and moved about quite independently on foot, living on the meat of game they killed or trapped, the roots, leaves, and berries of wild plants, and a small stock of half-ripe dates which they carried with them. Whether this was their normal way of life, however, or only a temporary expedient forced on them by circumstances is not clear. The language that they spoke was Tamaheq, which is a dialect of Berber spoken by the Tuareg.

The mythology of the nomadic Tuareg tells of a people known as the Issabaten (or Isebeten) who were living in the mountains of the Ahaggar when the Tuareg first arrived there; and one wonders if the little band Buchanan met may not have been perhaps the last independent survivors of some such ancient stock. The Issabaten were peaceful folk, organized in a series of social classes, and they were also supposed to be the originators of prehistoric Saharan art, but they are said to have had no camels or horses, and only a few donkeys, sheep, and goats. According to another version of the story, they had never even seen a camel, had no sheep, and were completely ignorant of the use of any kind of metal. They are often described as wandering hunters of mouflon who were finally adopted into Tuareg vassal tribes, among whom some of their supposed descendants are still distinguished as specialists in hunting and still hold exclusive rights, inherited patrilineally, to hunt in certain parts of the Ahaggar. A socio-economic organization of this kind is about what one would expect to find where a primitive nomadic hunting community has been overrun but only partially assimilated by a more highly organized pastoral nomadic people.

Another pattern of nonpastoral nomadic life, in which the wandering community returns periodically to a settlement or central base, was to be found not so very long ago scattered sporadically all the way across the southern fringes of the Sahara and beyond, from the Red Sea to the shores of the Atlantic. No more than fifty years ago a few such communities still survived as far north as southern Tunisia and in the hinterland of the Mediterranean coastal zones of Cyrenaica and Libya; but this pattern has since disappeared completely in most of the Sahara. Today it seems that only two tiny remnants remain, the Nemadi who are inland hunters, and the Imraguen who are coastal fishermen. Not half a dozen anthropologists have ever even seen members of either group, however, and unfortunately I am not among the lucky few who have.

The Nemadi are said to be divided into four small nomadic bands based on the extreme southwestern border of the Sahara, with their hunting ranges extending roughly two hundred miles northeastward into the most barren kind of desert country imaginable; and there are very few of them left, perhaps less than two hundred and fifty in all. Although the Nemadi are nominally Moslems they are very casual in matters of ritual, and apparently do not even observe the month-long fast of Ramdhan which is one of the most rigid obligations of Islam. And they still have pagan sorcerers including specialists in magic connected with hunting. Their social organization is patriarchal and they are said to observe Moslem marriage customs, but their women go unveiled. They seem to be endogamous as a rule, although I have not been able to discover just what the limits are within which marriages normally take place. On the other hand it has been said also that members of both sexes do occasionally marry Moors, in which case the newly married couple go to live with the husband's people, be he a Moor or a Nemedai (the masculine singular of Nemadi). Apparently Nemadi women sometimes marry French soldiers of the patrols charged with policing their territory, but this can hardly be a very common practice. Nemadi communities, rarely including more than three to five family units, are governed by elderly chiefs each of whom is chosen from among the direct patrilineal descendants of the supposed founder of his communal group. But these men seem to have little real authority excepting as advisors, for the degree of individual freedom is generally high. Each Nemedai has a sort of personal patron among the Moors, a man who will often lend him a camel for the big annual hunt and present him with a sheep or goat and a skinful of millet to help tide him over the winter season. In return the patron is given the skins of antelopes killed by his client, or a load of meat and some leather thongs. Some of the lesser Moorish tribes, on the other hand, pay the Nemadi to leave their flocks alone, and such payments are made customarily in Sudanese cotton goods.

Jean Gabus, a Swiss ethnologist who has spent some time with the Nemadi, has described them as being very variable in stature and black haired, but lighter skinned and straighter haired than are their Moorish neighbors. They have good teeth and big, flat feet, says Gabus, and a smooth, fast, gliding walk (as do most desert nomads). Several French authors have remarked that the women are often strikingly handsome and well built.

The Nemadi live a lonely life for they avoid the settlements and camps of others, and they have no slaves or parasitic groups attached to them. They have no houses either and only rarely a tent, but shelter themselves ordinarily with crescent-shaped windbreaks about ten feet across, which are made of small bushes with grass stuffed into the gaps between them. When a tent is used it is a curiously makeshift affair, consisting of several antelope hides sewn together into a sheet, about six feet square, the middle of which is supported by a single central pole while the edges are tied down. At night the supporting post is removed, and the tent covering spread directly over the occupants like a big blanket. Household furniture ordinarily consists of two or three wooden bowls, an earthenware pot or two, a wooden mortar and pestle and a flat stone for grinding grain (a "saddle quern"), a sheepskin rug perhaps, one or two straw pads for the baggage camel (if the family has one), and maybe a raised platform on which to place leather articles and the master's gun out of harm's way. Weapons include knives, spears, and sometimes a dilapidated gun.

Nemadi clothing is summary in the extreme, for men at work wear only a short kilt and singlet of leather or of cotton cloth, and a felt skullcap or a headcloth too skimpy to be called a turban. Reports dating back thirty years or more state that dog skins used to be worn in wintertime, and also that sometimes a whole antelope hide was worn, held in place by the skin of the forelegs tied together over one shoulder, and bound by a belt around the wearer's waist. One author, of somewhat doubtful reliability, has reported that the Nemadi sometimes wear iron bracelets (or arm rings?). Women simply bundle themselves up in big sheets of dark blue cotton cloth, but they leave their faces exposed. Although it seems that the Nemadi usually go barefoot, one author has written that they protect their feet occasionally with "flat sandals held in place by a thong which passes around the back of the heel and down between the first and second toes."

The Nemadi get most of their manufactured goods from sedentary Negro neighbors who live just south of them in the Sudan, for there they always find a ready market for products of the chase such as dried meat and particularly hides. These they exchange for cotton cloth and the firearms they prize so very highly, for millet, and for green tobacco which they smoke using the long bones of sheep as pipes.

Gabus says that each Nemadi hunter has three or four dogs which are purchased from the Moors, usually as pups but sometimes as fully trained adults. They look like coarse and rather heavily built sloughis but they are very expensive nevertheless; for a really well-trained animal is said to be worth as much as a two-year-old camel. Apparently dogs are also bought occasionally from Sudanese Negroes, in exchange for antelope hides. Males are often castrated to prevent their fighting and crippling each other, as they are very quarrelsome by nature and are also hungry most of the time. In view of the fact that without their dogs the Nemadi could never go on living as they do, it is only natural that they should attach great importance to them, and indeed dogs have come to be their most valuable medium of exchange among themselves. When a man buys himself a wife, for example, the bulk of the bride-price is always paid in dogs, usually four or five or even six, but sometimes, or so it has been said, as many as a hundred if the bridegroom's family is very rich.

In February 1951, Gabus accompanied a Nemadi hunting party on a fortnight's expedition of which he published an interesting description (in French). The group included nine hunters and two women, plus Gabus, his bodyguard and his interpreter, and nine camels carrying thirty-four *guerbas* of six and a half gallons average capacity (approximately two hundred and twenty gallons in all). The night before they started, the men acted out in ritual dances various phases of a successful hunt, and the elderly guide sharpened his knife ceremonially and sang incantations invoking choice parts of game animals. The normal rate of march was twenty to twenty-five miles a day, and the hunters, spread out over a wide area, moved on foot, usually from sunrise to sundown "without a pause," although when crossing the most barren sandy stretches (presumably empty of game) they traveled at night and rested in the daytime. Water was very scarce and so they supplemented their supply now and then with liquid squeezed from the stomach contents of animals they killed. Gabus says that the rumen of an adult addax antelope furnishes about half a gallon, which is acceptable to men and dogs alike.

The addax is the principal game animal of the Nemadi, followed by oryx, ostriches, bustards, and even, or so Gabus says, an occasional eagle. Gazelles are plentiful but are considered too fleet of foot to bother with. Antelopes are run down and pinned by the dogs, who then hold the animal until a hunter comes up and hamstrings it. This procedure is repeated three or four times until the herd takes fright and runs away, after which the hunters push the wounded animals along to where the baggage camels are and there finish them off with spears. Another way of hunting practiced by the Nemadi is for the hunter, with two or three dogs in leash, to stalk an antelope until he is within about a hundred yards of it, at which point the dogs are loosed and rush upon their quarry before it can get off to a good start. Apparently Nemadi hunters like to show off occasionally too, for General Diégo Brosset (writing under the pseudonym Charles Diégo) tells of witnessing a performance which was surprisingly like the "steer wrestling" one sees in rodeos. In this particular case the hunter's dogs immobilized a big male addax antelope, and the hunter then came up, seized the animal by the head, wrestled it to the ground, and drove its long horns into the sand so deep that its head was firmly pinned down, with the nose pointing at the sky. The hunter then arose, drew his knife in leisurely fashion, and calmly cut the animal's throat.

As soon as a hunt is over, all the carcasses are collected in one spot, skinned, and cut up into thin strips which are then dried in the sun; and finally the meat of each animal is bundled up in its own hide. Sometimes Nemadi men take their families hunting with them, in which case the women look after the baggage camels and the supply of water while the children help with the butchering and drying of meat. In dressing out an animal the Nemadi are careful not to touch its wounds "so as not to cause it pain," and its broken and empty marrow bones are carefully buried to prevent their being defiled by the dogs, presumably to avoid offending future victims and so causing them to refuse to let themselves be caught.

At the evening halt fuel is gathered when there is any to be found, and three tiny glasses of hot mint tea are drunk before any water or food is taken. The main course at supper is millet couscous,[1] precooked and then dried before leaving the home base. To this is added sun-dried meat, pounded to a powder, and hot water. By cooking the couscous before setting out the amount of water used in cooking on the march is kept at a minimum. During the evening the next day's hunt is never mentioned lest evil spirits be attracted and tempted to interfere.

Most authorities believe that the Nemadi are of Berber origin although they speak a dialect of Hassania, an almost classical form of Arabic. However they do have a very elaborate set of terms for game animals of different sorts, ages, colors, and conditions, and for various aspects of the chase, and this vocabulary is said to be rich in words which are clearly of Berber origin. Unfortunately no series of measurements or morphological observations and very few photographs of Nemadi are available.

[1] *Couscous* is a dish that Professor Earnest A. Hooton used to describe in his lectures as "a kind of Berber stew as opposed to Irish stew." The basic ingredient is wheat, barley, or millet flour, rolled into grains about the size of fairly big bird shot and steamed, to this are added, when possible, butter, stewed vegetables, and a very highly seasoned thin sauce. Meat is added by those who can afford it.

What photographs there are, however, show nothing to suggest that these people may not be a remnant of some archaic Berber stock that became Islamized and Arabized linguistically at a fairly early date, or that they could not just as well be a culturally debased remnant of some tribe of early Arab invaders. For all anyone knows at present either hypothesis may be right, although I am inclined to suspect that the Nemadi are indeed of Berber origin as has generally been supposed.

An enormous question mark remains at the end of this description of what seems to be the last surviving example of a very ancient hunting pattern of Saharan life. What kind of social organization and kinship system do the Nemadi have, and what are their noncommercial relations with the tribes that surround them? Apparently no one knows.

It is not surprising to find hunters in a hot desert, but one hardly expects to find fishermen there; and yet such are the Imraguen. The Imraguen, or Hawata (or Shnagla) as they are known in Spanish territory, are divided into a number of small nomadic and seminomadic groups which are scattered all along the Atlantic coast of the Sahara from about the level of the Tropic of Cancer southward nearly to the mouth of the Senegal River. Some authorities believe that they used to occupy the coast as far north as southern Morocco, prior to the last important Arab invasions of that region in the fifteenth century; and this seems reasonable enough in view of the fact that a few little groups of nomadic fishermen still survive there as a small and socially debased minority in the midst of some of the great Moorish tribes of pastoral nomads, such as the Ouled Delim. It is practically impossible, however, to reach any definite conclusions as to what the origins or the original territorial limits of the Imraguen really were, because the people who now go by that name have become so thoroughly mixed with various intrusive elements. The life of coastal fishermen seems to have become long ago a last resort for all sorts of neighboring groups and individuals of the interior who found themselves obliged to abandon other ways of life; and so today one sees occasional Spaniards and Spanish half-breeds among the predominantly

Berber population of the northern part of Imraguen territory, while in the central part there is an inextricable mixture of white and negroid freemen, war captives, slaves, and impoverished refugees, and, in the south, an overwhelmingly Negro and negroid majority. If one pins one's faith on linguistic evidence, it looks as though the original Imraguen must have been Berbers, for apparently Berber used to be their mother tongue although now it has been superseded to a great extent by Arabic, excepting in the technical vocabulary connected with fishing. Everyone is agreed too that Imraguen is a Berber word, the plural of *amrig* which may mean either a gatherer of food or one who makes use of a net, as in fishing.

The social organization of the Imraguen has never been described at all adequately and so remains something of a mystery. Apparently these people are divided into a considerable number of very small and widely scattered semi-independent clans (or tribes?) each loosely governed by an elder headman. Chieftainly authority seems to be very limited, however, for it is said that chiefs, or headmen, cannot even intervene in quarrels between fishing teams, who settle their differences by the simple expedient of fighting.

The material life of the Imraguen is a little better known than is their social system, but even so the picture is still far from clear except for rudimentary matters of detail. The economy seems to be based almost entirely on great schools of fish (chiefly mullet) which come close in to shore in August and stay there until April, when they disappear again. Fishing is usually done by men working in pairs and using a net of vegetable fiber, some fifty to sixty-five feet long and about three and a half feet across, which is held up by wooden floats and kept vertical by stone sinkers, or pieces of broken bricks or tiles. Mullet are caught in gill nets which have a mesh four fingers' breadth across, but nets of "very fine mesh" are also used sometimes for smaller fish. The usual procedure is for one man to hold his end close to the water's edge while his partner wades out and stretches the net across the path of an approaching school. Just as the fish reach him, the offshore fisherman swings around them in a sweeping circle which brings him back to the beach, and the two partners then haul in their catch. Sometimes two or three such teams set their nets at the same time, one behind another, so that any fish which escape the first are caught farther on. Normally, however, the run of fish is either too small or too concentrated for all the teams of even a small community to go out at once, and so they usually take turns, one at a time, in an order established for the day by drawing lots under the supervision of the oldest fisherman present. In addition to the fish caught in this way, porpoises are harpooned occasionally and giant sea turtles are taken too, when they come ashore on moonlit summer nights to dig their nests in the warm sand of a beach. The Imraguen are said to be inordinately fond of turtle eggs.

Boats are used sometimes in fishing but they are rare excepting in the north, where they can be bought every now and then from fishermen of the Canary Islands. A few are built locally, by specialists known as maalmin, but even so the materials used are almost all obtained from European trading posts. Apparently the fishermen along the southern and central stretches of the Imraguen coast used to have big dugout canoes, but it seems probable that there were never very many of them.

The fishing grounds of the Imraguen, or at least the fishing rights, are owned by nomadic Moorish warriors and Marabouts, who charge rent for them mainly in the form of fixed shares of the fish caught. Although the customary rate varies from place to place, it usually amounts to one fish for each cast of a net which brings in more than about half a dozen in all. Absentee landlords who live in the interior, however, and who appear to be in the majority, customarily settle for a yearly rent, paid at the end of the fishing season. Along the southern coast a typical annual payment consists of seventy dried fish, thirty-five roes, and a pint or so of the oil which is obtained by boiling fish heads. And a donkey may be included too, along with four or five yards of Sudanese cotton cloth. But no matter what form the rent—or tribute—takes, it never passes through the hands of a local chief or headman, but is paid directly to the landlord, or to an agent sent by him to collect it on the spot. In recent years this system has been breaking down to some extent, at least in the French part of the area where the government has been buying up the tribute rights of the Imraguen's Moorish landlords since 1917. But custom dies hard, and the Imraguen are weak whereas their Moorish neighbors are both strong and warlike, and so many landlords still collect tribute directly in addition to the payments they receive from the French authorities for having ostensibly abandoned rent collecting.

Most of the Imraguen are said to have no animals except donkeys, which they use mainly to fetch water for the camp. There are no good wells in the coastal strip where these people stay while fishing, but pools of water accumulated during the autumn rains constitute an adequate supply throughout most of the winter. As spring approaches, however, and the weather gets steadily warmer, water must be brought from permanent wells that lie some ten to fifteen miles inland. Thus the Imraguen are dispersed along the shore in scattered groups during most of the fishing season, but toward the end are forced back from the coast and draw closer to the permanent wells. In April, when the mullet disappear, they quit the coast entirely and move eastward to peddle their sun-dried catch in the camps of their Moorish overlords.

The Imraguen were first described by Robert Adams, a rascally mulatto merchant seaman,[2] who was captured by them when his ship ran aground in October 1810, somewhere in the general neighborhood of Cape Blanc. The people who captured Adams were "straight haired but quite black: their dress consisted of little more than a rug or skin round their waist, their upper parts, and from their knees downwards, being wholly naked. The men had neither shoes nor hats, but wore their hair very long: the women had a little dirty rag around their heads by way of turban. They were living in tents made of stuff like

[2] Robert Adams, whose real name may or may not have been Benjamin Rose, was probably an American citizen as he claimed to be. There can be no doubt that his account of his shipwreck and capture by the Imraguen is substantially true, although the story of his subsequent visits to Timbuctoo and Taoudéni appears to be false.

a coarse blanket, of goat's hair, and sheep's wool interwoven;[3] but some of them were without tents . . . . The men were circumcised, . . . Their mode of dressing fish was by drying it in the sun, cutting it into thin pieces, and letting it broil on the hot sand." After stripping the wreck these "Moors," as Adams calls them, buried their plunder and broke camp. "Adams, the mate and a sailor, Newsham, were left in the possession of about twenty Moors, (men, women and children,) who quitted the sea coast, having four camels, three of which they loaded with water and the other with fish and baggage. They travelled very irregularly, sometimes going only ten or twelve miles a day, but often considerably more, making upon an average about fifteen miles a day; occasionally going for two or three days without stopping except at night, at others resting a day or two, . . . Except one woman who had an infant, which she carried on her back, the whole party went on foot. The route was to the eastward, but inclining rather to the south than to the north of east, across a desert sandy plain, with occasional low hills and stones." The party finally reached a camp "where they found about thirty or forty tents, and a pool of water, surrounded by a few shrubs, which was the only water they had met with since quitting the coast," and here they also saw "some negro boys who were employed in taking care of sheep and goats." This was a camp of pastoral nomadic Moors. Of course the Imraguen seldom dress now as they did in Adams' day; but fishermen at work still wear a leather loincloth made of sheepskin, which is passed between the legs and held in place by a thong around the waist so that the ends hang down, in front and back, like little aprons. Sometimes the corners of these "aprons" are tied to the wearer's thighs which produces a result rather like an open-sided leather kilt. Ordinarily, however, the Imraguen dress much as do the poorer sedentary natives of the Sahara in general.

Most of the nomadic tribes of the Sahara, be they Moslems or "unbelievers," Arabs, Moors, Tuareg, or Teda, are pastoral communities whose routine activities are much alike simply be-

[3] The material of which Arab nomads and Moors generally make their tents.

cause of rigid conditions imposed by the environment. This makes it difficult to decide in what order they should be examined, but it seems best to start with the Tuareg, who have so often been described with really shocking inaccuracy, and then go on to consider the Teda, followed by the Arab Chaamba and finally the hybrid Moors. But first I would like to discuss a few basic traits which seem to characterize the pastoral nomadic peoples of the Sahara generally, as well as the ancient nomadic Bedawin [4] culture of Arabia as it was in the days of Mohammed.

Werner Caskel has stressed that ". . . a certain measure of anarchy is inherent in the Bedouins." "In this regard," he adds, "the Arab nomads and the Arabs generally are in sharp contrast to the Turkish nomads and the Turks in general, with their almost 'Prussian' discipline." And the same can be said with equal truth of the Moors, the Tuareg, and the Teda. Caskel sees this phenomenon as a function of an environment that forces major nomadic communities to break up during much of the year into relatively small constellations, made up of little scattered groups which nevertheless remain within a few hours' march of one another so as to be able to concentrate their forces quickly in order to ward off or avenge an attack on any one of them. And he has also called attention to the very important fact that "Bedouin economy is not self-contained but presupposes an economy of oases" within the same general area.

It has often been said that "treachery is peculiarly characteristic of desert nomads," and nearly everyone has read shocking accounts of merciless betrayals by such peoples throughout the world. But there is much more to this business of nomad treachery than is apparent on the surface. Underneath the often seemingly pointless brutality there lies a deep-seated idea, the dual code of ethics which is imbedded in the very core of all human society, extending from the family level upward through the level of the nation and beyond. This fundamental concept

---

[4] According to Coon (1958, p. 361), the word *bedawin* is an "incorrect but well-known plural of *bedawi*; it has become standard English." *Bedawi* means simply "a nomad." The spelling *bedouin*, borrowed from French, is still used commonly in English, but I will follow Coon nevertheless, except when quoting directly from authors who use the *ou* form.

stands out much more clearly in the relatively simple social structures of desert nomad tribes than in the complex patchwork patterns of highly developed sedentary communities, and that is why it is so often considered peculiarly characteristic of nomadic peoples. The late Sir Arthur Keith described it, with masterful clarity and precision, as follows.

"The members of a normal family, are prejudiced in favour of one another. . . . When children graduate from parental control to take their place in the life of their group, the family feeling or spirit expands so as to embrace all members of a group, as if the group had become their family. . . . It will thus be seen that the group spirit implies a discrimination between groups. A tribesman's sympathies lie within the compass of his own tribe; beyond his tribe, begin his antipathies; he discriminates in favour of his own tribe and against all others.

"The daily conduct of most men is based on a dual code: it seems so natural to them to love their friends and to hate their enemies that they believe that they are obeying only one moral code in doing so. . . . If a group no longer considered its own things much more precious than those of other groups, in no need of defence, then patriotism would be superfluous; if men and women behaved towards members of other groups as they did towards members of their own group, then all barriers between them would vanish and a general fusion would ensue."

But this would be against all human nature. The group spirit at whatever level, family pride or team spirit, community spirit, nationalism, patriotism, or religious unity, as the case may be, is a defense mechanism which man shares with many kinds of social animals including the great apes, and the continuous elaboration and extension of which have raised mankind above all other animals. But its cutting edges are being dulled progressively as the ever faster moving flow of human intercommunication dissolves more and more of the old barriers that have shut off human communities from one another for untold ages past. And so it is still found in a relatively simple and highly explosive form only among peoples who are still shut off to a great extent from quick and easy communication with others far away. This was the case among all the nomadic peoples of the Sahara until half a century ago, and it is still inherently the case with most of them as well as with much of the sedentary population of the area, even today. This is the key to the disturbing "mystery" of nomad "treachery," and also to the exasperating "deviousness" of the sedentary folk who live in desert cities and oases.

As the late Mr. Justice Holmes observed, in discussing the socio-legal structure of American society: "The ever-growing value set upon peace and the social relations tends to give the law of social being the appearance of the law of all being. But it seems to me clear that the *ultima ratio,* not only *regum,* but of private persons, is force, and that at the bottom of all private relations, however tempered by sympathy and all the social feelings, is a justifiable self-preference. If a man is on a plank in the deep sea which will float only one, and a stranger lays hold of it, he will thrust him off if he can. When the state finds itself in a similar position, it does the same thing." And, I may add, so do the nomadic tribes and sedentary communities of the Sahara, when they can.

Among Saharan nomads the spirit of merciless though "justifiable self-preference" used to find concrete expression not only in vicious attacks upon foreign intruders, but even more in endless raiding back and forth among the native tribes themselves. Because of the environment, because the "plank" of natural resources in the "deep sea" of the desert could "float" only a limited number of pastoral nomadic communities, the desert nomads were obliged to raid each other periodically in order to survive, in order to avoid getting "pushed off." Minor raiding, in the form of highway robbery, followed a familiar pattern. A handful of nomad warriors would conceal themselves beside the path of an approaching caravan, and then attack when least expected. In a matter of minutes they would gather together their booty of trade goods, arms, and animals, and be gone. This kind of short-range hit-and-run operation was indulged in by nearly all of the nomadic tribes occasionally, but was almost never practiced regularly as a routine economic activity.

Long-range raiding, on the other hand, did have a regular place in the economic patterns of many of the more powerful nomadic groups. And, although the number of warriors customarily taking part varied greatly from tribe to tribe, from as few as four or five to as many as fifty or occasionally even more, the general procedure was always pretty much the same. Success depended, of course, on the element of complete surprise, and on speed and efficient team work in collecting booty and getting away with it well ahead of the enraged victims bent on speedy vengeance. Also the target had to be far from the raiders' home territory, so as to increase the difficulty of immediate pursuit and also discourage retribution in the form of later counter-raids, or punitive expeditions. For this reason raiders usually directed their operations against some nomad camp three or four hundred miles away from home. Carefully avoiding all frequented trails, fertile areas, and watering points as much as possible, they would move cautiously across country, keeping to the roughest and most barren terrain where they were least likely to be seen by anyone who might report their presence and the direction of their march. Once arrived in the immediate neighborhood of their goal, they would settle down in hiding for a few days and study the routine comings and goings of their intended victims. When at last they saw that a herd of sufficient size and value had become separated from the rest, far enough away to be out of sight and hearing, the raiders would surround it quickly and hustle it off toward home as fast as they could go, taking the shepherds with them to prevent an immediate alarm. Unless the avenging owners of the stolen livestock could be left hopelessly far behind, as seldom happened during the first two or three days, the fleeing raiders followed an erratically zigzag route, if possible through particularly rough and barren country, so as to throw their pursuers off the trail. When very closely pressed, however, they would sometimes head deliberately for a sedentary oasis settlement where they would separate during the night and go off in different directions, mingling their tracks with those of ordinary commercial caravans. Raids of a roughly similar character were occasionally directed southward into the Sudan, where sedentary Negro villagers were seized and carried off as slaves to serve in the camps of their captors. In cases of this kind, however, pursuit was rarely a problem, for the would-be avengers very seldom had the necessary mounts.

Nomads who had been raided and had failed to overtake the fleeing robbers, usually sought revenge sooner or later by launching a counter-raid, or even a full-scale punitive attack, and this of course had to be avenged in turn; and so raiding back and forth between nomadic groups was both frequent and widespread in the Sahara as a whole. Warlike nomads also found sedentary settlements irresistibly tempting targets every now and then, especially after long periods of drought, so that small agricultural centers and even towns of considerable size were attacked and pillaged occasionally. To European authorities all such activities are intolerable, and so raiding has by now been suppressed completely except along the extreme western and southeastern edges of the desert, and even there it has been reduced as a rule to insignificant proportions.

One last characteristic activity which is common to most if not all of the nomadic peoples of the desert is the blood feud, based on the ancient legal theory of "an eye for an eye and a tooth for a tooth." The concept of reciprocal revenge is deeply rooted in the minds of desert nomads nearly everywhere, as is evident from the emphasis placed upon it in both the Old Testament and the Koran, and Saharan nomads by and large are no exception to this general rule. Blood calls for blood in a voice which can be disobeyed only at the cost of ostracism. When one man kills another otherwise than in battle, all close male relatives of the victim are in duty bound to seek out the killer and destroy him in his turn, after which it becomes the duty of his relatives to reciprocate in kind, and so on back and forth. Thus, in theory, a blood feud may go on indefinitely. In actual practice, however, "blood money" can usually take the place of blood sooner or later; in other words the thirst for blood revenge can be slaked eventually by payment, in money or livestock, of a variable sum corresponding to the importance of the victim whose death is being paid for. The exact amount is often predetermined by a

more or less fixed scale which has been established by local custom over a period of generations, but among some groups each
case has to be settled separately, by negotiation. When this occurs, the proceedings are usually presided over by a chief or "holy
man" who acts ordinarily as a moderator, rarely as a judge, between the opposing parties. If, as sometimes happens, a party
who have agreed to pay are too poor to deliver the blood price
all at once, they may borrow it and then proceed to work off
their new debt by paying tribute, and perhaps also rendering
certain specified services, over a period of years.

The blood feud system tended to promote periodic changes in
the structure of a nomadic tribe, because every now and then it
reduced drastically the economic rank and political power of
some kinship unit within the general framework of the community as a whole. It also led to periodic realignments of alliances
between kinship groups within the community, for those who borrowed became bound to their creditors, regardless of any previous allegiance. Thus, the blood feud was one of the most important obstacles to permanent political stability among and also
within the nomad tribes of the Sahara. It has been abolished
finally, however, and fairly successfully, throughout most of the
desert, and so has ceased to be a factor of any real importance
except historically.

Chapter 5

THE TUAREG

THE TUAREG of the Sahara proper, as I have defined it, are divided into three confederations, those of the Tassili-n-Aj-jer, the Ahaggar, and the Adrar-n-Ifoghas, distributed in that order from northeast to southwest, from the neighborhood of Ghadamès to the Sudanese frontier northeast of Timbuctoo. There are probably only about ten or twelve thousand of them in all, for the great bulk of the Tuareg, some hundred and forty thousand strong, now live outside the desert proper in the Aïr and the northern central Sudan. I will take the Ahaggar confederation as my Tuareg sample because this group seems on the whole to have remained the least affected by foreign influence, and also because I am familiar with it personally.

The Tuareg in general used to range over an enormous territory extending roughly as far north as Ouargla and Touggourt, eastward to Gatroun, westward to a little beyond a line running from Aoulef to Timbuctoo, and southward to below the great bend of the Niger River and the northern border of Nigeria. The eastern, northern, and western limits of this range have been slowly driven back over the last few centuries, first by ever stronger Arab pressure from the east, the north, and the northwest, and then by the gradual southward extension of European control. These steadily increasing pressures have produced a steadily increasing though fluctuating flow of the Tuareg population southward from the Sahara proper, through the Aïr and the Adrar-n-Ifoghas and into the Sudan. Under the stimulus of disaster in one form or another, this flow has occasionally become torrential for brief periods, as when, following the suppression of the 1916–18 rebellion, a great wave of Aïr Tuareg moved southward into British Nigeria and the main body of the Taitoq tribe left their home range in the northwestern Ahaggar for the country just west of Agadès. These movements were, however, only the latest major episodes in a general southwestward drift of which there is evidence going back at least as far as the eighth century, when the weight of Arab invasion first began to be felt.

The military administrative unit known as the *Annexe du Hoggar* covers roughly the territory that lies between Amguid and In Guezzam, and Djanet and Ouallen, and corresponds fairly closely to the present normal range of the Ahaggar Tuareg. This district is about the size of New York State, Pennsylvania, Virginia, and Maryland put together (an area of 146,300 square miles, with nearly 31,000,000 inhabitants in 1950), and supports a total native population of probably about 12,000, roughly the same as that of Swampscott, Massachusetts, or Gainesville, Georgia. Twice as many people work in the Pentagon Building alone as live in the entire Ahaggar.

Accurate population figures for nomadic peoples are always very hard to obtain, and in the Ahaggar it is practically impossible to arrive at anything better than very rough approximations. It is probably safe to assume, however, that there are about forty-four hundred Tuareg and four thousand Negro slaves in the area, plus some thirty-five hundred sedentary Haratin, a few small families of smiths, and a very small handful of Arab shopkeepers from the northwest who have settled in the largest sedentary centers.

The Tuareg speak various dialects of Tamaheq, which is a form of Senhadjan Berber. In Henri Duveyrier's words, "They are all thin, dry and sinewy; their muscles are like springs of steel." Physically they are the tallest people in the whole Sahara and among the tallest in the world. Men average only half an inch shorter than the average male American but individuals vary widely, from around five feet to about six and a half. They usually have a slim but wiry build with narrow shoulders and hips, small and rather flat chests, slender arms and legs, long, thin hands and thick, flattish feet. It has been said repeatedly that the arms of the Tuareg are exceptionally long in relation to their stature, but this is not true. Skin when unexposed is white, but what little one can see ordinarily is always deeply tanned. Faces are often more or less triangular, broad above and somewhat tapering below. Noses are thin and either straight or moderately convex. Hair is nearly always very dark, and light eyes are extremely rare although they do occur occasionally. Red-haired individuals with blue eyes and freckles are not entirely unknown. The foregoing description applies to Tuareg who are apparently unmixed racially, for those who are more or less visibly negroid (and they constitute a large minority of both the noble and vassal classes) vary accordingly. It has been stated emphatically, over and over again, that the noble Tuareg are racially purer than the vassals, but there is in fact no significant physical difference whatever between the two classes. Saharan Tuareg blood group distributions seem to be much like those of northern Berbers, and are curiously similar to those of the Basques (who live along the border between France and Spain) and the inhabitants of Geneva, Switzerland.

The Tuareg are divided into confederations as I have pointed out, and these are divided politically into tribes which are subdivided into clans and the latter into fractions. Socially the nomadic population is divided into three main classes, the Tuareg "nobles" and "vassals" and the Negro slaves. Rank seems to be essentially a quality of the clan rather than of the individual, for the Tuareg commonly speak of "noble clans" and "vassal clans," and, when one is in doubt about a person's social status, one does not ask what his rank is but what clan he belongs to. Also the tobol,[1] the symbol of chieftainship, is clan property and belongs to no particular family, although it is kept by the chief of the premier clan of a tribe in his personal abode.

The Ahaggar Tuareg confederation comprises three tribes, the Kel Rela, the Tégéhé Mellet, and the Taitoq, each headed by a noble clan which gives its name to the tribe as a whole.[2]

[1] A hemispherical drum made of half a big gourd with a skin stretched over the opening.

[2] Tuareg tribal and personal names are spelled in the literature in as many different ways as are the geographical names of the Sahara. Some of the variations reflect local differences in pronunciation, but most are due to the personal preferences of various transliterators.

Noble clans by definition outrank vassal clans, and so the chief of
a noble Ahaggar clan is usually chief of his tribe as well. The
tribes, each made up of a noble clan together with its satellite
vassal clans, are arranged in a fixed order of precedence, and so
the chief of the most noble clan (the Kel Rela) is normally chief
of the Kel Rela tribe and also paramount chief, or *Amenokal,* of
the Ahaggar confederation.

It is the men who govern at all levels of Ahaggar society. A
tribal chief is chosen from the premier clan of the tribe by a
clan council made up of the male heads of households, but he
must be confirmed in office by a council of male representatives of
all the component clans of the entire tribe, for his tenure depends
materially on the willingness of the tribe as a whole to pay him
tribute. For the same reason, the final confirmation of an amenokal rests with a council made up of male representatives of
all the clans in the whole confederation. Chieftainship is hereditary in the female line, however, passing in theory from an in-
cumbent to his eldest sister's eldest son; but the possible choice
falls in fact within fairly broad and seemingly rather indefinite
limits of degree of relationship, and so an undesirable heir-ap-
parent can easily be passed over in favor of a less direct heir who
is thought to be more suitable. A few early cases of father-to-son
succession are recorded in tribal traditions, but the circumstances
surrounding them have been forgotten. Brother-to-younger-
brother succession also has occurred now and then, but it seems
likely that the successor in such cases was regarded as inheriting
his right to the chieftainship through his mother rather than
through his brother, the former chief.

The position of an Ahaggar Tuareg clan is not firmly fixed
within the framework of the confederation. In times of crisis, for
example, a clan will sometimes break away from one tribe and
attach itself to another and more powerful tribe that is better
able to protect it. In the old days vassal clans were sometimes
swapped back and forth between noble clans, and so had their
tribal allegiance changed for them more or less arbitrarily. At
least one clan, the Ibotenaten, has been reduced from noble to
vassal status, in this case by a crushing defeat suffered in the

course of a blood feud. And so the distribution of the various clans within the tribal framework of the confederation tends to change gradually over the years, while internal tribal crises and intertribal warfare naturally accelerate the process.

Marriage is usually although not always within the clan but outside the first degree of cousinship and outside the camp community or fraction. A child of Tuareg parents inherits rank and privileges through the mother, regardless of whether she is a member of the father's clan or not; but the child is known as "such-and-such, child of so-and-so," the parent thus referred to being the father. Property is inherited from both parents, following the principle of Moslem law which provides that a male heir shall receive twice as much as a female heir who is related to the deceased in the same degree. Today a Targui, asked to give his ancestry, will recite the list of male forebears in his father's line, although in the fourteenth century Ibn Battuta wrote that descent was counted through the mother's brother, and that a man's heirs were his sister's children rather than his own. Oric Bates, citing Duveyrier, says that property acquired by force of arms used to be inherited by "the eldest son of the eldest sister of the deceased." Unfortunately, however, not enough is known about the underlying theory of Tuareg inheritance to make it possible to explain these seemingly contradictory statements. Marriage among the Tuareg follows a fairly rigid pattern. A newly married couple live in the camp of the bride's parents for about a year and then usually move over to a camp of the husband's people, but they sometimes settle permanently among the relatives of the bride if she and her husband are of different clans. A Tuareg camp is usually known, however, by the name of the highest ranking male member of the camp community. Children are normally brought up and continue to live among the group which their parents finally joined on a permanent basis, although boys are sometimes brought up by a maternal uncle. A widowed woman and her unmarried children are usually taken into the family circle of one of her brothers or married sons.

Boys are always circumcised, and the ceremony takes place at any time between the ages of five and seven; but there seems to be an "age group" factor involved, for all the boys in the camp who are about the right age are usually circumcised together in a single session. As for the young ladies, it is probably safe to say that most of them remain virgins until wed, even though the usual age at marriage is twenty to twenty-five for women and close to thirty for men. Monogamy is the universal rule and divorce is both unusual and generally frowned on. Adultery is probably no more common than it is in most societies where husbands and wives are frequently separated for periods varying from a few days to several months. Although an injured husband theoretically has the right to kill both his wife and her lover if they are caught in the act, in practice he merely repudiates his wife as a rule; and he may even decide to keep her regardless of her faults, in which case he appeals to the Amenokal who then fines the corespondent. The injured wife of an unfaithful husband simply packs up and goes back to her own people, unless she prefers to ignore the whole affair.

It has been said repeatedly that Tuareg women of the Ahaggar, young or middle aged, single or married, lend themselves freely to male guests as a general rule; but this is certainly a myth which seems to have grown originally out of a misunderstanding of the true nature of Tuareg social life. Premarital relations between the sexes are concentrated to a great extent in occasional gatherings whose main function seems to be to help young men and girls to get to know each other. These gatherings are of two main types, the *tendi* and the *ahal*. Tendis are usually afternoon affairs, held on various occasions of family rejoicing, such as the naming of an infant or the collection of the yearly rent from sharecroppers. The women of a camp begin a tendi by gathering around a tall wooden mortar (the tendi proper) over which a damp skin is stretched like a drumhead. Two light poles are attached to the skin, one on either side. On the ends of these two women sit facing each other, as on a see-saw, and vary the tone of the drum by resting more or less of their weight on the poles and more or less on their feet, which touch the ground. The rest of the women sit around the drum in a tight circle, one of them singing endless verses while the others clap their hands in time and add their voices in the chorus. While this is going on, young men from neighboring camps, dressed in their holiday best and mounted on their finest camels, begin to arrive in twos and threes. As they dismount, each goes to sit behind the lady of his choice, whom he proceeds to squeeze affectionately but unobtrusively. The women present are mostly young unmarried girls, with a sprinkling of widows and divorcees. Married women may attend only with the permission of their husbands, and they are expected to behave more decorously than the others. Any woman present, however, must get up and leave at once if her father, uncle, or older brother should appear. Singing and general conversation keep the gathering occupied until shortly before sunset, when the young men tear themselves away from their partners, remount their camels, and line up in two files, about fifty yards on either side of the women who remain huddled around the tendi-drum. For a while pairs of riders prance back and forth from one line to the other, showing off themselves and their animals to best advantage, and then at last one line comes forward in a body and proceeds to ride in a whirling circle around the seated women. Faster and faster they go, passing as close to the women as possible without actually touching them; and then suddenly one of the riders leans down, snatches the head shawl of a woman, and dashes off with it. All the other riders rush after him, and there follows a general scramble for the trophy which is finally returned triumphantly to its proud and flattered owner. And so the party comes to an end at last, and the young men ride off in the fading light of sunset to their respective camps.

Unlike tendis, ahals are held at night and usually have as their focal point some famous female musician, of noble family and often well along in years. The lady sits on the ground before her tent playing on an *imzad*, which is a one-stringed violin with a string of hair and a sounding box made of half a gourd covered with a thin membrane of skin. The high whining tones of Tuareg music, wailing on and on interminably in a persistent minor key, can be very irritating to European ears; and yet they are romantic in an eery sort of way when heard in the soft darkness of the desert night, fitfully illuminated by the flickering campfire around which shadowy crouching figures are more sensed than seen. The noble lady violinist plays on dreamily for a while, and then suddenly breaks into the stirring melody of some well known song of war or love, or a song that catalogues the virtues of a famous camel or some heroic warrior. A vocal soloist, who may be of either sex, usually sings the lyrics. Sometimes male singers also improvise flowery poetic songs describing their own prowess, ridiculing an enemy, or enumerating the personal charms of some particularly attractive lady in the audience. While all this is going on, the guests, who may number as many as a hundred on rare occasions, simply sit around and chat in ordinary voices or whisper sweet nothings in each other's ears. Occasionally, however, the men select a "sultan" and the women a "sultana," who put embarrassing questions to one and all and impose mock penalties on those whose answers are thought lacking in either tact or wit. Late at night the concert and burlesque interrogation come to an end, and a milk nightcap is passed around. Women then begin to wander off separately, each followed by two or three admirers with whom she settles down in some secluded spot. Once comfortably settled, she rattles on, talking and joking, while the young men take turns whispering in her ear and transmit mute messages by hand. One of them may trace a circle on the lady's palm and then touch the center of it, meaning that he wants to be alone with her. To this she may reply unfavorably by tracing a line along his palm from wrist to fingers; or she may trace that line and then retrace it in the opposite direction, meaning that he should leave with the others and return alone. When a young couple are by themselves at last, they may begin by kissing mouth-to-mouth, but more often they breathe up each other's noses, nostril-to-nostril. From here on things proceed naturally, sometimes going very far indeed, but rarely as far as many imaginative writers would have us believe.

In attempting to understand activities like the tendi and especially the ahal, many authors seem to have been led unwittingly astray by the conditioning of their own social environments. They tend to judge the manners and customs of others by their own. But, as one of my most knowledgeable colleagues once remarked, it seems to be a pretty general rule that in any given society, the greater the degree of sexual freedom customarily condoned, tacitly or otherwise, short of the ultimate in intimacy, the less often this extreme is reached in amorous play, at least among young people. Evidently, in trying to understand Tuareg women, Europeans often misunderstand them. The fact that these ladies can allow a very considerable degree of sexual intimacy and still avoid actual intercourse without resorting to violence seems to be due essentially to the simple fact that they are held in great respect by their menfolk.

Nearly everyone who has written about the Tuareg has dwelt at length on the concept of "courtly love" which permeates their whole system of intersexual relations, and yet no one has ever attempted to explain it beyond noting the obvious fact that it is at least superficially reminiscent of the attitude toward women which characterized the "courts of love" of the medieval troubadours. In the Sahara only the Tuareg seem to have made this attitude a basic element of their social structure, and so one wonders what special reason they can have had for doing so. In a remarkable analysis of the "courtly love complex" which flourished in southwestern France and southern Germany during the twelfth and thirteenth centuries, Herbert Moller has shown that it came into that area from Moslem Spain, and that it took root and grew because of a combination of local circumstances which enhanced the importance of women in terms of the prevailing socio-economic situation. The existing situation among the modern Tuareg is very different superficially, of course, and yet basically it is much the same. For example, a man can sometimes improve his social position, or at least that of his children, by marrying above himself, whereas a woman cannot; for, as I explained above, Tuareg children inherit the hereditary rank of their mother, no matter whom she marries. Indeed a man who marries a woman of higher rank than himself acquires in fact some of her prestige, much as does a prince consort, even though in theory his own inferior rank remains unchanged; and this state of affairs is exactly parallel to that which once existed among the upper classes of southwestern France and southern Germany. Therefore, while Tuareg women seldom marry beneath themselves, they can do so without losing either social or economic status; whereas a man can only marry at or above his own rank if he either hopes to maintain his hereditary status or aspires to climb up to a higher social level. Thus, Tuareg women obviously have more potential mates to choose from and so are dominant in courtship, while the whole adult unmarried male Tuareg population squirms eternally in the grip of an inescapable compulsion to cater to them in every possible way. In Moller's words "The great lady accepts" her admirer "as being worthy of her attention, but only at the price of behavioral restraint and refinement of manners. . . . She does not grant him the amorous 'reward' which he craves, but she gives him what immeasurably increases his 'worth': she rewards him with approval and reassurance," and this in spite of "a strong and sometimes morbid interest in matters of sexual frustration and fantasied compensations. . . . The symbolism of courtly love has apparently different layers of meaning, the common element of which is an anxiety regarding acceptance. . . . The range of this symbolism extends from the field of love and marital prospects to that of professional advancement; above all it refers to the deep human need of being accepted in congenial circles, that is in this case courtly society; and approval by courtly society implies the privilege of considering oneself superior." Here at last is a rational explanation of the truly courtly behavior which sets the Tuareg apart from all other Saharan peoples, and which has been the subject of so much irrational quasi-philosophical and pseudo-historical speculation. In fact the tendi and especially the ahal are simply organized manifestations of a system of tacitly formal attitudes which became publicly formalized in the Ahaggar, as they did in medieval southern Europe, by the development of courtly conduct and romantic poetry, "not read in privacy but presented at social gatherings" in response to "an abiding public interest."

Respect for women is also reflected in the Ahaggar in more material ways. A Tuareg bride, for instance, retains full title to all her personal property including livestock, while the husband pays all the family's expenses out of his own pocket although his wife may contribute if she feels inclined. And yet, even though women are treated with the greatest respect and deference, they can hold no office nor can they exercise any practical command beyond the very limited field of their own household affairs. They cannot appear in council, nor can they appoint speakers to represent them there. On very rare occasions a noble woman may intervene as an official peacemaker in a quarrel so serious that it might lead to a blood feud if allowed to go unchecked, and this can happen even in cases where the parties to the quarrel are not related to her by either blood or marriage, but only an older woman of very high rank, renowned for her intelligence, strength of character, and diplomacy can ever play such a role.

The picture I have just presented is full of gaping holes, but they cannot be filled in at present for lack of the necessary information. In spite of this one gets the distinct impression of a "double descent system," of the kind described by Gordon Gibson as "the utilization in one society of both patrilineal and matrilineal principles of affiliation resulting in two lineage systems cross-cutting each other." Among the Ahaggar Tuareg the patrilineal descent system draws the community together by providing channels of interaction between segments created by a matrilineal system which tends to divide the society into "separate corporate bodies." "The present function is in terms of a wide range of kin-like relationships leading to economic co-operation and to intermarriage among persons unrelated patrilineally. Double descent, therefore, permits a society" such as the Tuareg as a whole, who are broken up into "scattered and politically independent local groups, to maintain cultural uniformity and social cohesion." In other words, if the Tuareg were exclusively matrilineal, and not patrilineal at the same time, they would break up into a multitude of small separate communities. And under such circumstances it would be impossible for them ever to form cohesive major groupings of any kind or for any purpose.

It is not unnatural to jump to the conclusion, as several well known authors have done, that the ancestral Tuareg of ancient times were exclusively matrilineal and fully matriarchal as well, and that the patrilineal and patriarchal elements found in modern Tuareg culture were acquired relatively recently through Moslem influence, but this is not necessarily so. Gibson is inclined to think that the double descent systems found farther south in Africa evolved "as a whole," matrilineal and patrilineal elements being present together in a single complex from its beginning, and there is no good reason to suppose that this tentative assumption may not be equally applicable to the Tuareg. It is perhaps significant in this connection, however, that the concept of double descent is widespread among the Negroes of West Africa, whereas it appears to be unknown to the Saharan Arabs and the northern Berbers too. And this in turn makes one wonder if the Tuareg double descent system may not perhaps have been borrowed originally from the Sudan.

It is not surprising to find among a people like the Tuareg that kinship groupings and economic groupings coincide, for in an environment like that of the Ahaggar a family unit is obliged to be an economic unit too by force of circumstances. Each Tuareg vassal clan holds exclusive pasturage rights to a definite territory upon which no one else may enter, without express permission of the Amenokal, excepting that noble clans are always free to use the pastures of their own vassals as and when they please. But occasionally individual men also hold exclusive hunting rights in certain specified areas. Many Tuareg own garden plots in agricultural centers, and sometimes date palms and fruit trees of other kinds as well, all of which holdings are now parceled out to Haratin sharecroppers although some of them used to be worked by slaves. Since ownership of land is never outright in any of these cases, each leaseholder must pay rent in one form or another to someone or other at least once a year. Sedentary sharecroppers pay garden rent to nomadic landlords, while nomads pay pasture rent and garden rent as well to the Amenokal. Hunters pay their tribal chiefs for the privilege of hunting in specified preserves, even though their local hunting rights usually pass by inheritance directly from a father to his son.

The Amenokal of the Ahaggar is said to be "The Owner of the Land," by virtue of his position as paramount chief of a warrior aristocracy. I am inclined to suspect, however, that this may be an oversimplification of the case, for the land of the various tribes that make up the Ahaggar confederation is apparently treated as basically communal property, the title to which is vested in each succeeding Amenokal as an executive trustee rather than as a proprietor. This brings out the very important point that the Amenokal of the Ahaggar Tuareg is essentially a chief executive and not a true king or autocratic chieftain in the commonly accepted sense of those terms. And, theoretically at least, he can be deposed by popular demand although he normally continues in office until he dies.

The Amenokal and the noble tribal chiefs under him collect tribute from those over whom they have authority, but they are also supposed to protect these people by force of arms if necessary. When the warriors of a noble clan go raiding they often take the fighting men of one or more of their vassal clans along, and these vassal auxiliaries receive a substantial share of plunder if the raid is a success; and it is said that vassals also have an obligation to fight at the side of their noble masters in intertribal wars. It is in their own interest as a rule to do so anyway, if only to swell the ranks of those fighting to defend tribal interests which include their own.

Vassal clans pay tribute annually to their tribal chiefs or to the Amenokal, or both; and these payments usually include such things as dates, millet, congealed melted butter, baby camels, sheep and goats, manufactured articles of various kinds, a share of all merchandise imported by the clan as well as a share of the profits from any caravan commerce they may have, and about half of any booty they may capture in independent raids. Each vassal family used to contribute toward the upkeep of a particular noble family, while the nobles in their turn, men and women alike, were constantly begging from their vassals who could hardly afford to refuse them. But if this systematic begging became unbearable, as it often did, the vassals would simply pull up stakes and move quietly out of reach of their noble parasites. After each harvest each Hartani used to pay a third of a bushel (more or less) of grain to the Amenokal for each garden plot that he worked, in addition to the share of his produce which he paid to the local leaseholder. But much of this fiscal system has fallen into disuse in recent years, for the Amenokal together with his whole camp is now supported almost entirely by the French Government, which also contributes free grain weekly to many of the poorer nomads and Haratin. Thus the Amenokal and the higher nobles have no urgent need to press the collection of rents and tribute, while the sedentary and nomadic poor alike no longer need to pay either for armed protection or for economic aid. Once more it is the middle classes, the vassal Tuareg and the lesser nobles in this case, who suffer most severely from the stresses of political and economic change.

All Saharan nomads live primarily off their livestock, and livestock lives off pasturage. There are two main kinds of pasture in the Sahara: the permanent growth of wiry yellowish grass, little woody shrubs and thorny bushes that one finds scattered very thinly across much of the land and concentrated along dry river bottoms, and the small patches of thick, lush, emerald-green grass that flourish briefly in hollows here and there following rainstorms. Pasturage is always either very sparse or very scattered in the Ahaggar and so the nomadic inhabitants of the area must move often, for the supply in the immediate neighborhood of a camp is quickly exhausted. To make life still more difficult, water points are often few and far between, and it is not unusual to find good pasturage so far from any water that it cannot be used for more than a day or two, if at all. This combination of circumstances has made it necessary for the Ahaggar Tuareg to break up into small and highly mobile camps composed of fractions of clans, or even single families, and each of these units must move at intervals of usually somewhere between a week and a month and often over considerable distances, although always within the territorial limits of the tribe. As soon as a camp or constellation of neighboring camps is established in a new location, the headmen first arrange the daily grazing routine of the flocks and then set out at once to scout far and wide in search of the next pasture to be used and the next camp sites that their families will occupy. And so it goes the year around, and so the Tuareg of the Ahaggar are highly mobile nomads by force of circumstances, for they cannot survive otherwise in the region which they have made their own.

It is in the compelling forces of their environment that one finds the roots of the class system of the Ahaggar Tuareg. The nobles of a tribe together with the headmen of the vassal clans ride out in search of new pastures and at the same time act as military scouts, always on the watch for enemy raiders as well as for potential victims, alien camps or caravans which they can raid themselves. The vassals in their turn are responsible for the daily management and immediate protection of the flocks and herds, most of which belong to them anyway; and they also constitute an armed reserve that can be called up quickly in case a battle becomes imminent or a good opportunity for a quick raid presents itself. The slaves take care of the domestic service and household chores of the camps while their boys go out as shepherds with the flocks. Thus it is clear that the Tuareg class system is a necessity of pastoral life in the Ahaggar; for no pastoral community could survive there except as nomads, and no community of nomads can survive without a rigidly formalized division of labor and firm authority based on established rank.

In the light of what I have said it is obvious that Tuareg government has nothing essential in common with the feudal system of medieval Europe, to which it has so often been confusingly compared.[3] In the last analysis it is the vassals who

---

[3] The fundamental difference between the two systems lies in the fact that the basis of land tenure among the Tuareg is in no way like the *beneficium*, while the basis of personal allegiance is quite unlike that of the *comitatus*. The true feudal system of medieval Europe was based on the conferring of a specific privilege by an absolute ruler (or one of his vassals) on a less powerful neighbor in exchange for

have' the upper hand, for they can make and at least in theory break the mightiest of all the nobles, the Amenokal himself, and they can do so by peaceful means, again at least in theory. Ancient Egyptian records tell of a Libyan chieftain, Meryey, who actually was deposed peacefully and was replaced by his younger brother following a disastrous defeat in battle. Although the fact has not been recognized generally, it is some of the vassal clans that are the biggest numerically and also the richest on a per capita basis, which means that if vassal clansmen pay tribute to their noble "masters" it can only be because they choose to do so, because they find it in their interest to keep the nobles on their payroll so to speak. Thus, the Tuareg government of the Ahaggar is in fact a kind of republic (as opposed to a democracy) and not an absolute monarchy or true military aristocratic autocracy at all. It has been suggested that the present effective supremacy of the vassal clans may be only a recent development, resulting from the fact that the suppression of the slave trade and raiding deprived the nobles of their chief sources of revenue. This ingenious and attractive theory may perhaps be true to some extent, and yet I am still inclined to doubt it, if only because I can see no reason why the noble clans could not have maintained their supposed former strength on the basis of revenue derived from livestock and land rent, just as their vassals do to this day. In any case it is clear that the relative positions of noble and vassal clans have remained practically unchanged since the middle of the last century, before either raiding or the slave trade had yet been interfered with at all seriously.

Herds of camels and flocks of hairy sheep and goats are the main capital investment and so form the primary basis of Tuareg economy in the Ahaggar. The quantity and composition of the total livestock holdings have been variously estimated, but the following rough approximations are probably not far from the true figures: twelve thousand camels, two thousand sheep, twenty

some specified kind of continuing or periodic service. Among the Tuareg the relation between "noble" and "vassal" looks much the same at first glance, but this is an optical illusion, a case of merely superficial resemblance.

thousand goats, five thousand donkeys, and three hundred head of cattle (zebus) or thereabouts. Only some forty-five hundred camels are actually kept in the Ahaggar massif, while the rest are put out to pasture in the Tamesna region on the northern edge of the Sudan, roughly halfway between the Air and the Niger Bend. Most of the sheep are also pastured outside the Ahaggar proper, mainly in the country between In Guezzam and Kidal. The Haratin of the Ahaggar keep chickens too although only the eggs are eaten as a rule, but the Tuareg themselves eat neither eggs nor fowl, nor fish.

It has been said that the Tuareg have no special breed of riding camels but that likely looking animals are picked out early and given special training for use as mounts. The fact remains, however, that the young of famous camels are always the preferred choice, and are specially marked shortly after birth. The method of marking consists of pinching up three small folds of skin in a row, two or three inches apart, along the ridge of the nose, and then tying a thin leather thong very tightly around the base of each fold much as a string is tied around the opening of a toy balloon to keep the air in. After a while the thongs are cut away and three little round knobs, about the size of the end of your index finger, remain for the rest of the camel's life as a kind of hallmark of outstanding quality. Riding camels are very carefully and patiently trained from the age of about two years on, and males which are not considered worth keeping exclusively for stud purposes are usually castrated when about five years old.

Pastoralism is thus the central column of Tuareg economy in the Ahaggar while garden rent is one of the corner posts. Foreign trade is another corner post, and salt is the chief article of export. In April or May some of the Ahaggar Tuareg send their slaves to work for a while at the mines of Tisemt in the Amadror, and then, in July, they start south with their cargoes of salt. In the rich pastures of the Tamesna region they rest their animals for a while or exchange them for fresh ones, and then go on again to the commercial centers of the country just north of the Nigerian frontier. Here it is still summer and very hot, for the equator is still far to the south, but the heat is less scorchingly dry than in the desert, water is plentiful, and there are trees in whose shade one can rest comfortably. Trading begins in earnest late in October as a rule, but endless discussions and bargaining drag on for a month or two more. Salt as well as camels and donkeys, and dates imported from the north, are exchanged for millet and for a variety of manufactured articles such as cotton cloth and clothing, leather goods, household utensils, tools, and weapons. In January the Ahaggar Tuareg start the return trip northward, pause again for a while in the Tamesna, and finally reach their homes in March or early April. In the old days the Tuareg of the Ahaggar used to have active and regular direct trade relations with a whole series of other commercial centers in the desert to the north. Over the last thirty years or so, however, these commercial currents have been reduced to mere trickles by middlemen with trucks, who have gradually taken over delivery of the goods that used to come from the north by caravan. The trade still exists in a sense, but it has become indirect and its focus is now strictly local as far as the Tuareg are concerned.

In addition to their own trading activities, the Tuareg used to control caravan trade in general over a very wide area, and this was the third corner post of their economy. Barth wrote, a century ago, that in his day the Amenokal of the Ahaggar, Guémama, controlled all of the trade routes between Mourzouk and Timbuctoo, and it seems likely that this situation already dated back over a considerable period. The Ahaggar Tuareg used to control all trade in the southwestern Sahara too, as far west as Ouadane and southward into northern Nigeria, at least as early as the beginning of the fifteenth century. Their grip on much of this area was broken, however, by the Moroccans at the end of the sixteenth century, and they never seem to have been able to extend it again much beyond Aoulef in the northwest or southwestward beyond the neighborhood of Timbuctoo.

The Tuareg mechanism for controlling trade routes was based on the furnishing of guides and armed escorts to caravans passing through areas under Tuareg domination, and for these services there was a fairly uniform customary scale of charges based on the estimated value of a caravan's cargo and the reputed wealth of its owners. Some caravan leaders of course refused to pay the fee demanded and took their chances, while big caravans occasionally brought their own guides and guards along with them and small ones now and then tried to slip through unobserved. The Tuareg, however, succeeded in making such expedients unprofitable in most cases by raiding reluctant customers along the road. Thus a highly profitable protection racket was maintained for several centuries before the period of European domination.

The fourth corner post of the Ahaggar Tuareg economy used to be raiding pure and simple, and this activity was divided into two main types according to the chief object in view. Raiding for booty was practiced irregularly but fairly often, especially in times of hardship or in connection with intertribal feuds, and usually took the form of sneak attacks by small bands which stole livestock and promptly fled with it. The hottest days of summer were often the most favored period for this kind of operation, because the scarcity of grass and water at that season obliged potential victims to break up their camps and herds into small and isolated units which were relatively vulnerable to attack. Slave raiding, unlike raiding for booty, was practiced on a fairly regular basis. In the nomad camps of the Ahaggar the number of Negro domestic servants is usually almost equal to the number of Tuareg present, and this labor force used to be replenished when necessary by raids on Negro villages in the desert fringe of the Sudan and occasionally even on Tuareg camps in the Air, Tamesna, and Adrar-n-Ifoghas regions. I myself know a half-breed Tuareg freedwoman who was taken in this way from the Air not more than thirty years ago, and has long been happily settled at Tamanrasset; and she is by no means an exception. Thus raiding, the fourth corner post of the old Tuareg economy in the Ahaggar, was primarily a mechanism designed to keep the supply of livestock, both animal and human, at a satisfactory level in an area where the environment caused a steady normal decrease.

Pastoralism used to be the central column and crop shares, trading, protection, and raiding the four corner posts of Ahaggar Tuareg economy. With the coming of European domination, however, the last two pillars were kicked away, the third buckled and bent to a mere fraction of its former height, and the roof fell in along three sides of the economic structure and part of the fourth. The Ahaggar Tuareg presumably never lived a life of ease—no pastoralist can in such a rigorous environment—but their greatest perils used to be those of warfare. These dangers have been removed completely by the new European rulers of the area, and yet the Tuareg of the Ahaggar as a whole are undoubtedly in worse economic shape today than they ever were before. Their old culture, whatever one may think of it on the basis of modern European standards, was remarkably well adapted to conditions in their chosen homeland. The destruction of two of its five main material supports and the progressive weakening of a third have thrown their economic system so seriously out of balance that the whole edifice is doomed, and so the Tuareg of the Ahaggar as a nation, too stubborn to adapt themselves to any way of life other than their own, have at last added their name to the ever-lengthening list of vanishing peoples.

The extremely harsh desert environment of the Ahaggar caused its Tuareg inhabitants to adopt certain forms of social, political, and economic organization in order to maintain themselves as a reasonably stable and cohesive major community or nation, not only safe from the natural hazards of its habitat but also able to compete successfully with warlike neighbors and commercial rivals. And yet these special developments in communal organization are in a sense only secondary matters, for they obviously depend primarily on the ability of individuals and family units to survive at all; and individual survival is primarily a question of shelter, clothing, and food. The typical dwelling of the Ahaggar Tuareg is a leather tent, made pref-

143

erably of the skins of goats although sometimes those of sheep or even calves are used. A tent of mouflon skins is considered the height of luxury and elegance, but it is almost impossible to find enough to make such a tent nowadays. Once prepared, the skins are very soft and have a pleasing dull red brick color which is produced by rubbing them on both sides with a mixture of red ochreous clay and dried camel dung. After being prepared and cut down to rectangular form, they are sewed together with fine strips of leather. Anywhere from thirty to as many as a hundred and fifty may be used to make a single tent, but the first number is not far below the average. A finished tent of ordinary size weighs about fifty pounds.

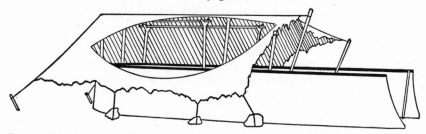

FIG. 3. Diagram of a leather tent of the Ahaggar Tuareg. (Part of the roof and the ends of the wall mats have been cut away.)

Tents are mounted on wooden frames of various closely similar types, the most common of which consists of three elements, each composed of two uprights with a horizontal member laid across their tops. The tallest element is set in the middle with one upright in front and the other in the back, and the two remaining elements are set up parallel to it, one on either side. The tent covering is then stretched over this framework, with its back and sides pegged down and the front left open, usually facing south. In good weather the overhanging front of the roof is stretched out horizontally to form an awning held in place by three supplementary posts, one in the middle and another at each end. The average tent is six to ten feet deep from front to back, ten to fifteen feet wide and four to five feet high in the middle, with the roof sloping away very gently on both sides and toward the back wall. The structure is completed by long strips of stiff yellow matting made of thin reeds, roughly three feet wide and up to twenty feet long, with simple geometric designs done in black or reddish brown ribbons of leather. These strips are set on edge around the inside of the tent so as to make an inner wall at the back and sides, and are extended out in front to form a sheltered enclosure which is usually semi-circular with the entrance opening in the middle. The little fore-court and the ground inside the tent as well are covered with clean sand or very fine gravel from the dry bed of a nearby gully. Tuareg camps are always very tidy and astonishingly clean. Both in the forecourt and in the tent itself the men's place is on the right as you enter and the women's and children's on the left, which is the reverse of the arrangement customary among Arabs. It has often been said that the men's place is on the east, the side nearest Mecca, but this is simply because tents are usually pitched facing south for the sake of warmth: it is always cool and often cold in the shade in desert mountain country except in summertime.

Household furniture and effects include sheepskins or rugs obtained from the north by trade, leather bags for food and personal belongings, saddles, bridles and weapons, wooden bowls, funnels and spoons and maybe an earthenware cooking pot or two, a wooden mortar and pestle or perhaps two sets of different sizes, and a *quern* [4] which may be either of the Neolithic saddle type or the small rotary model of the Roman Legions. The importance of spoons is particularly interesting because, until very recently at least, all Saharan peoples other than the Tuareg ate mainly with their fingers. Weapons and food are stored in the men's half of the tent and equipment connected with food and cooking in the women's half (although the actual cooking is usually done by slaves). A guerba full of water is

---

[4] A "saddle quern" is a long oval or rectangular slab of stone, with a slightly concave upper surface, on which grain is ground with another stone shaped usually like a slender rolling pin. A "rotary quern" consists of an upper stone shaped like a huge flattened doughnut with a small hole, set on a round, flat lower stone of the same size. Grain is poured into the hole in the upper stone which is then turned around and around (usually by means of a wooden peg inserted in one side), thus grinding the grain which runs gradually out around the edges in the form of flour.

hung from two long stakes just outside the forecourt. A brush windbreak built nearby protects the outdoor kitchen, and another windbreak, some fifty to a hundred yards away, shelters the family slaves. Sometimes in the hottest months, and particularly when a camp remains stationary for a considerable length of time, the tents are stowed away and replaced by zeribas. These are cubical structures, made usually of long grass laid over a wooden framework which measures roughly ten to fifteen feet across and eight to ten feet high. The Amenokal's camp was installed in zeribas when I visited it in November 1955, near the end of an unusually long period of drought.

Tuareg camps are always pitched in an inconspicuous spot, and always on high ground except on very rare occasions when the sky is cloudless and there is no possible danger of a sudden downpour that might produce flash floods. Each tent is occupied by a single family unit, ordinarily four or five individuals, and there are almost never more than five or six tents at the most in any normal camp; more often there are only three or four. In the camp of the Amenokal there are usually fifteen to twenty tents and often more, and one sees no flocks nearby, but this is a wholly artificial situation made possible only by the fact that the Amenokal and his personal retinue receive most of their supplies by truck from the nearest French Army post, and so can live in a way which would be impossible in the Ahaggar under anything approaching the normal conditions of nomadic life.

Although the little leather tent and the zeriba offer reasonably effective and comfortable shelter in an arid, mountainous environment like that of the Ahaggar massif, they solve only a part of the general problem of physical protection. Suitable clothing is also necessary to survive in such a place. In the old days the Tuareg used to wear leather shirts that reached below the knee and were sometimes elaborately decorated with fringe. Herodotus described Libyan women as wearing fringed garments of red leather some twenty-five hundred years ago, and Theodore Monod adds that some Tuareg women of the Niger Bend country still do so. Lyon wrote that leather shirts were worn by many of the Tuareg who visited Mourzouk while he was there in 1819, but Duveyrier found that they were already becoming scarce only forty years later. I myself have never seen leather clothing worn by Tuareg in the Ahaggar.

Tuareg men today wear very loose, baggy trousers made of dark indigo-blue or black cotton cloth, which are held in place with a braided leather cord by way of drawstring. The seat is baggy and hangs down well below the knees, the ends of the legs are sewed up so as to fit closely around the ankles, and there are no pockets and no fly. A loose, white cotton shirt, rather like a nightgown with very wide sleeves of medium length, used to be the standard undergarment, but the gandoura of Arab origin finally replaced it and is now being replaced in turn by the European type of shirt. The Tuareg gandoura is made of a huge rectangle of cloth, roughly seven to eight feet wide by eight to ten feet long. This is folded over on itself and the free corners are sewn together so as to leave the bottom and most of both sides open, a V-shaped opening for the head and neck is cut out of the fold at the top, and a large patch is sewed on inside so as to make a roomy pocket placed just below the left breast. The gandoura worn next to the skin, or directly over the undershirt, is usually made of white cotton, and a second one, of dark indigo-blue cotton cloth this time, is customarily worn over it. On gala occasions some of the Tuareg wear a third gandoura, made of very narrow vertical strips of Sudanese cotton cloth dyed a lurid pinkish violet, or of alternate strips of violet and white or dark blue, often with two large spiral patterns embroidered in coarse white thread, one over the left breast and the other on the back between the shoulders. This third type of gandoura has gone almost completely out of use within the last few years, but it is still worn occasionally and is considered extremely elegant. A Tuareg gandoura should be wide enough so that when the upper corners hang down freely they cover the hands, although they are usually rolled up over the forearms so as to leave the hands free and sometimes are folded over the shoulder, thus freeing the whole arm. A woollen outer garment is occasionally worn in cold weather. Lightweight blankets from the Gourara and the Touat used to be worn like giant shawls, but these have been replaced to a great extent by the burnous of the Arabs, a long hooded cloak made of wool or of camel's hair mixed with wool.

The Tuareg protect their feet with sandals of three main types. The true Tuareg sandal consists of a thick leather sole built up of two or three layers which are held together by ornamental stitching done in thin strips of bright red, yellow and green leather. Both ends of the sole are wide and cut off square, while the sides curve inward toward the center line. The sole is held in place by a long, narrow strip of rawhide which passes upward between the first and second toes, backward in a long loop around the heel and then forward again, and is attached indirectly to the sole on either side by short vertical loops. This type of sandal is very old and is almost never seen today except occasionally among groups who spend most of their time in rocky mountainous country. The second type is much like the first except that the sole is usually made of a single piece of leather the front end of which is folded back over the toes, thus protecting them from stones and thorns. It too is seldom seen today. The third type of Tuareg sandal has a large, thin sole, shaped roughly like a big figure eight, which extends out beyond the sole of the foot for at least an inch in all directions. It is held in place by a roll of thin leather that comes up between the first and second toes and is attached to the point of an inverted V, made of two very broad strips of thin leather whose rearward ends are sewn to either side of the sole just in front of the heel. This third variety is the standard footgear of the Tuareg today; and it is probably of Sudanese origin, for such sandals are almost always imported from the Sudan. Poor shepherds sometimes protect their feet with pieces of rawhide, held in place by thongs passing over the arch of the foot and around the ankle; but this is only a makeshift foot covering for those who can afford nothing else.

Before the introduction of modern firearms, the armament of the Tuareg was very distinctive and picturesque. It consisted of a sword, an arm dagger, a spear or two, two or three javelins, and a shield. The sword was about three feet long, broad, two-edged, and with a round point. The grip was always very small, barely big enough for one hand of not more than medium size, the pommel was a flattish oval cone, and the guard consisted of a flat rectangular crossmember covered with leather and set on at right angles. The best sword blades used to be imported, apparently from northern Italy, Germany, and Spain for the most part. Even today swords are still worn occasionally as symbols of prestige but they are almost never used.

The arm dagger was a foot long or a little more, with a blade sometimes made from a cut-down or broken European sword blade but more often of cheap wrought iron, made locally or imported from the Sudan. The hilt was always shaped like a cross, although the proportions varied a good deal regionally. This kind of dagger was used as a "stabbing knife," and was held so that the shaft of the hilt passed between the index and middle fingers, with one branch of the cross extending between the index finger and the thumb, and the other branch lying against the palm of the hand. The sheath was firmly attached to a strong, broad bracelet of leather, which was passed over the left hand so that the dagger in its sheath lay against the inner side of the forearm with the blade pointing toward the elbow and the hilt against the wrist.

The spear, which was used for throwing rather than thrusting, was made all in one piece from a rod of iron about seven feet long, with a barbed point shaped like a greatly elongated willow leaf. About a foot and a half of the other end of the shaft was flattened, with the butt flaring out like the edge of an axe. The best spears used to be imported from Ghadamès. The javelins were merely smaller spears, about a foot or two shorter, and with less flaring butts.

Shields were used for deflecting blows rather than for stopping them. They were large but light, and were made preferably of a single piece of oryx antelope hide, four to five feet long, about a foot and a half across the top and two and a half feet wide at the bottom. The top edge was cut out in a sharp downward curve, while the lower edge curved upward slightly. Tuareg shields were held in the left hand by a single vertical handle shaped like that of a suitcase. They were always ornamented with a standard design, nicked in the surface with the point of a sharp knife, which looks rather like an elaborate and highly stylized variation on the theme of the Christian orb-and-cross. Curiously enough, however, this standard pattern, which was always placed on every shield without exception, was often overlaid and partially obscured by pieces of red cloth, triangular or shaped like vertical rectangles with their long sides concave, which were held in place by bosses of white metal. No one seems to know what the underlying design really represents, and the Tuareg themselves refuse to tell, if indeed they have not forgotten.

Many Tuareg men wear arm rings which are made usually of a soft greenish stone, and are boiled in fat to turn them black and give them a lustrous finish. One ring, rarely more, is worn just above the elbow, usually on the right arm, sometimes on the left and occasionally on each. Some authors have maintained that these rings were used to crush an opponent's skull when one got a head lock on him, but it seems more logical to suppose that they were originally intended to protect the blood vessels and lower biceps attachment of the sword arm, just as black silk bandages have been used by student duelists in Germany. Arm rings are treasured heirlooms among the Tuareg; and there is something magical about them too, for powder scraped from the inner side of one and taken like snuff is the standard remedy used to stop a nosebleed. Young Tuareg ladies sometimes present inscribed arm rings to their fiancés. It is possible indeed that these rings are, or were originally, valued primarily for reasons of magical protection, much as iron arm rings are today by some Negroes of West Africa as well as by the nomadic Bedouin of the Syrian Desert. Although rings of iron apparently are never worn by the Tuareg today, two were found in the little fortress-tomb of their legendary ancestress, Tin Hinan, who lived probably in the fifth or sixth century of the Christian Era.[5]

By far the most distinctive and arresting article of Tuareg clothing and equipment, however, is the mysterious *teguelmoust,* the men's veil which has done so much to make the Tuareg so famous. The teguelmoust (or *litham* in Arabic) is actually a combination veil and turban made of a band of lightweight cotton cloth some ten feet long by a foot or so wide, preferably dark indigo-blue in color but often white or black nowadays. This band is wound around and around the head and face leaving exposed only the eyes and a small patch near the back of the scalp. The eye opening is made as narrow as possible on formal occasions, and its lower edge is often doubled over in the middle so as to draw the cloth tight across the bridge of the nose and thus prevent the veil from slipping down.

Self-respecting Tuareg still think it shockingly indecent for a man to let his mouth be seen by anyone to whom he owes the least formal respect. When eating or drinking, the left hand is slid up underneath the fold of cloth covering the face so as to hold it out away from the mouth without raising it above chin level, and the spoon, bowl, or glass containing food or drink is then passed up under the veil with the right hand in such a way that the mouth and even the chin remain concealed during the entire process. A Targui about to enter a camp other than his own must stop first and arrange his veil so that the eye slit is very narrow, for to do otherwise would be insulting and would place him in about the same position as that of a stranger ostentatiously whistling at the girls in a small American town. Indeed it may be taken as a general rule that a Targui will never show his face to anyone whose social standing he considers superior to his own. Minute changes in the arrangement of the veil are used to indicate changes in the mood of the wearer; and there are also many standard variations indicative

[5] And, after all, a black stone ring looks enough like a ring of iron to be perhaps an acceptable substitute in a land where iron is fearfully expensive. But here again there is danger in jumping to conclusions.

of social status and tribal or even clan affiliations. It is interesting to note that Ethiopian men used to wear big shawls which they arranged around their necks and shoulders in various ways each of which expressed a different mood of the wearer or his attitude toward the persons with whom he found himself. And even some Indians of the American Plains used to do much the same kind of thing with buffalo robes.

But when, where, and from whom did the Tuareg get the curious idea that men must all wear veils while women go without? All that Lyon, Barth, Duveyrier, Benhazera, Reygasse, Lord Rennell (Francis R. Rodd), Lhote, Blanguernon, Dupree, myself, and many others, have been able to elicit from the Tuareg themselves, over a period of a century and a quarter of patient effort, is that self-respecting men wear veils and always have, simply because it is the proper thing to do. Duveyrier, followed more recently by Francis Rodd and Henri Lhote, held that the teguelmoust cannot have had a utilitarian origin, because it is worn by men whose womenfolk habitually go unveiled in spite of the fact that both sexes are exposed to the same rigorous environment. Maurice Benhazera, writing fifty years ago, agreed with this theory, and cited as evidence the fact that Tuareg men questioned by him all denied flatly that the veil was intended to serve any useful purpose. Bissuel, however, stated that the western Tuareg went veiled as a matter of practical necessity seventy years ago. Other equally serious investigators have gone to extremes of both fantasy and caution. Barth, for example, suggested that the teguelmoust was designed "to imitate the shape of the helmet" of a medieval knight, while Claude Blanguernon, after noting that the veil is in fact a very useful protection against sun and wind regardless of what its chief purpose may now be, prudently declined to speculate as to its origin on the very reasonable grounds that there is no factual evidence at all to go on. Lhote has referred speculatively to a preposterous legend which says that the ancestral Tuareg, while living in the Yemen in southern Arabia, adopted the veil in order to look like women and so escape the unwelcome warlike attentions of their pagan enemies. It has been suggested also that Tuareg men hide their mouths because they think it shameful to expose either end of the digestive tract. But if this is so, then why do the women leave their mouths exposed?

The arguments advanced in favor of the theory that the teguelmoust cannot have had a utilitarian origin fail to convince me, for several reasons. In the first place men of all Saharan and many Arabian nomad tribes often veil their faces with a fold of the turban when out in the sun and wind or in a sandstorm, although being veiled or not seems to have no serious ceremonial implications for any of them except the Tuareg. And everyone who has traveled at all extensively in hot deserts knows that it is often advantageous to the point of being almost essential when on the trail to cover the head, nose, and mouth with light, loosely woven cloth; for such a covering not only protects the wearer from the sun and wind but also maintains a pocket of relatively moist air, kept humid by the breath, around the mouth and nostrils. This last function is of great practical importance for it protects the mucous membranes of the respiratory tract which otherwise suffer severely in an arid climate, even when the thermometer is only moderately high. Thus it it clear that the teguelmoust does have a very real practical value, regardless of what the Tuareg may say; and it is clear also that the men who wear it need it far more than do their womenfolk who go without.

It is not true that Tuareg women of the Ahaggar are exposed to the rigors of their environment either as much or in the same way as are their menfolk. The men are out and about a good deal of the time, riding here and there across the countryside on errands of one sort or another or on long journeys, while the women sit quietly in the shelter of their tents, gossiping, telling folk tales, doing fancy leatherwork, and teaching tribal lore and sometimes Tifinagh [6] to the children. Every family that is not miserably poor has at least two or three slaves to fetch and carry water, prepare the meals, and do the other daily chores, and so the mistress of a normal Tuareg household in the Ahaggar has no need to take a single step outside her tent

[6] The Tuareg alphabetic script, written Tamaheq.

except when camp is moved, or to visit with her neighbors, and to answer calls of nature. Although it is true that Tuareg women do not wear veils they are by no means alone in this respect, for the women of the other Saharan nomad tribes, Moslem Arabs included, seldom wear veils either except on the very rare occasions when they visit a sedentary settlement or town, and even then not always by any means. But Tuareg and other Saharan women alike all draw a corner of the head shawl (or turban cloth) across the nose and mouth occasionally as a simple matter of physical protection, and this has the same practical effect as putting on a veil. All this material regarding the wearing of veils and going without them proves nothing, but it does show that the teguelmoust may well have had a strictly utilitarian origin after all, quite apart from the unknown origin of the elaborate and rigid ceremonial quality with which its use has become imbued.

As for the date at which the teguelmoust was introduced among or developed by the Tuareg, there is only negative evidence to go on and very little of that. All I can say with any assurance is that it cannot very well be older than the introduction of cotton cloth, which is self-evident, and that it could easily have been derived from some quite ordinary type of turban, like that of the Arab Chaamba for example. Cotton cloth must have been introduced into the Sahara on a commercial scale very soon after the introduction of camel domestication had led to the establishment of a regular caravan trade with Egypt, if not before. There are indications too that it may have been known in the Ahaggar as early as the fifth century and perhaps even earlier, and yet there is no evidence in the literature that the Tuareg wore veils before the tenth or early eleventh century. As Rodd (now Lord Rennell) said: "It seems very strange that none of the classical and post-classical authors should have recorded a feature which so distinguishes this people from other races. There is no reference to the Veil until we come to the first Arab authors." Desert raiders remarkably like the Tuareg are known to have been in increasingly frequent and violent contact with Romans, Vandals, and finally with Byzantines,

from probably at least as early as the dawn of the Christian
era until the first wave of Arab invaders arrived some six centuries later, and after that they were in contact with the Arabs
for another three and a half centuries or so before anyone began to write of veiled men in the Sahara. El Bekri, describing
a major commercial center of the southwestern desert as it was
early in the 11th century, wrote of the inhabitants that "they
veil their faces as do all Berbers of the desert," while Ibn
Battuta, writing three hundred years later, said: "we came to
the country of the Haggar, who are a tribe of Berbers; they
wear face veils and are a rascally lot." But these simple matter-
of-fact statements too are very strange, for they seem to suggest
that even El Bekri took for granted that his readers were already familiar with veiled men of Saharan Berber tribes.

Tuareg women's clothing is less striking than that of the
men, and there is nothing at all mysterious about it. They wear
either a short cotton skirt that reaches just below the knees,
or a pair of baggy trousers, like those of the men but shorter.
Like the men they usually wear a white gandoura with a blue
one over it, but the under one at least is sewed farther up the
sides leaving open arm slits only a foot and a half to two feet
long. The costume is topped off with a shawl and a head scarf
of indigo-blue cotton cloth, the first measuring roughly nine feet
by six and the second about four by two feet as a rule. Lightweight woollen shawls, measuring as much as ten feet by six
and a half, and white or darkish pink in color, used to be worn
on festive occasions but have practically disappeared in recent
years. It is said also that Tuareg women sometimes wrap goatskin blankets around their shoulders in wintertime. Straw hats
with very high conical crowns and enormously wide floppy
brims, made of narrow interwoven strips of palm fronds, used
to be worn in summertime by women of rank, especially when
on a journey, but these too have almost completely disappeared.
Although Tuareg women never wear a veil (which is just as
well since many of them are extremely good-looking), they often
drape a fold of the head shawl loosely across the nose and mouth
when sitting out in the open or riding on the trail, simply as a

matter of physical protection. Young unmarried women and girls are inclined to be overcome with giggles when strange foreigners arrive in their camp, and then they hide their faces with the loose end of a shawl or with whatever piece of clothing is most handy, just as little girls do everywhere in the world.

Tuareg women sometimes plaster their foreheads and cheeks with mudpacks of red or yellow ochre, and smear their mouths with indigo and the region of the eyes with *khol,* a black pigment made of powdered antimony or charcoal mixed with grease. This lurid make-up gives fairly good protection against sun and wind, and the Tuareg consider it very beautiful as well, although to our eyes it makes the wearer look absolutely frightful. Men also apply khol profusely to their eyelashes, especially on gala occasions; but here again a practical element may be involved, for khol gives good protection against dust and glare, and is also very soothing to irritated eyes.

The Tuareg attach considerable importance to indigo-blue cotton cloth, a product which they get from the Sudan. This material is commonly known as *shegga,* and the most archaic and highly prized variety is made of a multitude of long strips about an inch wide sewn tightly together. A brand new piece looks black when seen at a distance or in a poor light, but in bright sunlight it has a dark purplish blue color with a coppery sheen like that of cheap carbon paper; and the indigo dye comes off on one's fingers at the slightest touch. Obviously anyone who wears clothes made of such material is soon stained with indigo from head to foot, and the Tuareg even rub it into their skins on purpose. Women often smear it on their foreheads, cheeks, and temples and around their mouths by way of make-up, and dandified men sometimes do likewise. The Tuareg claim that indigo not only protects human skin from the direct effects of sun and wind but also lubricates it and so prevents cracking, and they are quite right, at least up to a point. If they wash themselves only very rarely, it is partly to avoid removing the accumulated protective coating of indigo, the humble practical value of which has been greatly enhanced by its ever increasing fashionable value which has risen in proportion to the rising cost of indigo-dyed cloth. A dirty-looking, bluish skin is admired by the Tuareg as a symbol of prestige.

Much has been written about the reluctance of the Tuareg to wash, but it should be noted that in the desert one can go unwashed for long periods without either feeling dirty or developing a strong body odor. The air is so very dry that perspiration usually evaporates instantly upon reaching the surface of the skin, and so it is unusual for anyone to sweat visibly. Also most of the nomadic natives are in excellent physical condition in that they are very lean and wiry, and so they perspire relatively little.

Scarcity of water in the mountains of the Ahaggar is probably the main reason why the inhabitants of that region bathe so seldom. When an Arab nomad of the northern desert goes to town, the first thing he usually does is head for the public baths and get himself thoroughly steamed and scrubbed, but the Ahaggar Tuareg almost never visit any town big enough to have public or even private baths. A few permanent waterholes and a number of seasonal ones are to be found, however, scattered thinly through the Ahaggar massif, and the local Tuareg make use of such pools occasionally, although perhaps not quite as often as do the Tuareg of the Air, of whom Lord Rennell (Francis R. Rodd) wrote as follows. "In justice to my friends, I must admit that they washed their clothing, and especially their white trousers, very frequently, and when they washed their person, they did so very thoroughly from head to foot, with much rubbing and a prodigious splashing of volumes of water." It has been observed that the Tuareg of the Ahaggar, women as well as men, wash themselves with equal gusto when they wash at all, and this is not the kind of thing that one would expect of people who have any real dislike or fear of water as such. And finally it should be noted that among Saharan peoples in general, including the Tuareg of the Ahaggar, bodily cleanliness seems to correspond pretty closely to economic status, as it so often does elsewhere in the world.

Since I have already discussed slavery in the Ahaggar, a brief summary of the situation should suffice. The slaves, almost all

157

Negro captives from the Sudan, or the descendants of such captives, are chattels which can be bought, sold, and inherited. They do all the menial labor and housework around the camp and also act as shepherds. A slave can seldom marry without the permission of his master, who, however, usually advances the necessary bride-price. Nevertheless slaves are well fed and cared for as a rule, their children are brought up with the children of their masters, and custom forbids the freeing of those who are too old, too young, or too infirm to fend for themselves. A slave may even have a few goats of his own, although when he dies they are not inherited by his family but revert instead to his master or his master's heirs. Barth, writing a hundred years ago, noted as a striking exception that he saw slaves hitched to a plow and driven with whips in the Auderas Valley, some sixty miles northwest of Agadès. Although the slaves of the nomadic Tuareg, like those of sedentary communities in the Sahara, seem to have no tribal or clan organizations, they do have a strong feeling of corporate solidarity which finds expression now and then in nocturnal jamborees which are Sudanese in character.

Female slaves are often taken as concubines by Tuareg men of the Ahaggar, who prize them because they are less capricious and overbearing than Tuareg women and "because they have cool skins." The children of such unions are often recognized by their fathers but do not inherit from them, and, although free, they have a debased social standing little better than that of their slave forebears. Moussa-ag-Amastan, who was Amenokal of the Ahaggar from 1905 to about 1921, remained unmarried for some fifty years, during most of which time he lived with a bevy of Negro concubines and, for a while, with a young Tuareg slave girl named Harendou, whom he had captured on a raid into the Niger Bend country. Although this case was exceptional, it is by no means unique in the annals of the Ahaggar.

The smiths who live among the Tuareg present a familiar pattern of culture that characterizes many other groups of smiths and tinkers who are to be found living among a whole series of sedentary and nomadic peoples scattered all the way from Baluchistan through Arabia and on, southwestward and then westward, across the North African hinterland to the shores of the Atlantic. The general description of this pattern found in Chapter 3 leaves little more to add, except for a few matters of detail. Smiths of the Ahaggar usually live in small isolated groups of two or three family units each. Sometimes families follow the Tuareg about on their seasonal rounds, but normally they remain sedentary in one agricultural center or another, and go out only now and then for a few weeks or months to do general repair and reëquipment work in the camps of some nomadic tribe or clan. The men work wood and metals and are also barber-surgeons, while the women specialize in fancy leather work and embroidery. In addition to these functions and those previously mentioned, both sexes of the smith community act as go-betweens and spies in clandestine love affairs. They also engage in intertribal secret intelligence work. A major Tuareg chief may even have a smith as his most trusted though obscure counsellor and confidant, but this very rarely happens.

Smiths usually dress as do the poorer Tuareg. Although the men all wear the teguelmoust they arrange it in a sloppy fashion, and they seem to have no qualms about exposing their mouths in the presence of anyone excepting high Tuareg chiefs. They are endogamous and monogamous as a general rule, although a few have more than one wife and some of them marry Haratin or occasionally slaves. Ostensibly because of their lowly social status, but probably in fact more because of the fear of sorcery that they inspire, they come and go as they please, although in a cringingly ingratiating manner. Even those who have come to know me well still give me an impression of constant watchfulness and profoundly sycophantic tact, of the delicately oiled as opposed to the heavily greased variety. The smiths are, in the last analysis, the most perspicacious and cleverly adaptable of all Saharan peoples, for they have learned to live off and so outlive flamboyant warriors with their warlike retinues and grubbing gardeners alike. They have turned their status as "untouchables" to their own advantage and so remain untouched.

Physically the smiths of the Ahaggar cover the whole range of human variation between the true Negro type on the one hand and the Berber variety of Mediterranean on the other, but they seem to fall mostly within a highly variable category characterized in general by "European" features, combined with a dark yellowish brown or occasionally coppery skin, thickish lips, and curly or frizzled hair. They are very lean in build as a rule, but seem softer and much less wiry than the more active Tuareg.

And this brings me to another exasperating blank in the overall picture of Saharan peoples; for no one knows the true origin of the smiths of the Ahaggar. They themselves claim to have come from the northwestern Sudan and to be related to families of smiths who live there still. Benhazera, who knew them well fifty years ago, published an old Arabic text which states that "the smiths and the Fulani have the same mother." Walter Cline, on the other hand, maintained that the art of smelting iron was introduced into the western Sudan from across the Sahara by "camel-riding Berbers" from the north, and so suggested without actually saying so that the smiths may be of northern Berber origin. But no one really has any idea where they did come from, or when, where and from whom they first learned their trade. No one, so far as I know, has ever published measurements or blood analyses of a single one of them, and no one seems to have found out anything about their social organization or even their kinship terminology. Not a dozen photographs of their faces are available to students. Why? Simply because the Tuareg are spectacularly romantic whereas the smiths are not. The smiths of the Sahara as a whole, including those of the Ahaggar, have suffered the same fate that the Spanish gypsies might have suffered had George Borrow not been born; and, like the Spanish gypsies, they are disappearing fast. But there are other minorities among the Tuareg whose origins are almost equally obscure.

A number of vassal clans of the Ahaggar confederation are said to be of Arab or mixed Arab and Tuareg ancestry. The most reliable authorities all agree in lumping most of them together in a special almost tribe-like class known as the Issoquamaren, but do not agree entirely on just which clans should be included in this group. According to some, the Issoquamaren once claimed descent from a woman purchased in the Adrar-n-Ifoghas country by Arab invaders who came there straight from Mecca, about the middle of the seventh century, and finally moved northward to the Touat early in the twelfth century. The first part of this tale is very characteristic of marginal Arab schools of historical fiction, or rather fictional history, which are often no more reliable than the modern school of lecturers who tell us, for example, that the Tuareg are descendants of veteran crusaders who came to the Ahaggar from the Levant. This parallel that spans the centuries is funny, to be sure, but there is much more in it than just an amusing coincidence. It is a striking illustration of the fact that uncritical minds, Moslem and Christian alike, are always deeply moved by thoughts of the past glories of their race and religion. One must never forget the dangers of grotesque misinterpretation that result so often from the action of this powerful subconscious force. Indeed most of the Saharan peoples who have been converted to Islam stubbornly insist against all sense and reason that they are of Arabian Moslem origin. Other authors believe that the Issoquamaren are descended from Arab men and Tuareg women of the Tademait region, whence they were recruited as mercenaries by the Tuareg of the Ahaggar. Still others hold that they are descended from a group of Arab tribes of the Tidikelt and the Touat who were defeated and then assimilated by the Ahaggar Tuareg in the eighteenth century, or possibly before. It has been said too that the Issoquamaren enjoy a social status superior, at least in theory, to that of ordinary vassals, but in point of fact they are looked down upon as greatly inferior to "pure" Tuareg vassal clans. Although their clans and fractions have been parceled out among various supposedly pure Tuareg tribes of the Ahaggar confederation, they still seem to retain some remnants of the social structure of a single and united tribe. And since they have become rich in camels, they have regained in practical power and influence most of what they once lost in hierarchical prestige.

The Irreguenaten, another half-breed Tuareg group, are based on the Tamesna region, south of the Ahaggar, whence they move northwestward periodically, with their flocks and herds, across the Adrar-n-Ifoghas and back again. They are believed to have sprung from a series of marriages between Arab men and Tuareg women of the Ibotenaten clan. The descendants of these unions banded together and soon became so numerous, and so very rich in camels and in slaves, that they were finally able to establish a separate clan of their own. Although they are included in the general vassal category, they enjoy a nebulous but well recognized position of precedence in relation to most of the other Tuareg vassal clans. The social organization of the Irreguenaten is striking and important, for it includes the standard Tuareg system of double descent in a more highly developed and clearly defined form than can be found elsewhere. Although the group as a whole constitutes a single matrilineal clan, based on descent in the female line from a supposedly common Tuareg ancestress, this clan is subdivided into two patrilineal clans, the Haggarenin and Settafnin, membership in which is based on supposed descent in male lines from two male Arab ancestors. And this is very interesting as an example of a matrilineal clan structure that has been effectively split by Moslem influence into two patrilineal clans while still remaining basically a unit in the matrilineal terms of Tuareg social and politico-economic organization, and, to a great extent, in terms of internal economic organization too.

It should be noted that the partly Arab clans of the Ahaggar Tuareg confederation live for the most part outside the Ahaggar proper and are distributed in an arc that curves around its southwestern, western, and northwestern borders. The northwestern extremity of this arc continues curving eastward, then southeastward, and finally on southward around the territory of the Ajjer Tuareg confederation, while the southern gap in the perimeter of the resulting oval is closed by the zone of Negro-Tuareg contact in the southern Air. The Ahaggar massif lies at the center of this oval refuge area: it is a Berber island, so to speak, whose shores are continually swept by waves of the surrounding Arab sea, and, along its southern and southeastern coastline, by the negroid "Gulf Stream" of the Sudan.

The Tuareg in general have all embraced Islam; but for the most part, they are lukewarm and superficial converts. Their minds have been varnished, as it were, with Moslem doctrine, but the varnish has dried on the surface without impregnating their thought. There are some religious groups of Arab origin among the population, but they are very small and scattered, and their influence is relatively unimportant as a rule. Even the annual Moslem fast of Ramadhan, which corresponds to the Christian Lent, is not very generally observed, although in the middle of the fourteenth century Ibn Battuta noted that the Ahaggar Tuareg suspended raiding operations during this period. Arab Shorfa missionaries from Morocco first arrived in the Ahaggar probably in the late seventh or early eighth century, and there they soon set up a theocratic dynasty, the Imenan, who ruled both the Ahaggar and Ajjer Tuareg as a single confederation. About 1650, however, Goma, the last of the Imenan "sultans," was murdered by Biska, a noble of the Oraghen tribe of Ajjer Tuareg. There then followed a long period of anarchy and civil wars out of which finally arose, about the middle of the eighteenth century, the main framework of the present Tuareg political structure which I have already described. It is significant, however, that as recently as 1900 a Shorfa holy man exerted decisive influence in the electoral council of the Ahaggar confederation when that body found itself seriously divided over the choice of a new amenokal.

Since the Tuareg have no permanent buildings, they naturally have no mosques properly speaking, but when a camp stays put for a considerable length of time, a rectangular area, measuring usually some thirty feet by twenty and with its long axis running north and south, is laid off with lines of small stones. There is a sharp outward bulge in the middle of the eastern side, facing

Mecca. Within this "edifice" the men of the camp assemble for prayer, and so it does duty as a mosque. As in most Moslem communities, women never take part in religious ceremonies. It has been said that the Tuareg once had a Berber translation of the Koran, in the eighth and ninth centuries, but it was long ago destroyed or lost (if indeed such a text ever did exist) in the course of a violent religious reform movement.

The European conquest of the Sahara has done much to stimulate the Islamization of the Tuareg in general during the last hundred years, for Marabout and Shorfa families of the north have often found it advantageous to move southward and attach themselves to Tuareg tribes or clans whom they then proceeded to stir up against the French and Italian newcomers. And in this way the Koran became a kind of battle flag of local resistance to European penetration throughout the Sahara. The Camel Corps troops who have long maintained order for the European rulers of the desert, have always been recruited mainly from among Moslem Arab nomad tribes, notably the Chaamba, and their thinly scattered garrisons and outposts in Tuareg country soon came to serve as centers for the continuing diffusion of Islamic doctrine. And finally it has become less and less unusual for noble ladies of the Ahaggar to marry men of Arab Shorfa or Maraboutic families, sometimes from as far away as Ouargla. Thus racial and religious penetration have marched together into the Tuareg country, following the path that leads through adversity to political and biological union in a common cause.

The basic relation between the "living saints," Marabouts and Shorfa, and the warlike nomads of the desert was clearly stated in the Old Testament, as Monod has pointed out with keen insight and inimitable wit. In Esau and Jacob he recognized the pastoral nomad warrior and the holy man of the Sahara, where Marabouts and Shorfa families used to parley instead of fighting and bought off raiders just as Esau bought off Jacob long ago. In Monod's words: "The Marabout's soul is in anguish at this extreme but inevitable generosity which he imposes on himself, but he would a thousand times rather have anguish in his soul than brought into his body in the shape of a sharp javelin ending its whistling flight between his shoulders. But there are times when the Marabout gets his revenge for the humiliating brutality of the warrior. The latter is indeed too simple not to be superstitious, and so, with the roles reversed, there comes a day when he in turn will tremble before the religious chief and implore the blessing of the sorcerer on his raids; for who would dare undertake such an expedition without the magic formulae and the amulets which will assure success for the enterprise and personal safety in combat? The man of God alone confers, and not without a price, the power that is entrusted to him; and the man of the sword pays. It is indeed his turn." As a typical example of a nomad warrior buying the benediction of a holy man, Monod cites the transaction between Abram and Melchizedek, "the priest of the most high God," and he reconstructs the scene in imaginative but wholly convincing detail drawn from his own long experience among desert nomad tribes. After Melchizedek had invoked the blessing of God on Abram, the latter said: "How much will that be?" "Nay, my Lord is joking," replied Melchizedek, "It's free, I *give* my blessing; I *give* it to him." And Abram bowed down and said (thinking that after all if the blessing wasn't paid for it might not work, and knowing only too well moreover what his interlocutor meant by "gift") : "Harken unto me: I give the price of the blessing and of the amulets for my camels; accept it of me." And Melchizedek answered him: "Let not my Lord be vexed, and may he harken unto me: I do not sell him power, I give it to him. But if in return he chooses to bring me the tenth part of all that is his, what is that between us?" And Abram understood, "And he gave him tithes of all." Nothing could be more characteristic of desert nomads and revealing of the basic relation between them and holy men in the Sahara and elsewhere.

Clearly, the Tuareg of the Ahaggar had achieved an adaptation to their environment which was about as perfect as could be, in terms of social, political, and economic organization and of material culture, until the reforming forces of European civilization began to destroy the economic base and so to undermine the entire structure. And yet the origins of Tuareg culture remain a mystery. Although the Tuareg speak Berber dialects, and although their socio-political organization seems to be fundamentally the same as that of the Berber peoples of the north, their system of descent is quite unlike anything found among either the northern Berbers or the Arab tribes of the Sahara. On the contrary, it seems to be of a kind which characterizes a number of West African Negro tribes, notably the Mano and Ashanti, as well as several other Negro peoples who live still farther south. There are tantalizing hints too that the Tuareg may have been in touch fairly regularly with the eastern Roman Empire as early as fourteen hundred years ago; for the tomb of their legendary ancestress, Tin Hinan, contained gold jewelry whose style is suggestive of that area and age. Tuareg mythology also preserves the legend of a noble couple named Yunis (John) and Izubahil (Isabel), who are believed to have been imported in A.D. 1406 from Byzantium, to rule over the Air. And, finally, the distinctive one-piece iron spears and the equally distinctive wooden spoons of the Tuareg find their only close parallels (so far as I know) far from the Sahara, in the Island of Madagascar of all places! In short there is no lack of vague and mysterious hints as to the possible origins and evolution of Tuareg culture, but they are all so incongruous and incoherent that I can do no more at present than point out the fact that they exist, in the hope that some day they can be investigated properly.

Chapter 6 ~

THE TEDA

THE TEDA, of the southeastern central Sahara, used to be great raiders, operating over a tremendous area that extended from the Nile Valley to the Niger Bend and from the heart of the eastern central desert southward far into the Sudan, but that was before they were finally brought under control by the Turks and their Senoussi allies, succeeded by the French and the Italians, during the last century or so. Map 3 shows the approximate distribution of the Teda [1] in the Sahara. It has been estimated that they numbered about two hundred thousand some forty years ago, but the bulk of the population then lived, as it still does, south of the desert proper in the Sudan. Just as I chose the Tuareg of the Ahaggar, so I will use the Teda of the Tibesti as my sample in this case, for they seem to have been subjected to less outside influence than have their neighboring relatives.

The Teda of the Tibesti massif probably number between nine and ten thousand, some seven thousand of whom are said to be mainly nomadic while the rest spend a considerable though variable part of each year in agricultural centers here and there. The present range of the nomadic groups does not extend much beyond the limits of that Tibesti proper, and so covers an area of roughly a hundred thousand square miles or perhaps a little less.

Physically the Teda look a good deal like the Haratin although they are more slender, and the men have relatively long

[1] Pronounced Tedah, with the accent on the last syllable. These people are also referred to commonly as Tebu, Tibou, Toubou etc., but Teda or Teda-too is the name they call themselves by.

167

legs as well as long arms. Their average stature is just under five feet six inches, a good half inch less than the Haratin average and about two and a half inches below that of American men. They have small heads and faces, and their noses are usually broad but straight in profile. Their ears are often rather small and short, as those of Negroes usually are. Lips are often very thick but sometimes are as thin as those of any white man. Hair form varies from wavy to woolly, with the majority in or close to the latter category. The coloring of the Teda is normally very dark in all respects. It is surprising then to note that their ABO blood group pattern is about as different from that of the Haratin as it could be, and is also markedly different from the corresponding patterns of Arabic speaking peoples in general as well as those of Sudanese Negroes and of negroids generally. On the other hand, it is so much like Berber patterns that one cannot help but wonder if the Teda were not originally Berbers, however outwardly negroid they have become in relatively recent times. Today the Teda speak various closely related dialects which used to be classified as Sudanic but are now known technically as "Central Saharan." Nevertheless Teda speech seems to resemble most closely that of certain negroid Sudanese groups, and it is said to show no traces of Berber influence beyond what can be explained as due to contact with the neighboring southeastern Tuareg.

The Teda of the Tibesti are believed to be divided into some forty clans, and there are indications that these may be loosely organized into broader tribe-like groupings within some kind of unstable and ill-defined confederation. Rank seems to be essentially a quality of the clan rather than of the individual, just as it is among the Tuareg. At the top of the social ladder are the "noble" clans, the Tomaghera (or Tomagra), the Gunda, and the Arna, all of whom are said to have entered the Tibesti as conquerors from the southlands only a few centuries ago. Some say, however, that the Arna arrived relatively recently, from the Tuareg country to the northwest, and that it was they who first brought camels to the Tibesti. Next in rank are the "commoners" followed theoretically by the "vassals," but the differ-

168

ence between these two classes appears to be one of degree rather than of kind, and it may even have no other basis than a difference between the terminologies employed by different investigators. For the purposes of the present study I will lump "commoners" and "vassals" tentatively together in a single "vassal" class. After the Teda "vassals" come the *Azza* (hunters, smiths, and artisans), the negroid "serfs" (Haratin), and finally the Negro slaves, ranking in that order.

All the Teda of the Tibesti pay lip service at least to a paramount chief known as the *Dardai,* who is chief of the Tomaghera clan as well and used to be elected alternately from the three leading Tomaghera families by the council of that clan. The last of the independent Dardais was a man named Shaffai (or Shahai Bogar-Mi) who ruled from shortly before 1895 until he was defeated by the French and fled to Kufra in 1914. He surrendered to the French in 1920, was reinstated by them, and again ruled the Tibesti until his death in 1939, but this time he was only a feeble tributary puppet with very limited authority. During his first term in office, Shaffai used to receive tribute annually in the form of produce from the owners of gardens and of palm trees, toll fees from all caravans passing through his territory, and a share of all booty captured by the Tibesti Teda in their raids. Just as a major chieftainship is symbolized in the Ahaggar Tuareg confederation by a drum known as a tobol, so the authority of the Dardai is symbolized by the *kadmul* (or *debi*), a green turban which may possibly be of pre-Islamic origin. According to Teda tradition, the kadmul was inherited by an ancestor of the Tomaghera by virtue of his marriage to a woman of the Derdekishia, another noble clan in which the office of Dardai had been hereditary until then.

The political organization of the Teda of the Tibesti seems to be very elastic, and the positions of the various clans within it are even more unstable than were those of Tuareg clans within the framework of the old Ahaggar confederation. Apparently the Teda have long been politically in a state of kaleidoscopic fragmentation and recombination, because the various communal groups are often relatively isolated by the exigencies of their environment, because of a blood feud system which is elaborately formalized, and chiefly perhaps because the Teda have an extremely individualistic spirit so strong that it prevents their ever really uniting even in the face of an invasion. As Colonel Chapelle of the French Camel Corps once wrote, "they are incapable not only of uniting to carry out a joint policy but even of imagining such a policy."

Over the centuries many Teda clans have come into the Tibesti and others have moved away, obscure clans have risen to power and strong ones have faded back into obscurity again, old tribes have broken up in times of stress and their dislocated elements have recombined to form new groupings, and so on in a never ending series of piecemeal disintegrations and local reconsolidations. Even today many vassal clans are divided into two or more separate fractions, each attached to a different noble clan. But this is only part of a more general problem. The principle of freedom raised almost to the level of anarchy is so deeply rooted in the Teda philosophy of life that many families refuse to acknowledge anyone as their chief, while individuals frequently dispute the authority even of their own family headmen. And this is doubtless the main reason why so little is known about the tribal organization of the Teda, for its basic pattern is masked in ordinary times by the perverse eccentricity of individual fractions and family units, so that it becomes clearly visible only during those rare and fleeting periods when the paramount chief happens to be both an unusually strong and personally influential man.

Because of the centrifugal nature of Teda clan structure and the resulting tendency toward extreme fragmentation, administrative chieftainship seems to be lacking almost entirely at the level of the clan. Chiefs of clans exist, but they exercise real authority only as war leaders, or as spiritual guides and occasionally as judges; even so they are practically powerless except in times of acute general distress. Fractions of clans also have headmen, but almost nothing is known about their practical functions or the extent of their authority. True chieftainship seems to appear among the Teda only at the level of the tribe, which is a

unit made up of clans and fractions held together by ties of kinship or by geo-political considerations. Tribal chiefs are chosen
usually by a council of clan leaders; and yet, curiously enough, it
is said that they are named sometimes by the council of family
headmen of the vassal clan supposed to have been longest resident in the tribal territory. There seems to be no binding condition of lineage or seniority involved in the succession to chieftainship beyond the fact that the choice is customarily rotated among
a group of traditionally preferred families. The main functions
of a tribal chief are to negotiate agreements with neighboring
tribes and to lead the warriors in battle. And he also acts as
judge, although as such his function seldom goes beyond that of
a mere moderator who tries to bring about agreement between
opposing parties but is powerless to enforce any decision.

Men govern at most social levels in the Tibesti, and the inheritance of both rank and property appears to follow in a loose
and general way, the patrilineal pattern laid down in the Koran.
The rules governing the inheritance of property seem to vary a
good deal, however, from place to place. Estates are always
settled very quietly and even secretly, and Moslem "holy men"
are not allowed to have anything to do with such affairs. A matrilineal element appears to be present too, for a married woman
remains a member of the clan into which she was born, and her
grown-up children can always call on members of that clan for
help in such intercommunal matters as the recovery of stolen
livestock. The household unit consists of a "nuclear family," the
father, mother, and their unmarried children. Most Teda men
have only one wife at a time, although some have two or three.
Children respect their parents, the father absolutely and the
mother relatively; and older relatives in general are much respected too, especially grandparents and the father's oldest
brother. The father pays all family expense, including the price
of his sons' brides; but he can also beat his sons until they reach
the age of fifteen and his daughters even after they are married,
although he rarely does so. A mother can beat her sons only before they have been circumcised, but she can beat her married
daughters. Paternal aunts are treated almost as members of the

family, and are supposed to help around the house, but maternal aunts are looked on as family friends rather than blood relatives. Children of two brothers treat each other as though they were all full brothers and sisters, although the children of two sisters act as though they were unrelated. When the head of a Teda family dies, he is normally succeeded by his oldest son, but if none of his sons is yet of age, then his oldest surviving brother assumes the headship of the family on a temporary basis. Teda boys "come of age" when they are circumcised, between the ages of twelve and fourteen, and so are admitted to adult status. Several who are about the right age are often circumcised together, at the time of the date harvest, and such events are celebrated with goat sacrifices and feasts which not infrequently degenerate into drunken brawls. The actual circumcising is done by old men, smiths or Haratin, whose years and degraded social status are thought to make them magically immune. Girls too undergo a puberty ceremony which consists of shutting them up in groups for a few days, and tattooing their lips and gums blue, but they are not mutilated otherwise.

Mutual aid within the family to the fourth degree is obligatory in times of trouble, and relatives on both sides give animals to a couple who have lost their own. Even in normal times relatives help each other with their flocks, and with agricultural and date harvesting operations, much as do northern Berber villagers, but this cooperative system appears to be applied only within strictly limited segments of the community.

Blood revenge is a continuing hereditary obligation with no time limit. In retribution for a murder, the murderer himself must be killed together with one of his descendants or at least a relative. Only payment of the blood price can put an end to such a feud; but since the price of a rich man is thirty-five camels, plus goats, palm trees, and either cloth or cash to the value of another thirty-five, it is sometimes materially impossible to settle a feud by payment, even when both parties want to. The status of a murderer in the Tibesti is formalized to an extraordinary degree. After a man has killed another and has got a good head start on his pursuers, he stops to catch a goat (if he can find one), sacrifices it on a small pile of stones, cuts out a length of the intestines, and pulls the two open ends on over his feet like socks, thus hobbling himself. He then jumps up and down until the hobble breaks, whereupon he sets off again, magically freed. Soon, however, he will pause once more and draw a line across his trail, meaning "Follow me no farther or I'll kill you too!" As a final and lasting precaution the murderer takes to wearing an iron bracelet which is supposed to keep his victim's ghost from haunting him in dreams. A murderer also drops his own name and adopts another, chosen from a list traditionally reserved for such occasions. Regardless of this precaution, he never hesitates to announce proudly: "My name used to be So-and-so," which amounts to saying: "I have killed a man." In fact "murderer" is perhaps not quite the right word for the man I have just described; for his killing was probably done as a part of the normal process of the Teda code of honor, and so there is little likelihood that he was a murderer in the simple sense of the term as we are accustomed to use it. In terms of Teda social concepts, his status was perhaps more like that of a loyal but outlawed clansman in the Highlands of Scotland three or four hundred years ago.

The Tibesti Teda get married much younger than do the Tuareg of the Ahaggar, for a bride is seldom more than fifteen or sixteen years old and the groom only eighteen to twenty as a rule. The wedding is usually preceded by an engagement which lasts for several years, and a deceased fiancé is customarily replaced by a younger brother or some other close relative of his. A girl has little or no choice in the selection of her future husband, unless she happens to be an orphan, for her father must give his consent although her mother has no say. Boys apparently are free to choose whatever girl they like, provided she is of the same rank and no more closely related than the fourth degree of cousinship. In actual practice they usually pick a girl from outside their own clan. Young unmarried couples often run away in the face of parental opposition, and stay away until the girl is pregnant, after which the parents usually relent. If no pregnancy occurs within a fairly short time, however, the couple simply come home again and all is forgiven and forgotten. If a bride has not reached puberty, consummation is supposed to be postponed until her mother agrees that the proper time has come; but this rule is often ignored, and, even when a girl dies as a result, the bridegroom is not molested. It has been reported that a wife never pronounces her husband's name, but refers to and even addresses him as "the father of So-and-so," using the name of their oldest child regardless of sex: what childless wives do has not been recorded.

Monogamy seems to be the general rule among the Teda, as I have already mentioned; for in a random sample of two hundred and forty-seven married men it was found that only thirty-five had two wives and only seven had three. No man may marry a sister of his wife while the latter is alive, because of the firm belief that a woman will become sterile if she has intercourse, illicitly or even legally, with the husband of a living sister. When a man's wife dies, however, he may marry one of her sisters if his father-in-law is willing. Although residence is patrilocal as a rule, authorities differ as to the details; but it is generally said that a newly married couple usually stay on in the camp of the bride's people for a year or so following the wedding, and then move to the camp of the bridegroom's family, just as do the Tuareg. Chapelle, however, says that newlyweds stay in the bride's camp until their first child is born, and then can move away only if the groom pays a supplementary bride-price to his father-in-law. Probably the customs governing postmarital residence vary a good deal regionally. Both engaged and married couples avoid each other's parents as much as possible, which seems a wise precaution in view of the notoriously quick tempers of the Teda. And when a man has two or more wives he usually keeps them and their respective children in different camps or settlements, or at least in separate dwellings, as far apart as possible.

A married Teda woman retains full title to all her property, including household furnishings, livestock, and even palm trees, but it is managed by her husband and she cannot dispose of it without his consent unless she gets divorced. Teda couples rarely get divorced, but when a husband does divorce his wife she is then free to marry again without restraint. If, however, it was the wife who initiated the divorce, then anyone who wants to marry her must pay a bride-price to her former husband. In practice this secondary bride-price is often set so high that the woman finds no takers, and so finally returns in desperation to her former mate. Yet another brake is put on the freedom of a divorced woman by the custom which requires that any children born to her within five years after she left her husband be considered legitimately his. The children of a divorced couple stay with their mother as a rule until they are about two years old (the age of weaning), after which they go to live in their father's household. Nevertheless it is possible for a divorced father to buy his children back from their mother before the two-year period of her guardianship is over, although in order to do this he must give her a camel in payment for each one.

Teda custom decrees that a widow should marry a close male relative of her late husband, preferably an unmarried brother, although even a much younger nephew will do in the absence of anyone more suitable. But if the lady refuses to marry as she should within a year, then her family must return to her late husband's family the bride-price that they received for her, and she herself must forfeit her normal right to one eighth of her husband's estate. Under such circumstances her children too are taken from her, and are turned over in guardianship to a member of their father's family, usually his older brother. When, on the other hand, the man who is supposed to marry a widow declines to do so, her parents then try to find her another mate; and if they fail, as they often do when an elderly or unattractive woman is concerned, they try to engineer some kind of fictitious post-mortem divorce so as to avoid at least the obligation of giving up the bride-price. Teda wives may or may not be addicted to adultery, depending on which source one chooses to believe, but irregular activities of this kind are said to be punished only by a fine and relatively minor forms of personal vengeance. It is said that Teda men never take concubines, and even if they do take one now and then the practice is certainly exceptional.

The division of labor between the sexes in the Tibesti seems to be about the same as in the Ahaggar; except that men tailor their own clothes, or so it has been said.

Clearly, the social position of Teda women of the Tibesti is characterized by a curious mixture of restraint and freedom, and of Islamic and pre-Islamic attitudes. As was pointed out above, a Teda woman has practically no say in the choice of her mate. When married she must never eat in her husband's presence. And the blood price of a woman is but half that of a man. But even so, women are held in great respect in many ways, and enjoy privileges that are unusual by any standard. The birth of a girl, for instance, causes as much rejoicing as does that of a boy, which is rare in Moslem societies despite the Koranic ad- monition on this subject. And when a women is of noble birth, her sons inherit the right to use her family camel brand as well as that of their father's family. And, too, although a husband may beat his wife, he must pay her a fine if he wounds her, and repeated beatings are considered a legitimate cause for divorce. It is the wife who dominates the household insofar as internal family affairs are concerned, so much so that it is considered normal for her to strike her husband if he disputes her authority. When he is away from home, however, her authority becomes so absolute that she can move the camp and shift the family flocks and herds to a new pasture without consulting anyone, and can even deal in livestock in her husband's name. On the rare oc- casions when a man insults his wife in public, wifely authority finds expression in a surprisingly dramatic form of ritual public protest; for the offended lady promptly strips off all her clothes, flings them on the ground, and stalks haughtily away through the assembled bystanders, stark naked, to her tent. After a per- formance of this kind, peace in the family cannot be restored un- til the offending husband presents a substantial gift to his sulking spouse.

Teda women also fight among themselves quite commonly, and sometimes engage in regular pitched battles in which their menfolk seldom dare to interfere. They sometimes wear arm daggers too, and they are said to have worn swords as well until the practice was suppressed by the Turks about a century

ago. The importance of women appears again in historical mythology, for many genealogies are traced back to or through more
or less remote female ancestors. The key ancestor of the Foctoa
clan, for example, is said to have been a woman named Lehillé
Kyaidé-do, whose tomb can still be seen near Soborom, about
two hundred and fifty miles northwest of Faya (Largeau).

It is evident that the social position of Teda women in the
Tibesti is characterized by a number of customary privileges
that can hardly have arisen after the introduction of Islam into
the area. Indeed it is hard to imagine how such privileges, however deeply rooted they may be in pre-Islamic culture, ever survived the conversion of the Teda. The respect with which women
are treated generally, the authority they exercise at home, and
also the freedom they enjoy in expressing themselves publicly,
are all traits which simply cannot have arisen within the framework of an Islamic society. And there are vague hints too of a
system of double descent, and other striking reminders of Tuareg
socio-political organization.

Personal rank, for instance, depends on the clan into which
one was born. An individual apparently cannot rise above or fall
below the rank of his clan's hereditary class no matter what he
does, but the members of a clan can change in rank as parts of
the collective whole which may move from one class into another,
up or down, as the result of exceptionally good fortune or disaster. As in the Ahaggar, the noble clans themselves are not of
equal rank, while the relation between noble and vassal clans in
both areas may well be essentially the same. Even though it has
been said that the so-called "commoner" clans of the Tibesti are
distinguished from vassal clans by the fact that they pay no
tribute to secure the protection of their noble patrons, it is indeed difficult to believe that they produce nothing in return. And
the system of tribute payments to the Dardai during Shaffai's
first term in office is strongly reminiscent of the Tuareg tribute
system of the Ahaggar confederation. All this is very vague, for
the accounts of different authors are both fragmentary and conflicting. And yet such a constellation of parallels, involving such
basic and distinctive customs, certainly suggests that contact be-

tween the Teda and the Tuareg goes far back into the past, if indeed their two cultures do not have a common origin, at least in part. Again it is not easy to avoid jumping at conclusions.

The material life of the Teda also resembles that of the Ahaggar Tuareg to a considerable extent, for the economic organizations of both are based essentially on pastoral nomadism. Estimates of Teda livestock vary so widely that any I might cite could be accepted only as extremely rough approximations. Figures of two thousand hairy sheep, forty thousand goats or thereabouts, and perhaps five thousand donkeys seem to be about as reasonable as any. As usual, a few neglected chickens and dogs scavenge as best they can in the nomad camps and in sedentary settlements. The number of camels has been estimated at anywhere from fifteen hundred to eight thousand, but it probably varies a good deal anyway, in response to variations in the yearly rainfall. The Teda do not castrate male camels ordinarily, as most other Saharan nomads do, and so their male animals are exceptionally big and sturdy. Special care seems to be given stud camels too, for they are seldom if ever ridden and are never broken to carry even light loads. Animals are not only of practical value to the Teda, but are both used and avoided by them ritually. Sacrificial feasts, in which goats are killed and eaten ceremonially, are often held in connection with planting and harvesting, with marriages and circumcisions, and with housewarming celebrations when a new hut is set up. Fowl and their eggs, on the other hand, are taboo for adults in general, except in times of famine, just as they are among the Tuareg and the Moors. The Teda nomads of the Tibesti wander from pasture to pasture with their herds and flocks much as do the Tuareg, although they often stay in one place for as long as two or three months before moving on. Although pasture land appears to be considered ownerless in theory, each nomad clan has in fact its own range whose boundaries are established by mutual agreement with neighboring nomad clans; and this system naturally gives rise to frequent skirmishing punctuated by blood feuds and occasional pitched battles. Many Teda nomad families also own palm groves to which they return each year, in February as a rule, to supervise the pollination, and there they often remain until the crop is harvested, usually in August. Palm trees are said to be communal clan property, although their fruit is individually owned. Social activities reach their peak at the time of the date harvest, when the nomads, well fed again at last and resting in the midst of their plantations, hold marriage and circumcision feasts, each on as grand a scale as he can manage.

Estimates of palm groves again vary enormously, but it is probably safe to assume that there are about fifty-five thousand producing date palms in the Tibesti massif as a whole. Nomads also often own gardens in the agricultural centers; and title to these appears to be vested in individual families on the theory that title to the produce of cultivated land goes to him who first brought it under cultivation, and thence to his heirs. The usual garden produce includes wheat, barley, millet, maize, tomatoes, and onions, but the crops must be pretty poor in both quality and quantity, for it is said that the total grain production of the Tibesti comes to only about three hundred tons a year. The gardens are worked by Negro slaves or Haratin sharecroppers (serfs), supervised by the less physically fit members of proprietary families, who remain sedentary for considerable periods while their more robust relatives are moving about with the livestock. The nomads send butter and milk goats back to the sedentary overseers from time to time, and in return they receive as much garden produce as can be spared and also any goats that have gone dry.

The Teda love to give big communal parties, but guests are expected to bring presents in the form of livestock, dates, grain, cloth, clothing, jewelry, or even cash. These gifts are recorded, however, and the host in turn must make equivalent gifts to his guests when he attends parties given by them later on. This custom is found also among the Berbers of the mountains in northern Algeria. Reciprocal giving between individuals, often between husband and wife, is common practice among the Teda, and so it sometimes happens that different parts of a single animal or even of its milk production are owned by several different persons simultaneously. Naturally this is a fruitful source of quarrels adding to the general social confusion, especially when a question of inheritance arises.

In contrast to the general Saharan rule, nomadism in the Tibesti seems to be increasing while agriculture is on the decline; for sedentary folk there tend to become at least semi-nomadic as soon as they have acquired enough camels. Although several possible reasons for this phenomenon have been suggested, one of the main causes seems to be that the whole region has been growing more and more arid for the last half century at least. The gradual suppression of the slave trade has been an important factor too, for it has progressively reduced the supply of cheap labor available to cultivate the soil, a task that no true Teda nomad would ever dream of stooping to unless perhaps his very life depended on it. And, finally, the increased safety of the desert under European rule has encouraged many semi-nomadic groups to become full nomads.

The Teda nomads of the Tibesti used to derive most of their revenue from a far-flung caravan trade of their own, from protection fees extracted by them from the caravans of others, and from raiding, but all such activities have now become either entirely impossible or possible only so infrequently and on so small a scale as to be of very little importance economically. And yet in 1927 a Teda raiding party attacked the town of In Abbangarit, halfway between Agadès and In Guezzam and over six hundred miles southwest of the Tibesti, while as recently as 1951 a small band of Teda raiders ambushed a caravan and killed four Tuareg on the trail that runs from Bilma westward to Agadès. For many centuries the Teda also operated a flourishing caravan trade in slaves, but this has been wiped out completely as far as the Tibesti is concerned. A small external caravan trade still survives, based mainly on the exportation of goats, salt, dates, and dried tomatoes which are exchanged chiefly for millet, cotton cloth, and weapons, for tobacco, tea, and sugar, and for manufactured articles of wood and leather. The salt is extracted by evaporation from the water of brackish pools and marshes in the Tibesti highlands, while export dates are either dried in the sun or are stuffed into goatskins after their pits have been removed. Merchants engaged in this caravan traffic are rarely sedentary, and so trade and transport in the Tibesti are but two aspects of a single activity. The trade element of the external commerce of the area is still reasonably healthy, but the transport element was gradually broken down by the steadily growing competition of Arab caravans which, in their turn, are now fast losing ground to mechanized transport services operated by Europeans. Internal trade in the Tibesti has long been based on the exchange of milk products, dried meat, and skins produced by nomads for grain and other garden produce of the sedentary population.

Herodotus seems to have been responsible originally for the singularly persistent belief that the ancient ancestral Teda were cave dwellers. Some of the Teda of the Tibesti massif still do live in caves occasionally, or more often in the shelter of overhanging rocks where an artificial cave can be created by building a stone wall across the open front, but there is no good reason to suppose that shelters of this kind were ever regularly used by the Teda. Nomads of the Tibesti normally use two main types of shelter, a hut of skins or palm frond matting and the zeriba, which has already been described. The nomad hut is a sort of cross between a tent and a zeriba. The frame is made of sticks arranged in the form of a giant shoebox or an overturned boat, and is usually about fifteen to twenty-five feet long, seven to ten feet wide and five or six feet high in the middle. This framework is covered ordinarily with matting made of vegetable fiber, although the skins of antelopes are sometimes used. As a rule the entrance is at the left-hand end of the front wall, and is made by arranging the wall panels so that they overlap each other at that point, leaving a short corridor open between them. The opposite end of the interior may be closed off to form a little room where the women of the family can wash in private. When breaking camp the Teda remove the covering of the hut and take it with them, but they often leave the framework standing to be used when they come back again.

Sedentary and semi-sedentary Teda of the Tibesti live, as a rule, in circular huts, seven to eight feet in diameter, with walls of field stone laid up dry. These walls are anywhere from four to seven feet high and are surmounted by a conical roof of thatch or matting which is sometimes covered with earth. The doorway is usually very low, with wooden jambs and lintel, but it is sometimes of the offset type used in the huts of nomads. The interior is occasionally divided up by partitions made of matting set upon low stone walls. In front of the door there is often a small, rectangular forecourt, enclosed with low walls of stone, which may

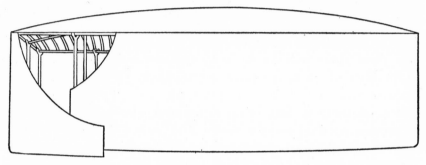

FIG. 4. Diagram of a Teda nomad hut. (Part of the entrance has been cut away.)

be roofed over with brush or left open to the sky, and which serves as a living room and parlor; and a small raised platform for drying dates and vegetables is usually to be found in one corner. This type of construction is strikingly reminiscent of the little hilltop fort known as "the tomb of Tin Hinan," at Abalessa on the western edge of the Ahaggar, which dates probably from somewhere between the fourth and sixth centuries of our era. The Haratin of the Tibesti live in cylindrical zeribas whose roofs are conical, and which are in fact just like the huts of the sedentary Teda except that they are made entirely of straw matting.

Teda household furniture normally includes sleeping mats, with light blankets for those who can afford them, a saddle quern, a small iron cooking pot, an earthenware pot or two, gourd containers with incised decoration, a long-handled wooden spoon, and a stirring stick with a short cross member tied on near the lower end. Basketry containers for milk and water are made by Teda women, and are waterproofed with grease rubbed into the inner surface. Pottery is made by the Haratin or slaves. Guerbas are present here as everywhere in the Sahara, and leather bags, made from the skins of goats, sheep, camels, and even cattle, are used for storing almost everything.

Apparently the most ancient basic garment of the Tibesti Teda is a leather tunic known as a *farto,* which is made of a pair of sheep or goat skins sewn together with holes left open for the head and arms and an open bottom like a skirt. Fartos are as a general rule worn with the fur side inside, at least in winter. When the temperature drops to freezing or below, as it often does in winter, two or more fartos may be worn at once; and over these there may be worn in addition a heavy robe, made of the skins of six to ten black sheep, cut down to rectangles of uniform size and shape and sewn together. Today, however, leather clothing is fast being replaced by cloth garments and blankets imported from the north. The Teda still seem to attach some sort of magical importance to leather clothes; for several Teda clans have a taboo which forbids the wearing of fartos under any circumstances, while men of the debased Azza class, on the contrary, always wear fartos and nothing else when engaged either in hunting or in performing ceremonial dances.

Well-to-do Teda men of the Tibesti nowadays dress much as do the Tuareg, except that trousers are usually a good deal shorter and the old-fashioned cotton shirt with wide sleeves has not yet been displaced by the gandoura as generally as it has among the Tuareg and the Teda of the Sudan. Two or three shirts are often worn at once by those who can afford them, the under one made of white cotton and the others of shegga if possible. But most of the Teda are so poor that a man rarely has more than a single set of garments, while a turban may be shared by two men who wear it turn and turn about.

The usual men's headdress is a combination turban and face veil, like that of the Tuareg but much less carefully arranged. However, occasionally one also sees a presumably older form of head covering—a leather cap which is made by folding a rectangular piece of hide over on itself, with the fur inside, and sewing up the edges. This type of cap fits loosely, like a paper bag, and covers the ears and neck while the corners of the top stick out like a pair of stubby horns. A red felt cap is also worn sometimes. Men seem to have little or no hesitation in exposing their faces under ordinary circumstances, although they often cover them when in the presence of strangers. In fact the Teda men that Lyon saw in the Fezzan in 1819 never wore veils at all, although a number of them came from the neighborhood of the Tibesti, and this makes one wonder just when the Teda did start wearing veils. Teda men usually wear sandals of the old-fashioned Tuareg type, made of camel hide for the rich and old truck tires for the poor. But they also have low rawhide shoes, with uppers of sheep or goat skin, and they buy fancy imported footgear when they can afford it.

The customary armament of the Teda includes a sword, of either Turkish or Tuareg type, an arm dagger which is worn point downward with the arm ring placed above the left elbow, a six-foot wooden thrusting lance with a long iron point shaped like a laurel leaf, and a quiver with three javelins, which are lightweight replicas of the lance and only about four feet long. The most distinctive Teda weapon used to be the *mouzeri,* a multibladed throwing knife shaped like a capital letter F or Y, which is said to be accurate up to sixty-five yards; but it has now gone almost completely out of use. Mouzeris were thrown horizontally from below waist level (much as a flat pebble is thrown to make it skip over water), and with enough force to stop a horse or even a camel running at full speed. Guns, mostly stolen from old Italian stocks, are fairly common in the Tibesti nowadays but are carried only by outlaws, at least in theory.

Teda women who are reasonably well off sometimes dress like Tuareg women, or they may wear long cotton shirts like those of the men except that they are often red in color. Usually, however, they wear a long rectangle of cotton cloth wound around the body, passing under the right arm and attached over the left shoulder with the end left hanging free for use as a head scarf. Shegga is again the preferred material if the wearer can afford it. Around the waist a braided leather cord or some more ornamental form of belt is worn. Teda women never veil their faces; and they use no make-up except a little khol around the eyes, and that only on festive occasions. Women of the servile Azza class wear leather skirts while working, and even noble Teda women of the Tibesti sometimes do likewise. A curious leather belt with a long fringe of thongs is also worn by Azza women, underneath their clothes when they are doing nothing in particular but outside when they are either working or dancing. And this custom seems to correspond to the ceremonial wearing of leather clothes by Azza men. By an extraordinary coincidence, if indeed it is a coincidence, similar fringed belts are found again over twelve hundred miles away to the northwest, in the Mzab, where as I have seen, men used to wear them during wedding celebrations.

The Negro slaves of the Tibesti seem to be comparable in general to those of the Ahaggar Tuareg. Sometimes they are well cared for, and may even be set free when they marry or their master dies, but often they are treated very badly. It has been reported even that their masters occasionally cut ligaments of their feet or toes, or drive thorns into the soles of their feet, to make it impossible for them to run away; but one cannot help wondering if such a practice would not reduce a slave's efficiency so much as to make it hardly worth while. Most freed slaves have become sedentary sharecroppers, and have been assimilated by the Haratin, who are known locally as *Kamadja*. It is said that slaves of the Tibesti used to have some sort of clan organization and even chiefs of their own, but no details of this system have ever been reported.

The Negro and negroid elements in the Tibesti population seem to be just about the same as those found in the Ahaggar, but Teda history and tradition are full of references to the supposedly Sudanese origins of various Tibesti Teda groups as well, including noble clans. Just where these latter groups came from originally, however, how they got to the Sudan in the first place and when, and what they did while there, are questions which cannot yet be discussed profitably for lack of sufficient information.

The smiths of the Tibesti seem to be much like those of the

Ahaggar on the whole although there is one basic difference; for here they are not a solitary parasitic group but form only one segment of a broad class or caste, known as the Azza, which includes several groups of occupational specialists, set apart collectively by their activities. The men of one group are hunters, tanners, and woodworkers, while their womenfolk weave basketry and also mats and nets of vegetable fiber. Azza hunters catch antelopes in traps, or hunt them with dogs in much the same way as the Nemadi. Sometimes, however, they employ a special technique which consists of surrounding an entire herd and driving it into nets made of sinew which are set up in series one behind another, so that even if an animal does manage to break through the first line or two, it is sure to get hopelessly entangled farther on. The men of another Azza group are tailors, while those of yet another act as resident minstrels and musicians. Azza women in general have the monopoly of pottery manufacture. A handful of Azza families are said to live the life of ordinary poor pastoral nomads, exercising no special manual trade, but they must be very rare exceptions.

The Azza smiths work metal but not wood, and they work only on commission, with raw materials furnished by their customers. Their products include all kinds of metal ware except swords and guns, which are imported from both the north and south. A powerful magic quality seems to be attached both to iron and to ironworking smiths in the minds of the Teda, who are said to believe, for instance, that an iron bracelet or arm ring protects a sleeper from any demons who may try to steal his soul.

The Azza as a whole have a number of non-Moslem taboos as well as some sort of clan organization of their own, but here again almost no details have been reported. They are also said to have a special dance in which the men wear old-fashioned leather shirts and perform "steps usually used only by women" (whatever that may mean); and this activity at least indicates a strong feeling of corporate solidarity. Before the establishment of French authority in the Tibesti, each Azza clan, and possibly each family, was bound politically and economically to a particular Teda clan or family, so that the primary function of the Azza appears to have been originally that of family retainers rather than that of a working class at the service of the community as a whole. They used to trade mainly, if not exclusively, with their immediate masters, to whom they also paid tribute, and they fought for their masters too though only as emergency reserves. The masters in return gave their Azza a helping hand when needed by feeding them in time of famine, fighting off their enemies, and recovering their stolen livestock. In fact the relation between the "noble" Teda and their Azza "vassals" was, until quite recently, very much more like the feudal system of medieval Europe than anything the Tuareg ever seem to have developed. Like smiths elsewhere in the Sahara, the Azza apparently have no language of their own, nor does there seem to be anything that sets them apart physically from the many other communities of Saharan smiths.

The early history of the Teda is still shrouded in mystery, for the little evidence that is available consists mostly of confused and incongruous folk tales from which it seems impossible to extract any clear historical meaning. The mythology of Teda origins, for example, often refers vaguely to an imposing white ancestor or an ancestral pair of white twins, brother and sister, or occasionally a lone white ancestress. More specifically it is said that the key ancestors of the Goboda and Mormorea Teda clans of the Tibesti, who are vassals respectively of the Tomaghera and the Arna, were Tuareg men from the Air. And it is said too that many Tuareg refugees and expatriate raiders have married into the Kindin fraction of the Goboda clan. Indeed, there can be little doubt but that the western Teda have been exchanging culture traits and genes with southeastern Tuareg tribes off and on since at least as early as the sixteenth century. I find myself again in a difficult position when it comes to trying to evaluate Arab cultural and physical influence on the Teda. I have already mentioned that the Tomaghera, the paramount noble clan of the Tibesti, are thought to have come from the Sudan, and the Tomaghera themselves admit that their ancestors intermarried with Arabs to some extent while in the southlands.

But is this a fact or is it just a bit of swank, a spurious claim to a place of honor in the hierarchy of Islam?

Some authors hold that the Teda were converted to Islam two or three centuries ago, but Lyon, a very reliable observer, wrote that as late as 1820 most of them were still pagan, while other authors say that the Islamization of the Tibesti did not get well under way until about 1880. The Teda must have been in fairly frequent contact, however, with Moslem Arab tribes for nearly a thousand years if not more, thanks to the caravan trade between northern Egypt and the western Sudan, and during the last century or so they have also been a target of determined missionary efforts on the part of the Senoussi. In spite of all this, however, Arab influence in the Tibesti seems to be but slight and largely superficial even now. Arab traders come there at the time of the date harvest, bringing with them cotton cloth and fancy clothes, manufactured articles and knickknacks and hard cash, but they are soon gone again. Itinerant Arab Marabouts come and go from both the north and south, but they are few and their visits far between. According to one author, there were no Marabouts living in the Tibesti in 1957; but another wrote that in 1953 there were nine of them, five of whom were members of the Tidjani brotherhood who had moved north from the Sudan. Of the remaining four, all followers of the Senoussi, one also came from the Sudan and the others from the north. Only one of the entire number, a Senoussist, was a Mecca pilgrim; but two Teda natives of the Tibesti had also gone on the Pilgrimage, making a total of only three pilgrims in the population of the whole area. It has been said that Arab Marabouts officiate "when possible" at Teda ceremonies such as circumcisions, weddings, and trials, and that they also act occasionally as scribes, but it is clearly implied that they are few and so are seldom to be found when wanted. It is said too that some Teda natives of the Tibesti act as part-time Marabouts, but nothing more appears to be known about them.

Oaths are customarily sworn on the Koran, and Teda women can so swear except when menstruating. And yet it is generally believed that he who swears falsely will die within a year's time, which is a pagan concept quite foreign to Koranic doctrine. Another clear survival of pre-Islamic pagan justice appears in the Teda custom of trial by ordeal, in which the defendant plunges his hand into a pot of boiling water and withdraws some small object from the bottom. If his hand remains unscalded he is vindicated.

All in all it looks as though the Teda culture of the Tibesti massif could be either a survial of some simple proto-Tuareg kind of culture or the impoverished and dilapidated remnant of a true Tuareg culture that has gone to pieces under the stress of an environment even more rigorous than that of the Ahaggar combined with the increasing pressures of alien peoples on all sides. Unfortunately, there is so little factual information available concerning the Teda of the Tibesti that one can arrive at no definite conclusions regarding them, except that they are obviously very well adapted to a singularly harsh habitat. As my old friend, Walter Cline, said in the preface of his monograph about them, written just before he died: "I had begun with the assumption that a realistic picture of northern Teda life could be drawn by synthesizing the accounts of European explorers. As I look over this picture now, the impression is not one of primitive simplicity—it is one of an unnatural blankness. I cannot believe that Teda culture is as featureless as it seems. Let us hope that some rugged young desert-lover will take my notes with him to Tibesti, learn the Teda language, fill in all the gaping lacunae—and return to his university alive."

Chapter 7 ~

ARAB NOMADS

The Arab nomad tribes of the Sahara vary considerably in their patterns of everyday life. Some of them are relatively independent of sedentary centers on which others depend to a far greater extent; some circulate regularly with their livestock over distances of several hundred miles while others rarely go more than forty or fifty miles from their home base. But all such variations on the main theme of desert nomadism are usually functional responses to environment, and involve no more than minor material details of the life of the group in question. The underlying basic character of nomadic Arab culture remains essentially very much the same everywhere.

The Chaamba of the northwestern central desert seem to be the best Saharan Arab nomads to examine here because, all things considered, they are the most typical. I will take the Chaamba Berazga (or Berezga) of Metlili as my sample in this case, for they seem to have been rather less affected by alien influence than have the other major subdivisions of the Chaamba. Their language is naturally Arabic. It is generally believed that the Chaamba came to the northwestern Sahara from Syria early in the fourteenth century, but this is hardly more than a guess. It is thought that their initial impetus carried them as far west as the piedmont country on the southern slope of the Atlas mountain complex south of Oran, and that they later moved from there southeastward to Metlili, probably about the middle of the fourteenth century.

There is no way of knowing why they finally chose to settle in such a forbidding region of the desert, whether it was for their own protection or primarily to prey on others, but the latter supposition seems likelier. Ghardaia, the youngest of the five cities of the Mzab, had been founded in or about 1053 and, together with its satellites, had already become the most important transfer point on the central one of the three great trans-Saharan trade routes between Barbary and the Sudan. It seems only natural that a vigorous and adventuresome nomadic people like the Chaamba should have leapt at the opportunity to establish themselves as freighters and bandits, alternately participating in and preying on the rich and concentrated commerce flowing both into and away from such a center. And Metlili is ideally situated as a base for operations of this kind. It is set below the level of an intricately dissected plain, on a spur that juts out from the eastern wall of a relatively fertile valley which forms part of the inextricable network of the normally dry drainage system south of the Mzab. It is only fifteen miles or so from Ghardaia, the Mzabite capital, it is easy to defend, and it is so well hidden that it can be seen from barely a mile or so away to the northwest and from hardly more than a few hundred yards in any other direction. Thus this little fortress-town became the political and commercial center of the Chaamba, at once their market, storage place, and arsenal, their caravan terminus, raiding base, and place of refuge and repose. It soon grew famous too as a haven for refugees and troublemakers from all over the northwestern quarter of the desert, and such recruits and their assimilated descendants soon helped to make the warlike Chaamba even more dreaded than they were at first.

The original Saharan Chaamba community, newly established in the region of Metlili, soon built up so much internal pressure, due to an increasing population, that clans and even tribes began to emigrate and reorganize themselves around other centers. The Mouadhi Chaamba, for instance, moved south to El Goléa, possibly in the sixteenth century, the Bou Rouba emigrated eastward to Ouargla, and other groups fled into the northwestern desert following the short-lived revolt of Bou Amama in 1881. Pressure sometimes built up in the new secondary centers too,

causing one group from El Goléa, for example, to move eastward to El Oued, and another to follow in the path of earlier
emigrants who had already gone westward from Metlili. The
western Chaamba were reinforced also by Chaamba emigrants
from Ouargla as well as by nomadic refugees from the piedmont
country to the north. And, finally, French military pressure in
the early years of the conquest of the Sahara, and gradually
increasing commercial pressure over the last fifty years or so,
have produced a fluctuating but substantial southward drift
among the Chaamba generally.

Some of the emigrant groups became autonomous, while
others attached themselves as semiautonomous or tributary allies
to Arab tribes already settled in the areas to which they moved.
In spite of this, however, and in spite of the fact that they
fought often with each other as well as with their parent group,
over matters of intertribal interest, the Chaamba as a whole retained a feeling of national unity so strong that they continued
to combine effectively in emergencies for the purposes not only
of mutual defense but also of reprisal. The famous massive
counter-raid of 1876, directed against Berber nomads of the
extreme northwestern corner of the desert, was a striking example of the willingness and ability of widely scattered and
politically independent Chaamba communities to join forces in
the interests of only one of their number.

Population figures on the Chaamba seem to be no more reliable than those on the Tuareg, and possibly even less so. The
estimates made in 1936 are certainly no more than very rough
approximations, but they are probably as good as any others
that are available. At that time the total Chaamba population
was estimated at close to twenty thousand with roughly eighty-
six hundred based on Metlili, forty-five hundred on El Goléa,
forty-six hundred on Ouargla, twelve hundred on El Oued, and
perhaps another eight hundred or so scattered around the
fringes of the great Western Erg.

Measurements of only nine Chaamba men have been published, and so I cannot say much about their physical characteristics beyond giving my own personal impressions gathered during

many months of observation in the field. Chaamba men in general seem to be of medium height, about five feet six or seven inches, on the average, although quite a few exceed the five feet eight or nine inches of the average American male. As a rule they are well proportioned, strongly built and lean, but very muscular in a sinewy sort of way. Rich men who have settled down or are semi-sedentary often become quite portly, but they are rare exceptions. There appears to be nothing distinctive about limb proportions or the size and shape of hands or feet. One day in 1954 an aged Chaamba chief, a famous Camel Corps hero of the Tuareg wars, pulled up his baggy trouser leg for my benefit and gleefully displayed bulging calf muscles almost literally as hard as steel. He explained with great emphasis that this particular type of overdevelopment is a distinctive racial characteristic of pure-blooded Chaamba nomads, and is never found even among their nomadic cousins of mixed ancestry. Probably my elderly friend stretched a point in his enthusiasm, but his demonstration served to emphasize another point which has often escaped notice. Nomadic camel men of the Sahara in general walk or trot along on foot beside their mounts much of the time, even on forced marches, and this practice has a marked effect not only on their leg muscles but on their posture and their build in general.

The heads and faces of the Chaamba vary a good deal in both size and shape. Unexposed skin is usually white or nearly so, except in individuals who show obvious signs of Negro admixture. Hair is most often wavy and very dark, but light brown hair does occur sometimes and occasionally has a faintly reddish tinge. Eye color is usually a very dark or even blackish brown, but I have observed a substantial number of eyes that are a curious, almost luminous, light brown which can be described appropriately enough by the romantic term "honey-colored." The ABO blood group pattern of the Chaamba is not markedly similar to that of any other Saharan people whose blood has been examined, but it is similar to that of Arab nomads of the Syrian Desert. Also the Chaamba and the nomads of Arabia alike have unexpectedly high percentages of B which are due in all probability to the presence of some Negro slave blood in the veins of most of them.

The basic unit of Chaamba social organization is the patrilineal clan, made up in this case of one or more extended families whose members are all believed to be descended from a single and more or less mythical male ancestor, from whom the clan takes its name. The Ouled Aicha clan (which belongs to the Ouled Fredj tribe of the Ouargla division) is exceptional in that its eponymous ancestor was a woman, but she is said to have been of Maraboutic origin, a fact which may have given her more than ordinary womanly prestige. It may be significant in this connection that the founding ancestor of the Ouled Fredj clan, the paramount clan of the Ouled Fredj tribe, is said to have been a Targui who emigrated to Metlili (and whose descendants later moved south from there to El Goléa, whence some of them finally moved north again to Ouargla), and so it is just possible that Tuareg influence may have had something to do with the incongruous appearance of this lone female key ancestress in the midst of an otherwise solidly patrilineal system of descent.

A Chaamba tribe is made up of clans whose key ancestors are believed to have been related or closely associated in some way, or of clans that have been brought together by force of circumstances, or of both. Noble clans exist, and in each tribe one of these is always considered more noble than the rest. Tributary nomad clans of the vassal type exist too, but they are few in number. The rank of a noble clan is based in theory on descent from a relatively early and famous ancestor or a relatively holy one, but clan rank can sometimes be changed considerably within the lifetime of a single chief if he happens to be outstandingly successful or the reverse. And tribes too differ in rank according to the relative ranks of their paramount clans. At the top of the Chaamba class system stand the warrior nomad tribes and clans, and the Shorfa and Maraboutic families. Next come the nomadic commoners and tributary "vassal" clans. Sedentary Arab clans come next, followed in order by the sedentary Zenata, the Haratin, and finally the Negro slaves, nomadic and sedentary alike.

All the Chaamba were probably united in a fairly rigid and formal confederation at the time of the founding of Metlili, but the groups which later broke away to settle elsewhere broke out of the confederation at the same time. The Chaamba still have a loose confederational structure of a sort, however, in that groups based on the same center constitute a single political unit in matters of external policy, a unit which is governed by the chief of the paramount tribe and a supreme council of tribal elders; but such regional groupings seem to be much less rigid and formal than are the confederations of the Tuareg, and they also appear to be functionally inert to a great extent except in times of serious emergency. In other words they hardly seem to fit the definition of the term "confederation" as I have been using it, and so I will refer to them instead as "divisions." The Berazga division of the Chaamba includes two nomad tribes based on Metlili. The first of these in rank, the Ouled Allouch, about four thousand strong, is divided into seven clans of which the Ouled Touameur ("children of Touameur"), supposed descendants of the mythical founder of Metlili, are considered the most noble. The Ouled Abd-el-Kader tribe, numbering some thirty-three hundred or so and divided into five clans, is headed by the Ouled Hanich, who are believed to be descended from Touameur's younger brother. The sedentary "tribe of the ksar" of Metlili includes one sedentarized Chaamba clan and four assimilated clans of immigrant aliens.

In addition to their class and lineage systems, the Chaamba used to have a well developed sof-like system based on two political parties, much like the two-party systems which are so characteristic of the sedentary commercial centers of the Sahara. This dichotomous political organization has now lost much of its former force among the Chaamba nomads, but the fundamental underlying spirit still persists. The tents of a single camp, for instance, are usually pitched in two more or less distinct clusters, and the men of these form two distinct groups in cere-

monial gymkhanas (*fantasias*) just as the boys form two opposing teams in their informal hockey games. A combat team of
warriors, on the other hand, usually includes men from one
party only. The two political groupings (or sofs) that find
expression in such ways are known respectively as Cheraga
(easterners) and Gharba (westerners), the former being traditionally progressive and the latter conservative in all things,
and they still retain a profound spirit of rivalry. The Ouled
Allouch nomad tribe belongs to the eastern party, but the nomadic Abd-el-Kader tribe and the sedentary clan of the Beni
Merzoug are both pretty evenly divided between the two. Thus
it appears that the two-party political system of the Chaamba
cuts across both tribal and clan lines, as well as the otherwise
fairly rigid social divisions of the class system.

In recent times the original clan and tribal structures of the
various Chaamba divisions have been considerably modified by
French administrative procedure. For example, the Chaamba
tribe which emigrated to El Oued used to include two separate
clans which were semiautonomous dependents of a local Arab
nomad tribe at the time the French arrived. In 1887, however,
the French government made these two clans independent and
set up the chief of one of them as a tribal chief with authority
over both. But this arrangement led to interminable administrative troubles, and so, in 1922, the new tribe was arbitrarily reduced to the official status of a single clan [1] and was reattached
administratively to the local Arab tribe. Similarly the two
Chaamba tribes of Ouargla were fused administratively into a
single tribe by government decree in 1927. Obviously such political manipulations inevitably make it difficult to learn much of
the details of Chaamba political organization as it was before
the arrival of the French.

Chieftainship among the Chaamba is theoretically hereditary in the male line, and this theory is respected in practice as

---

[1] Those who wish to look into the source material for themselves should bear in
mind that in French the term *tribu* is often used to designate what we call a clan as
well as what we call a tribe, whereas the term *fraction* may be applied either to what
we call a fraction or to a clan.

a rule although within very broad limits. The heir apparent of a clan chief is normally his eldest son, but a candidate for the chieftainship, no matter whose son he is, must be approved by the clan council of elders (*djemaa el kebar*). If the council agrees that the old chief's eldest son is not the man for the job, they may designate a younger son or a brother, or even a distant relative if necessary. The office of tribal chief normally devolves on the chief of the tribe's paramount clan, but the candidate must be approved by the tribal council of elders. Clan and tribal chiefs alike are essentially administrators, judges and negotiators of intercommunal agreements; they are seldom combat commanders. A war chief is usually named by a tribal chief in council, and is chosen solely on the basis of his personal reputation; and his authority is strictly limited in principle to the single operation for which he was picked out. Sometimes, of course, a spectacularly successful war chief acquires so much personal prestige and influence that he takes over the effective leadership of his clan or tribe and so succeeds in establishing a new dynasty, but this very rarely happens, and then only in times of unusual economic stress or political turmoil.

Personal rank in general depends in the long run on personal prestige, sometimes acquired directly but more often inherited patrilineally, and so it is essentially a matter of the individual and his forebears in the direct paternal line rather than a question of clan membership. The prestige on which personal rank is founded is most often based on the traditional renown of a more or less remote forebear, but an established reputation for good sense, accumulated wealth, and fame as a warrior are often important secondary factors. A Maraboutic background or Shorfa ancestry makes a man noble *ipso facto*.

Family organization is completely patriarchal, following the Koranic pattern, and so in theory women are scarcely more than chattels. In practice, however, the pattern varies a good deal according to the personalities of the individuals concerned. Even a powerful tribal chief will often turn secretly to his widowed mother (*el azhooza,* meaning "the old lady") for advice when he is seriously in doubt.

Marriage is customarily within the family, between the children of brothers, or at least within the clan. Girls marry between the ages of twelve and sixteen as a rule, and men between seventeen and twenty-five, depending mainly on their financial status. Weddings used to take place when the nomad tribes came back to their home bases in the early fall, and they were elaborate and luxurious affairs, but the Chaamba nomads are poorer nowadays and so usually marry quietly in the desert. Simultaneous polygamy [2] is general among all but the very poor, and it is not unusual for a man to have more wives at once than the four allowed by the Koran, while well-to-do men often take concubines in addition. Nomads of both sexes avoid intermarriage with Negroes, and with the sedentary population in general regardless of race, but older men sometimes take Haratin or Negro slave women as concubines and the offspring of such unions are automatically absorbed into the father's family. A widow is customarily taken to wife by a brother of her deceased mate, and the children of her first marriage then refer to this new husband as "father."

Birth feasts are now given only for male children, although it is said that they used to be given for children of both sexes indiscriminately. Boys are circumcised usually at the age of six or seven but there is an "age grade" factor involved, for if there are several boys in a single family they are often circumcised all at once, when the eldest reaches the age of ten or thereabouts. The operator is usually a Negro and is known as the *tahar,* meaning "cleanser." While the operation is in progress the patient is supposed to make a ritual demonstration of courage, by striking the operator for example, and when it is all over he must eat a piece of bread smeared with camel's dung so that "he will have the endurance of a camel." Boys are lodged in the women's quarters until after circumcision, but they begin to go out to pasture with the flocks as soon as they can walk.

---

[2] It is often useful to distinguish between "simultaneous polygamy," which means that a man customarily has two or more wives at once, and "consecutive polygamy," meaning that he customarily has two or more wives in succession but usually not more than one at any given time.

Those between the ages of circumcision and puberty form a separate intermediate group and live pretty much apart from the rest of the community. It used to be the custom when a boy reached the age of fifteen to give him a gun and a riding camel and allow him to join a raiding party. Thus "he received his baptism of fire which was his true baptism," and so achieved full adult status, an event that was celebrated by a feast when he returned from his first raid. But this custom has been dropped entirely since the suppression of raiding.

The over-all economic organization of the Chaamba is best exemplified by the Metlili division, which numbers about seventy-five hundred nomads plus roughly twelve hundred sedentary folk. The livestock is difficult to estimate, as is usual in such cases, and its numbers fluctuate very considerably from year to year under the alternating influences of effective rains and periods of drought. By way of a rough approximation, however, I would say that the nomads have probably about fifty-five hundred camels and eight thousand sheep on the average, with the latter concentrated mostly in the hands of the Ouled Allouch tribe. It is interesting to note that in 1890 it was estimated that there were some seventeen hundred camels in the Metlili area, for a human population of not quite four thousand as against the present population of well over eight thousand. The camels of the Chaamba are less refined in conformation and less fast than those of the Tuareg, but they are said to be more resistant to both thirst and fatigue. They are also less tractable, however, for the Chaamba are more brutal and far less patient with animals than are the Tuareg. The Chaamba also have a number of flocks of goats and a few donkeys, dogs, and chickens. Flocks and herds are customarily watered once a week during the winter months and every other day in summertime.

The nomadic Chaamba follow a seasonal round much like that of the Tuareg except that it is less variable and brings them back regularly once a year to their home bases. The Berazga division leave the bulk of their flocks out at pasture with a few shepherds and return to Metlili at the time of the date harvest, usually in September. In late December or early January they begin to move out again in order of wealth, the owners of the biggest herds and flocks going first. Shifting their tents from pasture to pasture they keep moving until June or thereabouts, when fixed camps of zeribas are set up, and in these the women and children stay with a few of the men while the rest either continue to move about with the livestock or return to Metlili to supervise the work in their gardens and date groves. In August or September the zeriba camps are broken, the nomad families return again to Metlili, and the annual round begins once more.

The nomadic range of the Chaamba as a whole used to extend from the Libyan frontier westward to the country of the Moors, just beyond the great Western Erg, and from the Mzab southward to In Salah and sometimes even as far southwestward as Ouallen, but it has been considerably reduced during the last half-century or so. Ordinary nomad camps are made up of anywhere from four or five to over thirty household units. Their average size is not much above the lower figure as a rule during the first or tent phase of the annual nomadic cycle, but is often a good deal bigger during the second or zeriba phase. Negro servants live apart in small and scrubby tents, set off to one side of the main camp. Household units of the nomadic Chaamba normally include four or five people, with five or six camels, a dozen sheep or so, a small flock of goats, two or three donkeys, a dog or two, and a few scrawny chickens. The women stay in camp, caring for the children, weaving, and doing the daily chores, often with the help of Negroes, while their menfolk are out guarding the livestock or scouting for fresh pasturage.

Most nomadic Chaamba families own palm trees or gardens, or both, which are cared for and cultivated by Haratin sharecroppers or Negro slaves (or freedmen), and they often own houses in the plantations and sometimes in the town as well. They very rarely occupy their town houses, however, but usually rent them, or use them to shelter members of the family who are not strong enough to travel with the flocks and herds. Poor nomads, who have only a few camels or none at all, often do not leave

Metlili until February or March and return again in midsummer, while a few members of their families stay in the plantations the year around and work in the gardens themselves without the help of slaves or sharecroppers. Dates are the principal food crop of the sedentary centers on which the Chaamba nomad tribes are based. In 1937 it was estimated that there were forty-seven thousand producing palm trees around Metlili and its auxiliary oasis, Seb-Seb, ten miles farther down the valley. Comparative figures for other Chaamba centers in the same year show that there were a hundred and seventy thousand palms at El Goléa as against an estimated seventeen thousand in 1873, and a million at Ouargla as compared with roughly four hundred and fifty thousand in 1892. These spectacular increases appear to have been due in the main to improved methods of well digging and irrigation introduced by the French administration. The gardens of Metlili produce most of the domestic plants that are to be found in the Sahara, with the emphasis on onions, carrots, tomatoes, and barley. Water for irrigation is drawn from pulley wells which vary in depth from about thirty-five to over eighty feet, depending on their location and also on the amount of rain that has fallen recently.

While the nomadic Chaamba are settled at their home bases during the autumn and early winter, they trade animals, milk products, wool, woollen garments, and skins for garden produce and imported goods such as grain, cotton cloth and clothing, tea, sugar and spices, tobacco, sulphur, tar, and manufactured articles. The latter include mainly jewelry and woollen clothing from Ghardaia and the north, hardware from Barbary and Ghadamès, and saddles, sandals, and other leather goods from the Sudan. In times of prolonged drought nomads are sometimes forced to sell the rugs and strips of tenting which their women weave for the family while out at pasture.

Before the coming of the French, the Chaamba used to have full control of all caravan trade passing over the central section of the north-south route that connected the Algerian coast with Timbuctoo and the western Sudan. In those days the western central Sahara proper was divided into northern and southern spheres of influence, separated by a line running roughly east and west through Ghadamès and In Salah. The country north of this line, between it and the territory of the Arbaa [3] and Ziban Arab nomad confederations of the extreme northern edge of the desert, was in the hands of the Chaamba, while the country to the south as far as the Sudan was controlled by Tuareg tribes. Just as the Tuareg in their territory operated caravans and imposed on the caravans of others a toll system enforced by punitive raids on those who refused to pay for their protection, so the Chaamba used to do in their own territory, and just as the caravan trade and protection system of the Tuareg have been largely destroyed by motorized competition and the suppression of raiding, so the similar activities of the Chaamba have been drastically reduced or eliminated entirely by the same factors. But the Saharan Tuareg still operate salt caravans on a small scale, and the Chaamba likewise still maintain a small caravan trade which supplies the oases of the northwestern desert in general with bulk goods from Barbary, such as grain from the Atlas Mountain steppe country of Algeria and sugar from the Tunisian port of Gabès.

In the old days big Chaamba caravans used to go regularly as far north as the high plateau country of the Atlas Mountain complex south of Oran and southward to the western Sudan, westward across the Gourara, the Tidikelt and the Touat, and eastward to Gabès, Ghadamès, and Djanet. Caravans heading north, east, and west went heavily armed and so were fully autonomous, but those going south had to pay toll fees to the Tuareg for the right to proceed beyond In Salah. Chaamba caravans are accompanied by professional camel men, rarely by the owners of the camels. The acknowledged leader, usually the oldest or most experienced camel man, is responsible for choosing the route and setting the hours of departure and of halts throughout the journey, and his authority is as absolute as that of the master of a ship at sea used to be. Well before sunset he picks a camp site for the night and the camels are unloaded. The men then collect fuel (usually dry roots or camel dung), cook,

[3] Usually though incorrectly spelt Larbaa.

and eat a leisurely supper, talk for a while, and finally go to sleep about ten o'clock. At dawn or thereabouts they rise and drink a little hot mint tea, camp is broken, and the caravan is on its way once more. There is a midday halt about an hour before noon, when the men drink some more hot mint tea, or milk, and the camels rest or browse but are not unloaded. Then on again, and so another day goes by.

Raiding used to be so important economically to the Chaamba that they had raised it practically to the level of an industry by the time the French arrived. It was a well-organized and highly formalized activity, with its own war chiefs and special rules, a dry land equivalent in fact of the maritime raiding organization of the Barbary pirates. And yet, curiously enough, it was the Chaamba raiding system that made possible the establishment (in 1902) of the French Saharan Camel Corps which finally put a stop to raiding in the western desert. This military police force is commanded by young French career officers, but the men are selected native volunteers. Their work is what Chaamba nomads have always known best and loved most dearly, namely the pursuit and destruction of bands of robbers and smugglers from rival tribes and especially their traditional blood enemies, the Tuareg and Moors. It was a Camel Corps patrol composed mainly of Chaamba, under the command of a French lieutenant named Cottenest, that broke forever the military power of the Ahaggar Tuareg confederation at the Battle of Tit on May 7, 1902. The Camel Corps quickly absorbed many of the old Chaamba raiders, and it still continues to attract young men of warlike families who would normally have become raiders in the old days.

The decline and final disappearance of raiding as a routine economic activity caused the Chaamba to expand commercially and extend their peaceful trade connections farther and farther beyond the limits of their own territory. Members of the sedentary "tribe of the ksar" of Metlili, notably the Shorfa, first began to go out as peddlers accompanying major raiding parties, but in time, as conditions grew steadily more peaceful, they began to set up little stores in sedentary centers all over the western desert. Together with a few commercially inclined Chaamba nomads, they gradually established themselves throughout the area extending from Djanet westward to Adrar and from Ghardaia southward through the Ahaggar. In 1925 a particularly enterprising chief of the nomadic Ouled Allouch tribe gave up his chieftainship, sold off part of his livestock to raise capital, and established a trucking line with headquarters in Ghardaia and branch offices at In Salah, Djanet, and Tamanrasset. In 1937 it was estimated that Chaamba of Metlili owned 80 per cent of all the shops in the southwestern quarter of the Sahara, and since then more and more of them have joined the ranks of emigrant shopkeepers each year. Chaamba store owners rarely become fully sedentary, however, for much of their time is spent on the road buying stock, often in the Sudan, and most of them also return briefly to Metlili once or twice a year. While they are traveling their shops are run by relatives or hired managers. In the last analysis it is the Chaamba's remarkable power of adaptation to a life of commerce and their aggressive expansion of external trade which, more than anything else, distinguish Chaamba culture from the cultures of all the other major nomadic peoples of the Sahara.

Few Chaamba nomads have been willing to give up the freedom of a wandering life, although a handful of retired Camel Corps soldiers, influenced by prolonged contact with European officers, have settled with their families at El Goléa. But once a Chaamba nomad does make up his mind to settle down, he soon becomes well adapted to sedentary life and may even take on, in the words of Capot-Rey, something of the air of a gentleman farmer. He never tills the soil himself, for that would be hopelessly degrading, but he is efficient and astute in the management of his plantations and his labor pool of Haratin sharecroppers and Negro slaves and freedmen. Aside from the Chaamba who were brought to Ghardaia as mercenaries and then decided to stay there, a few Chaamba Berazga families have also settled in Melika and, to a lesser extent, in other towns of the Mzab.

Nomads everywhere, who have not settled down, naturally require some kind of shelter which offers suitable protection from the weather and at the same time can be moved with reasonable ease. This does not prevent different nomadic peoples from developing or adopting different and more or less distinctive forms of shelter. The tent, or *khaima,* used by the nomadic Chaamba is essentially the same as that used by the nomads of Arabia: it consists of strips of rough and heavy cloth sewn together edge-to-edge and arranged usually (though not always) with their long axes parallel to the long axis of the tent, running from end to end over supporting posts. These strips, made of goathair mixed with wool, are usually about two and a half to three feet wide and of variable length, and they are woven by the women, on horizontal ground-looms, during those seasons when the family is moving about with its livestock. The material is not degreased and also swells up when wet, and so it is practically waterproof. Different tribes and clans use slightly different standard patterns and colors, so that one can often tell at a glance before arriving at a camp what group its inhabitants belong to.

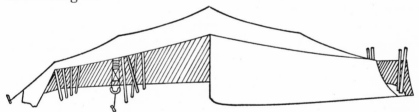

FIG. 5. Diagram of a Chaamba tent. (The right-hand front corner has been cut away to show the cooking area.)

The average khaima is twenty to thirty feet long, about six feet high in the center and ten feet deep or so, and is divided in the middle by a curtain (running from front to back) which is made of the same material as is the tent itself. As one stands facing the khaima, the women's and children's quarters are to the right of the central curtain, protected and concealed from view by a second curtain stretched across in front of them. And at the right-hand front corner there is often a small cubical annex, open to the sky, where the women do the cooking. The left-hand half of the tent is the men's domain, and serves not only as sleeping quarters but as a living and dining room and as a parlor for receiving guests. The sides of the khaima are pegged down all the way around when the weather is cold or stormy, but they can be rolled up in hot weather to allow free circulation of air. The only serious disadvantage of this kind of tent is that it is heavy and difficult to handle, especially when wet.

The zeribas which the Chaamba sometimes occupy in summertime are cubical in shape, and are made of scrubby bushes or palm fronds tied to a framework of sticks. It is said that some of the western Chaamba nomads also make semi-spherical wicker frames and cover them with light woollen blankets; but I have never seen any myself. One wonders if this curiously un-Saharan form of hut may not have been introduced originally by traveling traders who had seen similar huts in the Sudan, or if it could possibly be a degenerate copy of the Teda nomad tent. Very poor folk sometimes hollow out a circular area in the ground, build a little wall of stones around the edge, and cover the whole with a roof of brush, thus producing a kind of semi-subterranean hovel not unlike the round huts of the sedentary Teda, although much cruder. Semi-dugouts of this kind are found, however, scattered sporadically all over most of the central and western desert, and so it seems hardly possible to find out where they originated.

The usual Chaamba household furnishings include guerbas for water, a heavy wooden couscous bowl, a few earthenware pots and nowadays some imported hardware, a small rotary quern, and thick rugs which are placed on the ground with the smooth side up so that they can be swept more easily. There is often a ground loom beside or even in the tent and sometimes a vertical loom as well. Tenting, woollen clothes (gandouras and burnouses), and saddlebags are usually woven in the camps, and rugs may be too or they may be bought from nomad tribes of the southern slopes of the Atlas Mountains, particularly the Ouled

Nail who live in the steppe country to the northwest and north of Laghouat.

Chaamba clothing is not basically different from that of the other major nomadic peoples of the Sahara, but it is distinctive in matters of detail. The traditional Chaamba male costume includes a longish undershirt of white cotton cloth, like that of the Tuareg except that the sleeves are shorter and less voluminous, but this garment is fast giving way to the cheap European cotton shirt. Trousers used to be much like those of the Tuareg except that they were somewhat shorter and less baggy, but today they are usually baggy only in the seat and around the thighs, while the legs are fairly close fitting below the knee. They are made of medium weight white cotton cloth as a rule. A gandoura of white cotton or lightweight woollen cloth is worn over the undershirt, and it too is less voluminous than the Tuareg model, for it is only a little wider than the extended elbows of the wearer. A burnous, usually of white wool, is worn over the gandoura, and an extra burnous or two, often made of brown or gray camel's hair more or less mixed with wool, may be worn in cold weather or on ceremonial occasions by the well-to-do. The sedentary and semi-sedentary Chaamba often wear a kshabia in cold weather. Although this garment is undoubtedly of Roman origin, the Chaamba probably got it from the Mzabites who all use it, and who in turn doubtless brought it south with them from Barbary a thousand years ago.

The typical headdress of Chaamba men is a white turban of flimsy cotton cloth arranged with a loop hanging down below the chin so that it can be pulled up easily to cover the nose and mouth. This type of veil, if it can be so called, seems to be a purely protective device with nothing ceremonial about it. The standard footgear of the nomadic Chaamba used to be rawhide boots about ten inches high, laced over the arch of the foot up to the ankle and left open above, but this early form has been considerably modified by European influence. Today smooth red or yellow leather is used ordinarily for the boot itself, while the soles are often made from pieces of old truck tires with the startling result that miles of desert trails are now stamped with the trademarks of American and European rubber companies. Sedentary Chaamba, and rich nomads when they come to town, usually wear low laceless shoes of Mzabite manufacture.

The characteristic arms of the Chaamba used to be oriental swords and daggers, and guns made in the urban seaport centers of Barbary or imported through them from Europe, but these have been replaced by modern firearms and knives of local manufacture. Camel men and shepherds always carry heavy sticks three or four feet long, which are very formidable weapons in their hands.

Chaamba nomad women normally wear a light undershirt and trousers which are much like those of the men but are less bulky. They used to wear a simple draped and belted tunic of cotton or light woollen cloth, caught up over one shoulder or both and held in place with a brooch or two, or with long thorns; but nowadays they usually wear one or more voluminous belted dresses of cheap and garishly printed cotton cloth, which come down to just above the ankles and look a good deal like the dresses worn by peasant women in central and eastern Europe. Sedentary women of Metlili go without trousers as a rule. The customary woman's headdress is a small colored scarf or two, hardly more than a rag, wound around the head like a turban with one end hanging down over the right ear. The standard outer garment, seldom worn except as a protection against cold or on very rare occasions when visiting a town, is the haik. When a woman is wearing one for reasons of fashion, it covers her entirely so that nothing can be seen except her feet, but in cold weather, when it is worn only for physical protection, it is draped around the shoulders but not over the head or face. In fact Chaamba nomad women almost never bother to conceal their faces when they are away from settlements as they are nearly all the time. And, although they seem to avoid their menfolk as much as possible, this is probably a matter of deference rather than ritual modesty.

The sedentary "tribe of the ksar" of Metlili is a heterogeneous community. It includes a sedentarized Chaamba nomad clan, a Shorfa clan that immigrated from Morocco long ago, three refugee groups of northern origin, two of which are Maraboutic families formerly attached to the Arbaa nomad confederation, and finally a handful of immigrants from a sedentary Arab clan of Ouargla. The Shorfa and Maraboutic holy men, in addition to their mercantile activities, cater to the nomad's need for charms and ceremonial services just as do the holy men of nomadic groups elsewhere. A dozen or so sedentary families of Metlili are said to be descendants of Mzabites from Melika (about half a mile east of Ghardaia) who abjured the puritanical doctrine of their people and fled from the Mzab five hundred years ago or thereabouts. In addition there were seven Jewish jewelers and merchants from Ghardaia settled at Metlili twenty years ago.[4]

Well-to-do families of the Chaamba Berazga have always had Negro servants, who used to be obtained in the Sudan by professional raiders, brought north in commercial caravans, and sold in the slave markets of In Salah and the Mzab. Although the Negro slaves of the Chaamba were freed many years ago by French decree, their material status, like that of the freed slaves of the Tuareg, remains very little changed in practice. Freed Negro slaves and their descendants accompany nomad families on their seasonal wanderings, doing the household chores and helping out occasionally with the flocks, while others stay in sedentary centers cultivating the gardens of their masters and making basketry. They act as sorcerers and magicians too, just as smiths do among the Tuareg; for they are makers of amulets, love potions, and insidious poisons, and they also practice sympathetic magic and necromancy and cast powerful spells on victims near and far. They appear to have a communal organization of their own, but nothing seems to be known about it beyond the fact that they hold secret ritual reunions of some sort in addition to the usual overt festive gatherings. The negroid Haratin of the Chaamba country, who are the sedentary gardeners, constitute only a minor element in the population as a whole; and they seem to be able to move rather more freely from one center to another than can their cousins who live farther south. Indeed, young

---

[4] However, only one, whose wife and children lived in Ghardaia, was still doing business there in 1950, and he too had left by the time I returned there in 1954.

Haratin men sometimes act as free itinerant peddlers, wandering about among the nomad tribes from camp to camp exchanging tea and sugar for milk products and wool.

I have already pointed out that Chaamba men not infrequently take Negro or negroid Haratin concubines, and that the children of such unions automatically become members of the father's family. As a result of this there is a considerable negroid element in the racial composition of the Chaamba generally, although it still appears to be substantially less among the Berazga than it is among the other Chaamba divisions and most of the other Arab tribes of the Sahara. As is the case with the Zenata, negroid admixture seems to be least among the most fully nomadic groups, and, as among the sedentary white population of the northern desert in general, it is apparently most in the highest and lowest social ranks of the sedentary and semi-sedentary economic and religious aristocracy. Also there has certainly been some inter-breeding between the Chaamba and the northwestern Tuareg, but it has just as certainly been infrequent and always on a very small scale. If there is any Tuareg blood at all in the veins of the Chaamba Berazga it must be very little indeed.

Chapter 8 ~

THE MOORS

THE TERM "Moor" has been used in so many different senses that I must redefine it before proceeding further. When I speak of Moors I am referring to the basically white and mainly pastoral nomadic population of the Spanish Sahara and of the French Saharan territory which adjoins it on the east and south, extending inland to about 7° West Longitude and southward to the Senegal drainage system. Almost nothing is known about the peoples of this area prior to the middle of the seventeenth century, and very little more is known until less than a hundred and fifty years ago. In Chapter 3 I explain how the Tadjakant, once warrior nomad lords of the far western desert, came increasingly under the influence of both Arabic and Sudanese cultures until at last they were practically destroyed as an independent and united people by neighbors who had remained pastoral nomads in the desert and so had retained their warlike vigor. These neighbors were the Moors whom I am about to describe. It is not yet absolutely certain that the Tadjakant should be excluded from my Moorish nomad category, but I will do so tentatively because they have long been both heavily negroid and almost completely sedentary. As my main Moorish sample I will take the nomads of the western central part of the Spanish Sahara, and particularly the Ouled Tidrarin, because they seem to have been affected relatively little by recent foreign influence.

Such vague and shifting shadows as one can glimpse through the mists of western Saharan history seem to suggest that the modern Moors are both physically and culturally products of mixture between Arab invaders and nomadic Berber tribes that the invading Arabs found already living along the northern and northeastern borders of what is now the Spanish Sahara. Moorish medieval history and tribal tradition both preserve the story of the Almoravide Emir, Abou Bekr ben Omar, who raised an army in southern Morocco some nine hundred years ago and launched a victorious missionary war across the western Sahara into the Sudan. His troops are said to have included Arab warriors, scholarly holy men of mixed Arabic and Berber ancestry, and pastoral nomadic Berbers. The first two groups were classed as nobles, whereas the third is said to have been relegated to tributary vassal status because its members were neither learned nor particularly valiant. Even if this story is not historically accurate, it still defines a system of social categories which is characteristic of the Moors today; and so there can be little doubt that herein lies the key to the problem of how the main framework of modern Moorish social organization came to be.

Many Moorish myths that deal with tribal origins tell of ancestors who came into the central Spanish Sahara from the south. The Ouled Tidrarin, for instance, are all supposedly descended from a common ancestor named Hannin, otherwise known as Tidrarin meaning literally "man of the mountain," from the Berber word *adrar* which means "mountain" and is used also to designate the region in which Ouadane is located (as well as other places). And there is still a ruined building at Ouadane known as "the fort of the Ouled Tidrarin." All this would seem to indicate that, although the Moors came originally from the northwestern desert, some of them at least migrated southward to the fringes of the Sudan and then finally moved north again, into what is now the Spanish Sahara.

The story of the Ouled Tidrarin tribe is a good illustration of the confusion that characterizes even recent Moorish history. In the eighteenth century the Ouled Delim, by then one of the most fully Arabized of all the major Moorish tribes, entered a period of rapid expansion. It is said by some that they attacked the Ouled Tidrarin and reduced them by force to the status of tributary vassals; but others say that the Ouled Tidrarin voluntarily sought the protection of the Ouled Delim against bands of raiders who were constantly making off with their livestock, and that the new protectors took advantage of this situation to force payment of tribute on an annual basis. In any case the Ouled Tidrarin decided to stop paying in 1877, whereupon the Ouled Delim attacked them, and there then ensued a long series of ambushes, skirmishes, and occasional minor battles. Some say that it was the Ouled Tidrarin who finally persuaded the powerful Rguibat nomads to come in on their side; or it may be that the Rguibat came in on their own initiative because of a blood feud. Then the Ouled Delim in turn restored the balance of the opposing forces by bringing in the Ait Lahsen as their mercenary allies, and finally almost all the central Moorish tribes got involved in one way or another. In 1892 the Ouled Delim persuaded the Rguibat to withdraw from the war, ostensibly on the ground that it was really none of their business in the first place. Hostilities then gradually petered out over a period of years and the Ouled Tidrarin returned at last to their old status as tributary vassals of the Ouled Delim. The history of the Moors is made up almost entirely of a tediously repetitious series of vague and confused stories of this kind, with the result that one can be sure of very little except that the status of a clan or tribe could and occasionally did shift under the stress of compelling circumstances, and that it is now practically impossible to discover just what these circumstances really were in any given case. Thus there is little hope of finding out much about the socio-political structure of the Moors as it was more than a century or two ago. Its main outline probably has not changed greatly since about the end of the fourteenth century by which time the impact of Arab invasion seems to have been pretty well absorbed, but even since then there have surely been many communal disintegrations and regroupings and innumerable minor and even major shifts of power balance of which we can never hope to learn.

Arab influence on Moorish culture seems to have been greatest in the field of language, for most of the Moors now speak a form of Arabic which is remarkably pure on the whole although characterized by the retention of various Berber expressions and turns of phrase. Practically pure Berber still survives, however, here and there, mainly among scattered Maraboutic vassal groups which become more numerous the farther south one goes, and whose members are usually bilingual, in Berber and Arabic.

Although a good deal of field work has been done on the physical characteristics of the Moors, most of the results have not yet been made available. What has been published, however, makes it clear at least that the Moors are rather like the Tuareg on the whole except that they are shorter, averaging only about five feet five inches in height. They are thin and wiry, their heads are long and relatively narrow as a rule, and their faces are usually oval, with long and rather narrow noses and narrow jaws. The nasal profile is most frequently more or less convex, often straight and rarely concave. Lips vary a good deal but are most often medium in thickness. The most common skin color is said to be yellowish brown. Hair is usually curly although both straight and woolly hair are sometimes found. Hair and eyes are almost always very dark, but light hair and light or even blue eyes do crop up occasionally. The ABO blood group patterns of the Moors seem to vary a good deal regionally. Although they are much like those of the eastern mountaineers of Barbary in general, they are still surprisingly negroid, even among tribes like the Izarguien who are noted for their general outward resemblance to northern Berbers. Men are said to be more numerous than women which is in striking contrast to the situation usually found in the Sahara and in the world in general. Apparently this is due to the simple fact that Moorish men usually outlive their women, a fact as curious as it is inexplicable for the time being.

The social structure of the Moors is difficult to analyze because of the relative independence of communal elements which has resulted in a loose and fluid kind of organization, seemingly rather like that of the Teda although somewhat less chaotic. The basic unit is undoubtedly the patrilineal clan, which, as in the case of the Chaamba, is made up of supposed descendants of a common ancestor from whose various sons the different fractions of the clan are usually believed to be descended. Clans are strictly patriarchal in theory, as is apparent particularly in times of stress when aid is customarily sought from the paternal kin, but in good times when all is well there appears a secondary tendency to strengthen relations with the maternal side of the family. A pregnant wife, for example, often goes to live temporarily with her mother, although a newly divorced wife who happens to be nursing an infant usually stays on in her former husband's household until the child is weaned. A bride, previously married or not, brings her personal property including livestock with her and it remains her own. And a matrilocal element crops up too occasionally. When a woman of the Rguibat, for example, marries a man of another tribe, the couple frequently set up housekeeping among the bride's people who thereupon adopt the groom as one of their own; and this has happened often enough for it to be said that only one Rguibi in ten is "pure" in terms of tribal ancestry. Thus Moorish women still enjoy much more social importance and freedom than would normally be accorded them in a strictly Moslem society. It has been noted moreover that women's names appear occasionally in the traditional genealogies of the southern and central Moors, and that they appear more and more frequently the farther back one goes. Women today have no overt authority, however, beyond the limits of their own households, and even there it is the men who rule.

The nucleus of a Moorish tribe is made up of clans whose key ancestors are supposed to have been related or closely associated in some way, and the tribe as such is usually known by the name of its paramount clan. Additional clans often used to attach themselves to strong tribes voluntarily as tributary vassals, for it was customary for a group that had incurred a blood debt it could not pay to attach itself in this way to a richer and more powerful group which could pay off the debt at once and then recover the cost gradually in the form of annual tribute. Clans could also be brought into a tribe as tributary vassals simply by conquest. Thus, a Moorish tribe is, or was until very recent times, a rather fluid and unstable constellation of satellite clans bound by politico-economic ties to a core whose elements were held together by ties of kinship, real or mythical as the case might be. Similar situations seem to exist in the eastern desert too, as among the Hassaouna, a tribe of mixed Berber and Arab origin. Although the Moors no longer have any supra-tribal groupings that can properly be re-

ferred to as confederations in the strict sense of the word, neighboring tribes are sometimes loosely associated in regional divisions roughly similar to those of the Chaamba. In the old days
true confederations did exist, based mainly on blood debt alliances in all likelihood, but they seem to have broken up following
the partial suppression by European authorities of the old blood
debt and tribute systems.

Moorish tribes differ in rank, as do Moorish clans, but their
relative relationships are not permanently fixed for they can move
either upward or downward in the socio-political scale, as the
result of exceptionally good or bad fortune. For example, a clan,
or even a minor tribe, can be raised in rank by being admitted to
permanent membership in an alliance headed by a more powerful
group, usually as a reward for help in war. Some authorities believe that collective rank among the Moors is primarily a matter
of "population dynamics," in other words that the bigger a clan
is the better chance it has of becoming noble; but others have
pointed out that vassal clans are sometimes over twice as big as
noble ones in some of the most powerful nomadic tribes. Thus,
mere numbers can hardly be the deciding factor in determining the
rank of any given group of Moorish nomads. Wealth in livestock
does not seem to be the deciding factor either, for some vassal
clans are far richer in this respect than are their noble masters.
In fact it looks as though an efficient fighting organization, together with the strong leadership and rigid discipline which this
implies, is the only thing that can surely raise a nomadic Moorish
community above others of its kind. It is also possible, although
apparently less likely, that some of the noble Moorish clans may
actually be subordinate to their vassals in terms of ultimate
sovereignty, just as noble clans are among the Tuareg of the
Ahaggar; but here again not enough is known about the situation
to warrant any definite conclusions.

The clearest evidence as to the relative positions at any given
time of the various elements in a composite nomad community,
such as a tribe or a confederation, can usually be found in the
system of tribute payments. Among the Moors, however, such
systems are seldom simple, because tribute may be paid for one

or more of a variety of reasons. Weak groups pay stronger ones for armed protection as well as for economic assistance in times of serious hardship, and also sometimes for the purpose of refunding a blood debt which the stronger group has paid on their behalf. Rich groups, on the other hand, often pay economically weaker ones which are nevertheless more warlike and therefore useful as mercenaries. Merchants also pay tribute at times for the right to take caravans regularly back and forth across the territory of a certain tribe. Even some of the Maraboutic clans pay for protection, and so are known as "Marabouts of the shade," although others, known as "Marabouts of the sun," have remained independent and defend their own interests when necessary. And yet even a tributary Maraboutic group still retains a certain degree of preëminence in terms of political power, as is illustrated by the fact that when a member of such a group is brought to trial he need furnish only half as many witnesses as a warrior nomad noble is obliged to produce.

Payment of tribute is not ordinarily made collectively by one group to another but is handled rather at the family level, each family headman of the tributary group making a predetermined annual payment to a specific family headman of the warlike protectors. But the situation is sometimes complicated by the fact that a warrior's right to tribute payments can be sold by him to another of his own kind, so that in an emergency he can raise capital on short notice if he must. Usually, however, he prefers to go begging among the tents of the tributary dependents of his kinship group rather than liquidate such a source of regular income. And finally it is clear that the Moorish tribute system as a whole offers many opportunities for serious abuse on the part of the warlike aristocracy, and so naturally the latter not infrequently impose on their vassals increasingly onerous exactions over and above the terms of the original tribute agreement. And this in turn leads every now and then to all but interminable conflicts, of which the revolt of the Ouled Tidrarin was a typical example.

Government among the Moors follows roughly the same basic pattern as that found among the Chaamba, except that religious chiefs, always closely associated with some religious brotherhood, are relatively numerous and often very powerful. Indeed it has been said that the chiefs of major Moorish divisions used to be chosen exclusively from Shorfa clans. Clan and tribal councils play a relatively important role too, for not only do they designate the successor of a dead chief but they continue to exert a considerable degree of influence over him after he has assumed office. Although it is the chief who usually initiates new policies and directs their applications, the council retains the power to veto his decisions. It is often difficult and sometimes practically impossible to bring together the full council of a major clan or tribe, simply because the tents of even a single clan are often widely scattered, but the Moors have solved this problem by establishing a system of communal subcommittees which have enough authority to deal with all but the most important questions of internal policy and government.

Secular chieftainship tends to be hereditary, but only in a loose and general way; for, although an administrative chief is chosen preferably from among the close male relatives of his predecessor, proven ability, age, wealth, and personality are the final deciding factors. War chiefs, like those of the Chaamba, are named solely on the basis of proven ability, and then only for the duration of a single operation. Religious chieftainship, on the other hand, is usually hereditary in the male line, and so there have arisen here and there powerful holy families which are practically dynastic in character. The most famous and also the most influential of these is the family of El Ma el Ainin ("The Water of the Twin Springs") who live in the northern part of Moorish territory.

The governmental system I have just described sounds so neat and reasonable that one would naturally expect it to work smoothly, but it does not. In fact the spirit of personal rivalry among the Moors is so intense that candidates for a vacant chieftainship can seldom bring themselves to bow unprotestingly before an unfavorable decision of any council, and so council meetings called to name a new chief often degenerate into armed brawls. Even after a new chief has been chosen and officially installed in office, it is not at all unusual for disappointed relatives to rise in armed revolt against him. Indeed, political murder used to be so common in the southern part of Moorish territory that paramount chiefs there almost never died natural deaths before European control over the area became firmly established.

The independent character of Moorish socio-political units is expressed again in the governmental system by the fact that each tribe has a law code of its own, established and modified when necessary by the tribal council. These special codes are limited mainly to matters of police policy and procedure and are, of course, fitted into the general framework of Koranic law. Councils also act as courts of law in criminal cases, and are then presided over by Marabouts who have a thorough knowledge of the tribal common law. If the plaintiff and accused belong to different tribes, the councils of both tribes sit jointly in judgment, but, if they cannot agree, the case is taken before some member of the holy family of El Ma el Ainin, who are looked on as the supreme court of the land. It has been said that the Rguibat have a divisional council, known as The Council of Forty, which not only acts as a supreme court in criminal cases involving members of two or more tribes but also has absolute authority over a whole division in matters of general policy, such as a question of whether to go to war or not.

The social class structures of most of the Saharan nomad tribes are much alike except in matters of detail, and that of the Moors is no exception. There are four main levels in Moorish society, the uppermost of which consists of predominantly Arab Shorfa and warlike nomad clans, and Arabo-Berber Marabouts. Next come the tributary vassals, the nomadic fishermen of the coast (the Imraguen), and the pastoral nomads of the interior, as well as the few sedentary and semi-sedentary Moorish groups. Next in rank are the itinerant entertainers and the smiths, followed by the Haratin, the freedmen, and finally the slaves. Personal rank appears to be regarded as primarily a matter of the group rather than of the individual, for when one asks what a man's rank is, the name of his tribe or clan is normally given in answer; but it is said also that famous warriors have occasionally been ennobled individually, as a reward for some special service or out-standing act of bravery.

The first step toward adult status and the full privileges of hereditary rank is circumcision. Boys are usually circumcised at the age of about six or seven in the north and four or five in the south, but there is also an "age group" factor involved, for in a single camp all the boys who are about the right age are usually circumcised at once. They are then kept on a meat diet until their wounds are healed. After circumcision a boy passes from the parental control of his mother to that of his father, who then proceeds to school him in the arts of riding and the use of arms. At the age of twelve or thirteen he begins to veil his face occa-sionally and starts to take an open interest in the opposite sex. Surprisingly enough, Moorish girls are subjected sometimes to an operation corresponding to circumcision,[1] a practice unknown elsewhere in the Sahara but common enough among the Negroes of West Africa, from whom the Moors may have acquired it.

Marriage is almost always within the clan, the preferred union being between the children of brothers or between a man and his brother's daughter. Except for this uncle-niece type of union, however, the marital prohibitions of the Koran are rigidly ob-served, while marriage with anyone below one's own rank is very strongly discouraged. Couples often get engaged when they are mere children, but such engagements are often broken off amicably before the parties reach marriageable age. Girls marry at about eighteen as a rule, while men usually wait until they are a little older. Consecutive polygamy, wherein a man has several wives in succession but seldom more than one at a time, is common, al-though nomads tend as a rule to have fewer wives than do seden-tary and semi-sedentary folk. But it is not uncommon either for a man to keep his first wife always, and to take in addition a whole series of secondary wives, one after another.

Infidelity is frowned upon by the Moors, so much so in fact that it is sometimes raised above the strictly family level and treated as a matter of communal concern. A husband whose wife commits

---

[1] This operation, known technically as "excision" or "female circumcision" con-sists of cutting out the clitoris and the *labiae minorae*.

adultery may flog her or lock her up for three days, or he may simply dismiss her. But when a husband and wife are both known to be involved in adulterous activities, they may be put to death on the theory that they are endangering the basic social structure of the community, in other words that they are setting an intolerably bad example. Divorce is less common among nomads than among sedentary folk, but it is never difficult. A woman can buy her freedom, for example, and then remarry after only three months' time. If she has any male children, the father must pay for their maintenance, but he can also keep them with him if he wants to. A widowed woman normally goes to live with one of her sons, or even with a son of her deceased husband by a former marriage if that son's own mother is dead.

Religion among the Moors is a complex affair, in which many pre-Islamic pagan beliefs and practices survive beneath a fairly hard but generally thin coating of Islamic doctrine. Although all Moors are nominally Moslems, they are not usually strict in their observance of traditional Islamic ritual. Boys begin to observe the annual fast of Ramdhan at the age of seventeen, and girls at fifteen, but neither sex seems to be very conscientious about it at any time. Although Julio Caro Baroja wrote that major religious chiefs whose authority extends beyond the limits of a single tribe supposedly have to make the pilgrimage to Mecca in order to consolidate their positions, he added that there was not a single pilgrim among the Ouled Tidrarin when he visited them seven years ago. And there also seem to be numerous survivals of pagan ritual. The Ouled Tidrarin, for instance, are said to celebrate exceptionally good harvests with a curious sort of strip-tease dance, a thoroughly pagan performance which begins with the young men and women lining up in two ranks facing one another. First a boy steps forward, places a present of sugar and tea or trinkets on the ground, and retires to his place. Then a girl steps out between the lines, lets her clothes fall to the ground, picks up the present, and goes back naked to her place. After this has been going on for a while, to the accompaniment of much whooping and yelling, self-restraint begins to crumble and eventually nature takes its course. Such doings make one wonder just what the day-to-day premarital relations between the sexes may be like, but so far no one who knows the Moors well—and there are few who do—has even mentioned the subject.

Moorish economy is based primarily on pastoral nomadism, which in this case depends on sedentary centers to a lesser degree than elsewhere in the Sahara. The country of the Moors is exceedingly barren for the most part, and agricultural centers and oases are very few and very poor, as is illustrated by the fact that as recently as 1950 it was extremely rare to find even a thousand date palms in any one place in the Spanish Sahara. A few oases in the French part of Moorish territory have as many as ten to fifty thousand palms each, but they are so far south as to be almost outside the desert proper. Partly because of this situation, the nomadic population is always widely scattered, and in bad seasons the tent units of even a single family may be obliged to camp tens of miles apart much of the time. The problem of finding pasturage and water close together is even greater than in the Ahaggar, and so it is not unusual for a young man to be sent with baggage camels to fetch water for the camp from sometimes as much as thirty miles away or even more. Under such circumstances every member of the camp community naturally has to work hard all the time. Herding and agricultural labor when out at pasture are men's work, while women set up the tents and take them down again, make leather cushions, sandals, and belts, and cords of hair or leather, and weave fancy saddlebags and tenting material.

A comfortably well-to-do nomad family ordinarily has somewhere in the neighborhood of twenty-five camels, fifteen sheep, and forty goats, and, although figures vary greatly, even the poorest families usually have at least two or three goats each. Extreme exceptions do occur, however, as in the case of one tribal chief in the south who is said to own some five hundred camels, five hundred head of cattle, two thousand sheep, fifty donkeys, and two or three horses, all of which make up approximately a third of the livestock of his entire tribe. Sheep are of the woolly northern variety for the most part, while the goats are like those found all over the Sahara. The southern Moors have an elaborately complex nomenclature for sheep, which used to be their basic unit of exchange and had fixed values in relation to camels, donkeys, and cattle, so that livestock in effect took the place of a fairly elaborate monetary system. In describing camels the Moors in general use Arabic age and color terms (except possibly their term for gray: Moorish is *edjan;* the Tuareg Berber is *yendjelan*), which suggests that camel domestication may be a relatively recent development among them. Indeed, some authorities believe that they did not begin to use camels extensively until as late as the sixteenth century, although that seems almost incredible. In 1946 the number of camels in the Spanish Sahara was estimated at roughly a hundred thousand, but in 1950 there were only a little more than half as many left, a striking illustration of the disastrous effects of prolonged periods of drought. The Moors also have a few donkeys, dogs, and chickens. According to Robert Adams, horses were common enough in his day (1810) to be presented as rewards to European captives who accepted conversion to Islam, but there are now almost none left among the northern and the central Moors and not many in the south.

Conservational nomadic pastoralism, trade, agriculture, and raiding are, or were until very recently, the four main pillars of Moorish economy. I will not embark here on a general discussion of the pastoral practices of the Moors since there is nothing particularly distinctive about them except the systems of lending and collective labor. Loans of livestock constitute an important conjunctive mechanism which binds together different social segments of a nomadic Moorish community. Rich men often lend animals to their poorer neighbors, sometimes for purely material convenience and sometimes as a form of charity, while owners of very large herds and flocks often lend parts of their holdings to less prosperous relatives, and so disperse their property for greater safety. A borrower enjoys free use of the animal that is loaned and of such of its products as he consumes himself, but he must reimburse the owner for products that are sold and must also pay some sort of depreciation fee if he is able. Loans are made for periods of anywhere from "three days to three generations," but the terms are always agreed on in advance. Although livestock loans are very common, they often lead to serious quarrels, especially when a borrower dies and the problem of inheritance arises. The principal activity involving collective labor is sheep shearing, which is done by the men of a nomadic community working on a cooperative basis. The visitors who gather at a camp to help on such occasions are fed by the women of that camp, and a good time is had by all.

The nomadic Moors follow an annual round in much the same manner as do the Tuareg, but with a general tendency to move westward toward the seacoast in the spring and autumn, northward in the summer and south in wintertime. Those of them who, like the Chaamba, own garden plots and palm groves in sedentary centers, return to their plantations each year at the time of the date harvest, usually about the middle of July in this case. Ostrich drives, carried out on horseback, used to be a popular accessory source of nomad income a century and a half ago, but they are now of little or no importance, due to the disappearance of ostriches from most of Moorish territory. Nomads trade in local markets, offering camels, goats, wool, and sometimes barley in exchange for garden produce and imported goods and foodstuffs. And for this reason, a few members of each nomad tribe usually remain permanently at some sedentary center, where they act primarily as brokers and butchers but also as bakers and interpreters.

Caravan trade on a really big scale was an important element of Moorish economy until the extension of motorized transportation made such operations relatively unprofitable. Big caravans used to go regularly once a year from the northern Spanish Sahara southward right across the desert to Timbuctoo, and back again. A vivid description of one such expedition, about 1800, has been preserved in the memoirs of James Riley, a shipwrecked American sea captain who lived for several years in slavery among the Moors. The caravan he tells of numbered over a thousand men and four thousand camels, the latter loaded with all sorts of merchandise including weapons, silk, salt, spices, tobacco, and even amber. Nearly a month after setting out they were stopped by a sandstorm and wisely remained camped for two days, until it passed, but even so over two hundred camels and nearly three hundred men were lost. And from then on things went from bad to worse. After crossing one particularly long waterless stretch, with the loss of roughly three hundred more camels and another hundred men, the caravan finally reached a major watering point only to find the wells completely dry. The leader then announced that all but three hundred of the remaining camels must be killed, so that the surviving men could use their blood and liquid squeezed from their stomach contents in place of water until the next wells were reached. Everyone agreed with this in principle, but no one was willing to sacrifice his own baggage animals and abandon his own merchandise, and so a bitter argument arose. At last the "oldest and most judicious men" began killing camels anyway, according to the leader's orders, and this started a fight in which everyone soon became involved. The leader himself was among the first to fall, followed by two or three hundred men and some five hundred camels; and the blood of all these victims, human and animal alike, was drunk by the survivors. Finally, of the whole caravan that had started out, only twenty-one men and twelve camels reached Timbuctoo alive.

This disastrous expedition was an extreme case, of course, but it does show the kind of thing that could happen to almost any caravan, given only a little unusually bad luck. Riley goes on to tell how one of the fortunate survivors returned home from Timbuctoo under what were doubtless much more normal circumstances. This man joined a north-bound caravan, made up of about fifteen hundred men and four thousand camels together with two thousand Negro slaves, which traveled northward without incident clear across the desert to El Goléa and thence onward to Touggourt. There traders bound for Tripoli and Tunis turned off toward their respective destinations and the others continued westward to Morocco, dropping off along the way a party of merchants who headed north across the Atlas Mountains to Algiers.

Today the Moorish caravan trade still extends all the way from Marrakech, in southwestern Morocco, southward to a line running roughly east and west between the mouth of the Senegal

River and the Niger Bend, but most of the merchants engaged in it belong to Maraboutic and other tributary vassal clans. Live-stock and wool, the chief articles of export, are exchanged mainly for dates, rice, grain, and various manufactured articles from the north and the northeast, while leather goods and millet are obtained from the Sudan in exchange for salt. Slave trading has been largely eliminated in recent years and the volume of caravan trade in general has been much reduced, especially in the north. The chief source of salt is at Idjil, where 3,466 camel loads of eight or nine bars weighing about forty-five pounds each (making a total of about six hundred tons in all) were taken out in 1950. Trade in weapons used to be mainly in Jewish hands, and the men engaged in it paid individually for the protection of powerful Moorish chiefs, but this kind of commerce has broken down too under the increasing pressure of European rule.

There is said to be a slowly growing tendency among the nomadic Moors to settle down to a semi-sedentary commercial life, but it has not yet made any very substantial progress except perhaps in the south. Agriculture is practiced by some Moorish nomads in much the same absentee landlord manner that characterizes the nomadic Chaamba. Since it is considered shockingly degrading for a nomad to cultivate the soil (except when out at pasture), the plantations are worked on a crop sharing basis by sedentary Haratin and Negro slaves and freed-men. The landlord furnishes the land and water and normally receives half of the crops produced. Nomadic Moors also practice agriculture themselves occasionally in the course of their wanderings, and the produce of this activity is treated as communal property. The water of heavy rains sometimes collects in hollows in which rich pasturage springs up as a result, and Moorish nomads often plant barley, millet, and even water-melons in such places when conditions are suitable. Small temporary dams are built when needed to keep accumulated rain water from running off, and the soil is tilled with primitive iron-shod plows which many nomad families carry with them as part of their camp equipment. Only men handle the plow and do the sowing and reaping, all of which tasks are usually performed, as shearing is, by cooperative gatherings much like American "husking bees." The grain harvest is stored in subterranean silos shaped like huge bottles, lined with straw, covered with sand or stones, and watched over by a paid guardian who is usually a shepherd as well. A single silo of this kind may hold anywhere up to a ton or thereabouts, and is owned collectively by the members of a clan or tribe.

Curiously enough, it is not considered degrading in any way for a nomadic Moor to till the soil in the manner just described; and in point of fact it is a practical necessity for him to do so because of the relative scarcity and poverty of sedentary agricultural centers in the far western desert. Apparently a Moor retains his honorable nomad status and the social dignity that goes with it just as long as he doesn't settle down and devote himself primarily to gardening. As long as nomadic livestock raising continues to be his principal occupation and chief means of livelihood, it doesn't seem to matter much what secondary activities he may engage in occasionally on the side.

One of the most important elements in Moorish economy used to be raiding on a major scale. This was an elaborately formalized activity among the Moors, organized much as it was among the Chaamba, and it was practiced so regularly and so often that it seems to have become an integral part of the normal pattern of relations between groups. Livestock stealing, sometimes even between clans of the same tribe, used to be so common as to be in effect almost an industry. In the winter of 1919-1920, for example, a Rguibat raiding party crossed the western desert to Tahoua in the Air, nearly fifteen hundred miles from their home base. The round trip took eight months and the raiders lost about a third of their number along the way, but they brought back much booty. Raids naturally gave rise to blood feuds, and these to reprisals and to more blood feuds and counter-raids, and so raiding became a self-perpetuating activity for reasons quite apart from its economic basis. It has not yet been completely suppressed by any means although it has been brought more or less under control, especially in the central and southern parts of Moorish territory. Even today, however, nomadic Moors look on Camel Corps troops as enemy raiders, for the distinction between robbers and policemen apparently escapes the Moorish mind which automatically oversimplifies the situation by reducing it to the proposition that "Anyone who isn't for us is against us."

The eastern Moorish tribes also used to be engaged in almost continual conflict with the westernmost Chaamba and Tuareg who were their neighbors, and all three parties raided each other endlessly back and forth, but this was stopped at last by the establishment of French control over Tuareg and Chaamba territory through the mechanism of the Camel Corps. The equipment of a typical Moorish raider consisted of a camel or, very rarely, a horse or mare, a saddle and a guerba or two, a gun with bandoliers of cartridges, and a dagger. Young warriors used to borrow or rent equipment, customary rates being a third of the booty for the camel's owner, another third for the owner of the gun and a sixth for whoever provided the ammunition.

Driven as they are constantly by sparse pasturage, scanty water, and their insatiable love of preying on each other, the Moors seldom stay anywhere very long. Therefore they require a shelter which is readily portable and at the same time strongly made, and so they use the khaima, the same Arabian kind of tent that is used by the nomadic Chaamba. It seems practically certain that this type of tent was introduced into North Africa from Arabia, which leaves one wondering what kind of shelter the ancestors of the Moors used before the arrival in their midst of the first Arab invaders. It could easily have been either the Tuareg type of tent or the tent-like hut of the Teda, but unfortunately there seems to be no way of finding out what it really was. The modern Moorish tent is usually made of strips of goathair, mixed with camel's hair or wool, which are woven by the women of a camp acting cooperatively, although tents of the southern Moors are sometimes made of the skins of goats or lambs. A light lining of cotton cloth is hung inside occasionally for better insulation. Tents are usually about twenty feet long, very rarely as much as forty feet in length; and the women's and children's side is on the left as you enter, just as it is among the Tuareg, which is the opposite of the usual Arab arrangement as found among the Chaamba. Tent furnishings include ground mats of esparto grass covered with rugs or with blankets made of goat- or sheepskins sewn together, leather-covered fringed cushions, wooden dishes, bowls, spoons, and milk funnels, a wooden mortar and pestle and a small rotary quern, some cheap metal kitchenware perhaps, a baggage rack made of sticks tied together and the ever present guerba.

Moorish clothing is much like that of most other Saharan nomads except in matters of detail. Boys go naked until they have been circumcised, and girls until they are seven or eight years old. According to James Riley, most Moorish men used to wear kilts of camel's hair cloth or goatskin, while rich men wore gandouras of blue cotton cloth, and sometimes, as a shawl, a light woollen blanket measuring about twelve feet by four. Adult male clothing nowadays includes baggy trousers which often reach only to the knees (and may be made of either white cotton cloth or shegga), a shirt that reaches just below the knees, and a voluminous gandoura or two of medium length, the outer one preferably blue, gathered around the waist with a belt. Well-to-do men sometimes wear a large fringed shawl, also preferably blue, in wintertime, but more often they use burnouses or even cloaks made of skins. Shepherds wrap themselves in sheepskin blankets in cold weather. The typical men's headgear is a voluminous blue turban which may or may not be arranged so as to cover the face, but the Moors seem to attach no ceremonial importance to it and often remove it altogether when engaged in manual labor. Moorish men let their usually curly hair grow fairly long (unlike the Tuareg, Teda, and Chaamba who shave most or all of the scalp), and arrange it so that it sticks out bushily in all directions, thereby giving them a startlingly wild and ferocious appearance when they have their turbans off. The reasons for this are practical, however, as well as aesthetic, for if the Moors did not arrange their hair in some such way, they would have to keep their heads covered when working in the sun. Men also paint their eyelids green sometimes, for reasons which remain unknown. The

Moors used to go barefoot in the old days, but now they all wear sandals, similar in type to the modern Tuareg variety, which they import from the Sudan. Their typical weapons used to be muskets, spears, and oriental swords and daggers a century ago, and they have not changed much since except that the firearms are of modern types.

Formerly Moorish women wore shirts much like those of Tuareg women except that they were made of camel's hair and had a roomy inside pocket, on the back of one shoulder, in which to carry a baby. Captain Riley wrote that "the breasts of middle aged women become so extremely long, lank, and pendulous, (being in appearance not unlike a wrinkled stocking with a small bunch at the bottom,) that they have no other trouble in nursing the child which is on their backs, when walking, than to throw up their breasts over the top of their shoulders, so that the child may apply its lips." Nowadays female costume consists of short, baggy trousers worn underneath a long, belted tunic or two (the outer one preferably blue, as usual), together with a big blue shawl which can be arranged so as to cover the head and conceal the face. Sometimes a separate head shawl, also blue, is worn in addition. Women occasionally use a kind of combined turban and face veil, not unlike that worn by Tuareg men but rather more like the sloppily arranged turban worn by Teda men of the Tibesti. They rarely veil their faces, however, except in the presence of distinguished strangers. Moorish women also perfume themselves with herbal extracts and smear their eyes, hair, hands, and feet with various mineral and vegetable substances, much as Tuareg women do.

The blue cloth that figures so prominently in Moorish costume is most frequently dark indigo shegga, but bright sky-blue cotton cloth is often used today, just as it is beginning to be used among the Tuareg. The Moors obtain shegga in the Sudan in exchange for salt mined in the southern part of Moorish territory. Just how and why the Moors, and the Tuareg as well, first came to have such an overwhelming preference for blue and preferably dark blue cloth, as opposed to cloth of any other color, remains a mystery. Although the material is invariably shoddy and soon wears out, the cost is relatively high, and so such cloth has come to be a sign of wealth and hence a symbol of prestige; and yet it is by no means clear whether or not this was the original reason for its popularity.

The Moors are musical, but unfortunately their musical activities have received very little attention. About all that seems to be known is that they have a distinctive double-headed drum, the *toba,* and also a very unexpected instrument, the *ardeen,* which is a small upright harp with ten strings. The lyrics of secular songs are Berber as a rule, while those of religious ones are Arabic, which is natural enough in view of the fact that Arabic speech and Moslem doctrine came together into the Sahara.

Although the descendants of the Arabs who first overran Moorish territory, from the north and the northeast, succeeded in consolidating their conquests for good and all before the seventeenth century, most of them finally lost their separate identity and became submerged in the mass of Berbers whom they had converted and subdued. Shorfa clans still survive, however, among the more Arabized Moorish tribes and divisions, and it is probable that some of them at least have valid claims to descent from the conquering Arabs who introduced Islam into the western desert. Curiously enough it seems that the majority of Moorish Shorfa clans are still basically Berber except for their religious quality, and they also appear to be characterized by a strangely fervid spirit which one ordinarily associates only with very recent converts. The Rguibat tribes in general claim to belong to one huge Shorfa family and they are generally treated as such, although it is well known that the Rguibat as a whole are actually no more than an assemblage of heterogeneous groups which became united in their present form only a little over two hundred years ago. The semi-mythical ancestor from whom they took their name was Sid Ahmed-er-Rguibi, a pious man who is said to have come from Barbary in 1503 or thereabouts as a Moslem missionary to the valley of the Draa in southwestern Morocco, where he married an Arab woman. Noble Rguibat clans claim direct descent from his numerous grandsons, the mother of one of whom, incidentally, is thought to have been a Negress. And yet, in spite of their semireligious prestige, the real power of the Rguibat seems to reside essentially in their great strength as a well-organized fighting force, and this, in turn, doubtless rests mainly on their wealth in livestock and their closely knit political organization. Here is a good example of how the quality of being Shorfa, of being or of being supposed to be holy because descended directly from the prophet Mohammed, is of real positive value only when in the hands of individuals or groups strong and efficient enough to make practical use of it.

Maraboutic clans are the principal guardians of pre-Islamic Berber speech among the Moors, as I have already pointed out; and this, and their usually tributary vassal status, together with their concentration in the south, suggest that they may well be relatively pure remnants of Berber tribes that were conquered at the time of the Arab invasion of the northwestern desert. Some authorities believe that the Arab invaders remained illiterate warriors for the most part, while many of the conquered Berbers became learned holy men, and this is probably correct. But how such people ever came to be looked on as a religious Moslem elite remains something of a mystery in the feeble light of what little is known about them. There are indications, however, that the Moors often regard Marabouts as sorcerers rather than as holy men in a strictly religious sense, which goes far toward resolving the dilemma. For example, when a drought lasts so long that there is danger of disaster, a Marabout is sometimes tied up hand and foot and beaten or left out in the sun until he promises to bring rain promptly, or until rain comes. Sometimes the Marabout is stripped and beaten by moonlight, which suggests that there may be a residual element of moon worship involved in such proceedings. One is reminded of the status of *sadhus* in northern India. Both ritually and economically the ordinary functions of Moorish Marabouts are very much like those of holy men among the Chaamba, for not only are such men the repositories of learning as well as the makers of amulets and spells, but they are often enterprising shop-

keepers and merchants too. Some Maraboutic families are sedentary and nomads come to them from near and far to buy charms
and cures for man and beast alike, while others are retained by
nomad groups and accompany them on a permanent basis so as
to be always readily available in case of an emergency.

Jewish traders and artisans used to be numerous and influential in that part of the western Sahara which lies along
the eastern edge of Moorish territory, but unfortunately almost
nothing seems to be known about the details of their doings
either before the terrible massacres of 1492 or since. If there
are Jewish merchants still active anywhere among the Moors,
no one has described them, and so I can only assume for the time
being that they are now either absent or so few as to be of
negligible importance, both socially and economically. Although
a considerable number are thought to have fled into the southern
part of Moorish territory late in the fifteenth century, no trace
of such people is to be found there now. Probably a few refugees from Tamentit did actually settle down among the southern
Moors, but they or their descendants must have been either
killed off or converted and absorbed eventually into the bulk of
the local population. And, no matter what the answer to this
interesting question may be, there is very little chance that anyone can discover it at this late date.

The smiths who live among the Moors seem to be much like
those found among the Tuareg of the Ahaggar; for the men
work wood and metals while their women do fancy leatherwork
and some embroidery. All are much feared as sorcerers and
magicians, for it is said not only that they can cause a victim to
bleed to death merely by staring at him, but that they can also
break with ease bonds which are strong enough to hold Marabouts and even Shorfa. And yet, like smiths among most other
Moslem peoples, they are universally despised as well as feared.
Some Moors say that the smiths are descended from a Jew who
was captured in 629 by the Moslem faithful at the Battle of
Jaibar (an oasis town a little north of Medina, in Saudi Arabia).
The story goes that once this captive had been converted to
Islam, he took to manual labor by way of penance for his former

heresy, and he is also said to have married a Negress. Thus his supposed descendants are considered triply despicable, because they work with their hands and are of mixed Jewish and Negro ancestry. The smiths are organized in fractions and clans which pay tribute to Moorish masters much as do vassal Moorish groups, but that seems to be all that is known about their sociopolitical organization. They are nomadic for the most part and move about with nomadic Moorish clans and tribes. Racially they appear to vary all the way from bush Negro to only faintly negroid Moorish morphology and coloring.

Wandering entertainers seem to be perhaps of somewhat more importance among the Moors than they are elsewhere in the Sahara. Most of them come from the southern part of Moorish territory, on the northwestern edge of the Sudan. Each of the "bards," the principal class of entertainers, normally has a Moorish patron whose praises he sings in the manner of a medieval European troubadour, and more or less fulsomely in proportion to his patron's openhandedness. Bards are usually accompanied by their wives, both physically and musically, which is contrary to the usual practice of minstrels elsewhere in the desert. They are regarded with a mixture of admiration, disdain, and fear, and they have an unenviable reputation for being scandalmongers and troublemakers generally. A common Moorish saying goes: "Better Negroes than smiths: better smiths than bards," and this is malicious irony, for Negroes are in fact considered the lowest form of human life.

The Moors have Negro slaves just as do the Tuareg, but they have relatively few of them: in a random sample of a hundred and fifty Moorish families it was found that only twenty-three had slaves. Although men apparently outnumber women by nearly four to three among the Moors, the sex ratio among their slaves is exactly the reverse. This curious discrepancy may be only a recent development, however, for the excess of females in the slave population has been explained as due to the necessity of raising male slaves on the spot now that they can no longer be imported. Negroes and negroid persons of inferior status are not allowed to join in the festivities of their Moorish masters, but they hold dances of their own which are Sudanese in character. There are two main categories of slaves among the Moors. Those who are born in a Moorish household are not sold as a rule, and they may even acquire a special favored status as milk-brothers of their masters since Negresses often act as wet-nurses for Moorish infants and occasionally a Moorish woman will nurse the male infant of a slave. Such slaves are not infrequently set free, even when young if they are well -behaved, and it is said moreover that some of them can buy their freedom although it has not been explained how this is done. Slaves who have been bought, on the other hand, are often sold again, and they enjoy no special privileges but are mere chattels. In the old days they used to be obtained mainly from salt merchants who purchased them in the Sudan or captured them in raids there. Slaves who have been freed usually remain on good terms with their former masters, and occasionally even rise to the status of tributary vassals. But a freedman's property reverts to his former master if the freedman dies leaving no heirs of his body.

In spite of the disdain with which Negroes are regarded and the repugnance with which mixed marriages are looked upon by Moorish nomads, it is clear that many aristocratic Moors have a distinct "touch of the tar brush," although it seems on the whole that they have perhaps as little Negro blood as any of the major Saharan nomad groups I have described. One author who has worked among them points out that here, as elsewhere in the Sahara, Negro blood often enters into noble lines through the agency of female slaves and their half-breed offspring; but the fact that male slaves are sometimes allowed to sleep in the women's and children's end of their master's tent may also be relevant in this connection. Conversely it is apparent, from the few photographs available, that some of the lowly smiths have more than a little Moorish blood in spite of the ironclad rule against marriage with a person of inferior rank.

In sum, the Moors seem admirably adapted to their extremely harsh environment, but they also seem to have been rapidly approaching a point of economic stagnation if not decay by the time they first began to come under the control of European powers.

Their essential spirit of disunion, expressed in endless feuding, raiding, counter-raiding, intertribal, and even intratribal wars, seems to have blocked effectively all avenues of economic or political expansion on a grand scale. The Moors are proud and war-like nomads and are, in a sense, the best example of a Saharan pastoral nomadic population, for they came under European control only in 1934 and that control is not yet fully effective by any means. But, on the other hand, they have been for centuries more exposed to foreign cultural influences, both in the north and south and along the Atlantic coast as well, than have any of the other Saharan nomad peoples. And they are, in addition, a mixed lot both culturally and physically. They use an Arab kind of tent but the occupants arrange themselves therein according to Berber custom; they have embraced Islam but still indulge communally in pagan rites; and indeed they show a curious mixture of Arab and Berber and of Islamic and pre-Islamic elements in nearly every facet of their very special way of life. And finally the great Moorish tribes which constitute the aristocratic autocracy today are all relatively recent upstarts whose past is woefully obscure, and who, in the course of their violent and meteoric rise to power, have destroyed the social, political, and economic systems of their predecessors so thoroughly that hardly a trace remains. Thus the Moors are of interest chiefly for their value as a striking example of how the nomadic desert tribes of the Sahara can change both physically and culturally, and presumably have been changing for millennia, with a fluidity and speed that have been all too seldom recognized.

Chapter 9

HEALTH AND DISEASE

IT IS NOT yet possible to present well-rounded pictures of either the nutritional or pathological condition of the Saharan population as a whole, or even of any one of its major geographical or ethnic subdivisions, for the harshness of the environment and the extremely scattered distribution of the inhabitants have made it impossible so far to carry out general medical surveys except on a very limited and local scale. Public health services and private medical facilities alike are still completely absent in most of the desert; and even in the French Sahara, where they have made far more progress than elsewhere, they are only just beginning to recover from what, until three or four years ago, had been a chronic shortage of both personnel and equipment. There is hardly a member of these services who has not distinguished himself outstandingly by tireless and selfless devotion, but, by the same token, only a tiny handful have had a moment to spare from their daily routine work, and so it has been materially impossible for them to accumulate and organize the masses of data necessary for the compilation of modern "public health surveys." Sedentary peoples of the southern agricultural centers subsist mainly on the produce of their gardens, chiefly millet, sometimes barley, and also vegetables and occasionally fruits. The few who can afford it own goats whose milk, both fresh and sour, is drunk and is also used to make butter and cheese. Meat is very rarely eaten, and the diet as a whole is usually deficient both in variety and quantity. Eggs are eaten now and then, as are hedgehogs, lizards, and locusts.

Farther north, in the oasis towns of the central zone of the Sahara, diet is usually more varied but still often deficient in both

237

quantity and variety except among well-to-do landlord and merchant families. Wheat and barley [1] are eaten in the form of couscous, gruel, unleavened bread, fritters, and thin pancakes which are baked on heated flat stones. Millet and sorghum are used occasionally. Dough is sometimes mixed with onions and tomatoes before being baked in loaves. Those who can afford to, dip their bread or pancakes in a hot sauce seasoned with red peppers, or in butter which is similarly spiced or, more rarely, sweetened with sugar.

Dates are a staple almost everywhere in the northern and central zone of the Sahara except in the far west, where producing palms are scarce. They are eaten in their natural state or in the form of a pounded paste which, in turn, may be mixed with rancid butter or with whole wheat flour now and then. Although dates are very nourishing, they seem to promote tooth decay, as Leo Africanus noted in the sixteenth century.

A highly seasoned soup known as *shorba,* made with vermicelli and such vegetables as are available, fresh or dried, is another staple dish throughout the desert, although most of the vermicelli used is imported from the north. An edible paste, known as *kaboosh,* is made of cheese, butter, and spices pounded together. Eggs are eaten occasionally and are boiled hard, fried, or made into omelets. And the milk of goats, sheep, and sometimes camels is drunk, sweet or sour.

Livestock is valuable chiefly for its milk or as a means of transportation, and so meat is eaten only once or twice a year by ordinary sedentary folk in the oasis towns. It appears most often as an ingredient in couscous, but is also cut into cubes which are wrapped in fatty folds of peritoneum and roasted on skewers. Sometimes it is fried, in animal fat or vegetable oil. Barbecues of sheep, goat, or even baby camel are very popular but

[1] At Ghardaia and elsewhere in the northern Sahara grain is threshed communally in the following way. A circular threshing floor of hard-beaten earth is prepared near the edge of the gardens, and on this the cereal is spread. Four lines of mules or donkeys, five to ten animals abreast, are then arranged on the floor so that they radiate from its central point like the spokes of a wheel. This "wheel" is then driven briskly around and around counter-clockwise, to the accompaniment of a perfect pandemonium of whooping and yelling.

are reserved for ceremonial occasions such as circumcisions, weddings, the welcoming of distinguished guests, and the great feast that marks the end of the month-long fast of Ramdhan. Meat is often preserved in the form of "jerky" (strips smoked or dried in the sun), which is cooked by boiling with vegetables and spices. Chickens and pigeons are cooked in the same way, or are incorporated in couscous. I have already mentioned that dogs and cats are sometimes eaten, but only ceremonially, or so it seems. Small game animals such as gazelles, foxes, fennecs, jackals, and hares, and also wild birds, are caught in traps or snares. Lizards, hedgehogs, and small rodents are eaten too, as are locusts when they descend on the plantations as they do periodically. Boiling hot mint tea, heavily sweetened when sugar can be had, is a mainstay of Saharan diet everywhere.

Unfortunately it is impossible at present to arrive at anything like precise estimates of the average daily caloric intake of a typical individual in any given Saharan community. Approximate mean figures have been worked out, however, for the sedentary population of In Salah, and these can be accepted as reasonably accurate and so probably significant in a general way. They are as follows: dates, 1,485; cereals, 527; sugar, 200; fats, 140; greens, 120; all of which makes a total of not quite 2,500 calories a day.

In the urban centers of the northern desert diet is again more varied except among the very poor. For example, the typical daily menu of an average upper middle class Mzabite family of Ghardaia is as follows:

On rising: coffee with milk and unleavened bread made of whole wheat or barley.

About 9:00 A.M.: three miniature glasses of very hot mint tea, heavily sweetened, and fritters.

About 11:30: three quarters of a pound of dates and half a pint of buttermilk.

About 1:00 P.M.: shorba, fresh vegetables, and salad greens, more mint tea, and peanuts for desert.

About 4:00: more mint tea, or coffee, and perhaps some peanuts or fritters.

239

About 8:30: couscous, followed by mint tea or coffee and peanuts or a little pastry. For variety the couscous may be taken at noon and shorba in the evening.

In spite of the very small number of Jews in the Sahara, Jewish diet is interesting because it is markedly different in some respects from the diets of Moslem communities who live in the same environment and are at the same economic level. Upper middle class Jews of Ghardaia eat approximately as follows:

Breakfast: coffee with unleavened bread.

Lunch: an alcoholic aperitif (usually anisette), followed by a very highly spiced dish of fresh vegetables, cooked in oil and then boiled or steamed, and finally mint tea.

Supper: more aperitifs, followed by couscous or shorba, preserved meat fried in oil (three or four times a week), mint tea and sugary cakes.

Meat is preserved by being dried, then fried and finally packed in earthenware jars with a mixture of oil and mutton fat. Saharan Jews drink heavily: in fact it is almost a ritual for men to get at least moderately intoxicated every Saturday morning, after services in the synagogue, and then sleep off their hangovers in the afternoon. The favorite beverage today is anisette, but before the coming of Europeans it was a kind of brandy made of dates, which is still brewed clandestinely in order to avoid the liquor tax.

The Saharan Jews also have a whole series of food taboos in addition to those which are observed by Jews in general. Camel meat is forbidden as well as pork, and the meat of animals with claws, notably dogs, cats, and jackals must be avoided. The meat of horses, mules, and donkeys is forbidden too. Fowl may be eaten only when killed by a rabbi, who cannot delegate his authority in this respect. And, as is true among Jews everywhere, meat and milk or milk products must not be eaten at the same meal. Still other Saharan Jewish food taboos are based on sympathetic magic. Mutes, for example, may eat no tongue and the blind must not eat eyes. If several of a family are born lame, none may eat meat from the leg or foot of any animal. And if there have been an unusual number of stillbirths in a family, then all the members must refrain from eating liver; although what liver has to do with stillbirths is by no means clear. Various sedentary Saharan groups besides the Jews have more or less similar taboos, but practically nothing is known about them.

Children of the sedentary peoples of the Sahara in general are breast-fed for anywhere from eighteen months to two years after birth, but they often begin to share the food of their elders little by little within a year or less. If a mother is unable to nurse her infant, recourse is had to a wet nurse or a goat, since goats are thought to be much better for this purpose than are ewes. Preserved milk of European preparation is avoided as a general rule on the ground that it is "unnatural."

The diet of Saharan nomads has been described in no more general or complete a fashion than has that of their sedentary neighbors, and so I can hardly do better than consider it in terms of the four major nomadic groups whose social, political, and economic organizations I have described. Even in these cases it is not possible to construct either complete or fully accurate pictures, but at least reasonably good rough outlines can be established.

Among the Teda of the Tibesti, barley, millet, wheat, and maize are the chief staples when available. Grain is ground on saddle querns and then is usually boiled or roasted. The most common cereal dish is *aseeda,* which is a kind of mush seasoned with sour milk. Dates are usually dried, and then are often crushed, mixed with flour, and rolled into balls. Dom palms, which grow wild in most of the Sahara, are sometimes cultivated in the Tibesti, in the midst of the date palm plantations. Only the sweetish rind of their fruit is edible however, and this is reduced to a powder by being pounded between stones. It is seldom eaten when other foods are plentiful.

Wild seeds, roots, and fruits, such as figs, are important foods in the Tibesti because cultivated plants are either scarce or absent in much of the area. Colocynth (*Citrullus colocynthus*), the favorite seed-producing plant, is gathered by Teda women in October, but it is sometimes cultivated also on a small scale. The

241

seeds are very bitter and violently purgative in their natural
state, and so require elaborate preparation to make them edible.
First they are dried, stuffed into sacks, and trodden to loosen the
husks. Next they are winnowed, mixed with the ashes of camel
dung, ground on a saddle quern, and winnowed once again. Then
they are boiled with tamarisk leaves, washed over and over in
cold water, dried, and finally stored away. The finished product
is usually cooked by roasting. Colocynth flour ground up with
dried dates is used as an iron ration on the march. Various other
wild seeds also are ground up and eaten in the form of mush,
gruel, or flat cakes. The berries of a bush known as *dji,* rather
like currants, are preserved for future consumption by being
pressed into round loaves. They are eaten both as a delicacy and
as a famine food.

Goats and sheep are kept mainly for milk and butter. The
milk of goats is a staple article of Teda diet, although camel's
milk, which is far more costly, is preferred. Milk is usually drunk
sour; for as soon as it is drawn it is put into waterproofed baskets which are never cleaned and there it promptly curdles. The
supply of milk is always scanty, however, except after heavy
rains, and so most of it is reserved for children as a rule. Butter
is a standard article of trade as well as of diet.

Livestock is ordinarily too valuable to be killed, and so meat
is rarely eaten except on festival occasions, but when fresh meat
is available, the Teda gorge themselves on it. Goats are
slaughtered only for feasts, and camels only when they become
too ill or too infirm to work. Their meat is preserved by jerking,
and is then prepared for the pot by being pounded up. Bones
and sinews too are sometimes ground up, boiled, and eaten, while
ground dry bones mixed with freshly drawn camel's blood, and
even broth made from old sandals or other articles of leather
are standard famine foods. Generally speaking, however, the
Teda of the Tibesti are mainly vegetarians, by force of circumstances rather than from choice. Game is not eaten in the Tibesti
to any great extent, although lizards and skinks are common articles of diet. Mouflon, gazelles, and antelopes are sometimes
trapped, and this is done mostly by members of the despised

Azza class. Some of the southern Teda are said to be inordinately fond of dried fish which they import from the Sudan, but
apparently fish is not traded as far north as the Tibesti.

Tobacco is chewed, usually mixed with natron, and is sometimes smoked in pipes made of camel dung which burn progressively along with the tobacco in them. Heavily sweetened tea is
extremely popular nowadays although it was introduced probably not much more than a century ago, but only the very well-
to-do can afford it. Poor folks make a tea-like brew from the
leaves of a wild plant known as *atiafunu*. At the time of the date
harvest the Teda usually cut down several palm trees and brew a
highly intoxicating wine from their heart pulp, and drunken
orgies then become the order of the day until the supply of wine
is exhausted. Determined efforts of the French administration to
suppress this practice have succeeded only in making it clandestine.

The Teda of the Tibesti have an almost endless series of food
taboos, many of which, however, seem to be restricted to a single
clan, and to be based on some memorable event in the mytholog-
ical or factual history of the group. Thus, members of the Terin-
téré clan eat no ostrich meat, supposedly because once upon a
time an ostrich helped one of their ancestors to escape pursuit.
The Mahadena, on the other hand, never eat liver of any kind,
simply because "it resembles clotted blood." Among the Teda in
general, only boys not yet circumcised, and girls who have not
reached the age of puberty, are normally allowed to eat birds
or eggs (apparently ostriches are not thought of as birds). But
eggs and chicken broth as well are sometimes given to adults as
medicine, which only serves to emphasize the magical quality
attached to them.

The Tuareg of the Ahaggar subsist mainly on the milk and
milk products of their goats, camels and occasional hairy sheep.
One of their chief food staples is a dried cheese (*tikamarin,* or
tikomaren), nearly as hard as stone, which has an abominable
smell but keeps almost indefinitely. It is usually prepared for
eating by being pounded up and mixed with various boiled dishes.
In winter many of the Tuareg live exclusively on cheese (tiko-

maren and also a more ordinary kind) and camel's milk, plus a few wild seeds and roots occasionally; and when times are exceptionally hard, whole tribes may go for as much as two years with practically nothing else to eat. Curiously enough, camel's butter seems to be used only as a hair dressing, and only by the women.

Cereals (maize excepted), wild plants, fruits, vegetables (mainly dried onions and tomatoes), meat of domestic animals and game, and the various dishes made from these ingredients, are roughly the same among the Ahaggar Tuareg as those found among the Teda of the Tibesti, but they occupy a relatively minor place in Tuareg diet. The basic cereal dish of everyday is *assink,* a gruel made by boiling grain, usually millet, and adding sour milk or butter. Couscous was a rare luxury dish a hundred years ago and is still scarce, because expensive. Cakes made of flour, milk, butter, and honey are reserved for feasts. Rice has long been imported from the Sudan, but it is costly and consequently scarce. Fresh vegetables are almost never eaten. Dried dates imported from the north are popular, but not everyone can afford them.

Meat is usually roasted, on skewers or otherwise, or is stewed, preferably with raisins and ground dried dates. A dish known as *abatool,* much like a Scottish haggis, is prepared by stuffing the stomach of an animal with its intestines and hot stones, and burying the whole in a bed of coals. Animals were not barbecued until quite recently, but were cooked whole by being split open and laid flat in the hot sand and ashes underneath a fire. The standard iron ration for the march consists of jerky, cakes made of a mixture of dried dates, flour, butter, and pepper, and the inevitable stony cheese, all of which are pounded up together and mixed with water, hot or cold according to circumstances. Uncooked millet flour is eaten by riders on forced marches. Tea, coffee, sugar, and tobacco snuff (for chewing, or, more precisely, "dipping") are highly prized luxuries which few Tuareg can afford. Tobacco is not smoked, however, and all alcoholic beverages are avoided, following the precepts of the Koran.

The Tuareg of the Ahaggar ordinarily eat one good meal a

day, in the evening, when on the march, and two, with the main
meal at midday, when in camp. Most of the time they live
barely above the starvation level, although, like the Teda of the
Tibesti, they gorge themselves on fresh meat whenever an occasion offers. Even the most wealthy and influential do not hesi-
tate to beg insistently for tea, sugar, and tobacco. Duveyrier
considered Tuareg food "delicious," but he was a romantic
soul. Even such hardened old Saharans as Maurice Reygasse,
not to mention my tenderfooted self, have found it all too often
revolting in the extreme. But this is probably no more than a
function of the fact that meat and cheese are so precious to the
Tuareg that they keep them long after they would have been
either eaten or thrown away by people having access to a more
abundant and varied food supply. Tuareg diet then is based
primarily on dairy products and grain, plus dried dates once in
a while and meat only occasionally. On the whole it seems to
be deficient in quantity more often than in quality, judging by
the appearance of the Tuareg in general.

The Ahaggar Tuareg also have a series of food taboos, but
no really satisfactory explanations for any of them have yet
been found. Fowl and their eggs must not be eaten even as
famine foods, except by children. A century ago Duveyrier reported that Negro slaves who had recently partaken of such
things were not allowed to use communal drinking vessels. A
thoroughly reliable friend, who is a member of the Agou-n-
Téhélé clan of the Ahaggar confederation, told me that hens'
eggs are not eaten because they are made of the unclean refuse
that hens live on, and that the meat of birds is avoided because
it is "cold" and therefore causes sickness. I could not learn, however, just what was meant by "cold," for my informant, asked
to define this term, merely repeated it several times impatiently,
as if to say that any fool should know its meaning without having
it explained. Certain large lizards are said to be taboo because
they are "maternal uncles" of the Tuareg. Fish are taboo for no
known reason: possibly they are thought to be "cold" too.

The nomadic Chaamba eat much as do the Tuareg except that
their diet is much richer in dates, grain, and vegetables and

contains little in the way of preserved foods. In the evening they take their one substantial meal of the day, which consists usually of shorba, dates, and a nourishing but heavy and rather indigestible unleavened bread (*kessra*) which is baked in the hot sand under the camp fire. This meal invariably ends with the three traditional miniature glasses of scalding hot tea, the first only slightly sweetened, the second flavored with mint and with more sugar added, and the third made almost sickeningly sweet and syrupy. The tea is poured from a considerable height which reaerates it to some extent, and the drinker sucks it up noisily, thereby cooling it and aerating it some more. It is always very strong.

Couscous is eaten sometimes, but is so expensive that it is usually reserved for feasts. Fresh meat, also costly and therefore rarely eaten except on festive occasions, is either barbecued, broiled, cut up and roasted on skewers, or boiled. Baby camels are sacrificed and barbecued on the occasion of the annual autumn harvest festival. Camel meat is preserved ordinarily by being cut into long, thin strips, salted and sun-dried, and the resulting jerky is used chiefly as an iron ration. Gazelle meat is usually broiled over a bed of coals or boiled and mixed with couscous. Lizards of all kinds and sizes are eaten roasted, and locusts too are eaten in season, raw, roasted, or fried. During the fall and early winter, when the Chaamba nomads are settled at their home bases, they eat much as do the sedentary folk of the northern urban centers of the Sahara. Their food taboos, aside from the regular Koranic ones, seem to be few and relatively unimportant on the whole. The Chaamba Berazga, for example, have a taboo which forbids the eating of camel brains or tongue, but so far I have not been able to discover any reason for this curious prohibition. Chicken, eggs, and lizards are all eaten freely, in sharp contrast to Tuareg and Teda practices.

There is nothing particularly distinctive about the diet of the nomadic Moors, which seems to be roughly intermediate in character between the usual Tuareg and Chaamba diets. Milk and milk products are always the main staples, while cereals are important too but only seasonally, in the spring and early summer. Domestic fowl and eggs are forbidden foods, just as they are among the Tuareg and the Teda; and yet various kinds of lizards, including those which are taboo among the Tuareg, are eaten freely. The Moors do have one distinctive dietary characteristic however, and that is their superstitious attitude toward milk, an attitude which they express in a whole series of minor ritual observances. As an example, the froth on a bowl of freshly drawn camel's milk must be removed gently, with a stick, for to blow it off would surely bring bad luck. Unfortunately, however, no one seems to know just what it is about milk that inspires so much awe in Moorish minds.

In summing up my discussion of the diets of the nomadic tribes of the Sahara, it can be said in general that all these people live primarily off their livestock, and off the wild flora and fauna native to their territories. Most of them have also come to depend secondarily, to a considerable extent, on the agricultural produce of their sedentary neighbors. And in addition, pastoral nomads fill out their diet with imported staples, mainly grain and dates, and luxuries such as tea, coffee, sugar, salt, and spices, all of which were made readily available to them in the first place by their mastery of the trans-Saharan caravan trade. Highly organized food procurement systems of this kind must, however, be comparatively recent developments in terms of the ethnological history of the Sahara. The few surviving groups of hunters, food gatherers, and nomadic fishermen, notably the Nemadi and the Imraguen, may have preserved earlier dietary patterns, dating back perhaps even to pre-neolithic times. But only future archeological investigations can reveal just what the methods of food procurement and the eating habits of Saharan peoples really were before the dawn of written history.

In Chapter 1, I described the main problems of water supply in the Sahara, and little remains to be added here. Unfortunately the published data on drinking water available in the area before the arrival of European drillers of modern wells are very scanty and incomplete, but what little information is available indicates that water from the old-fashioned wells and foggaras was seldom suitable for drinking purposes, according to modern hygienic standards. Often it was unpleasantly rich in magnesium and various calcium salts, and even in sulphuric acid now and then, and it was often seriously polluted. A sample of drinking water taken at Ghardaia in 1929, for example, was found to contain two hundred colon bacilli (*Enterococcus coli*) per liter. Wells are polluted commonly by infiltration, sometimes by creatures that fall into them accidentally, and occasionally by human bodies. Foggaras are polluted mainly by animals that fall down the open mouths of their vertical shafts and drown in the main channel. Natural pools, such as one finds in the rocky ledges of mountain massifs, are often polluted by the droppings of live animals and the bodies of dead ones, as well as by travelers who stop to bathe in them. In view of all this, it is easy to understand the high rates of gastro-intestinal disturbances which characterize so many Saharan groups, while on the other hand, one can only be surprised that the peoples of the desert generally are as free from infectious waterborne diseases as they appear to be. The drilling of modern wells as a regular procedure is a fairly recent development in the Sahara, for although a few artesian wells were drilled at places like El Goléa as early as 1891, the first modern wells in the densely populated Mzab date only from 1938.

In spite of the Saharan climate, which is a very healthy one on the whole, the life of an individual native is often eventful medically, and it always begins in a very Spartan manner. Childbirth in the desert seems to conform to a fairly uniform pattern everywhere, and proceeds usually about as follows. When the expectant mother finds that her time has come, she kneels on the ground with her knees spread wide apart and her hips resting on her heels, and holds her body upright by clinging to a cord or belt that is attached either to a nail in a wall of the house or to a roof-pole of the tent, as the case may be. Beneath her there is spread a plaited mat, a thin woollen blanket, or (most often) a thick layer of clean fine sand, onto which the infant is ejected. The mother is usually attended and assisted if need be by an elderly matron, who is normally a professional midwife among sedentary folk but more often an aunt or some other close relative where nomads are concerned. Aristocratic women of the nomadic Tuareg are said to insist, as a matter of pride, on being left completely alone while they give birth, and women of the impoverished Haratin too often give birth alone by force of circumstances. It is not particularly unusual for a poor nomad woman to break away from a moving band, give birth beside the trail, rest up for an hour or two, and then hurry on to rejoin the others.

Accidents during delivery are not uncommon. Multiple births seem to be relatively rare by world standards, but when twins are born, it is not unusual for one of them to waste away and die from undernourishment. Binding of the belly is not practiced, and so umbilical hernias are common everywhere. Saharan mothers usually recover very quickly after giving birth. Custom requires as a rule that the mother get up and walk at least a few steps on the first day, but unless the family is on the march, she should enjoy complete rest for seven days, and remain secluded at home for about forty days in all, after which she is expected to resume her normal activities. Puerperal fever is only moderately common in northern sedentary communities and very rare among the southern nomads. Female sterility, on the other hand, is common, and seems to be caused usually by venereal infections. Natural abortions too are not uncommon, and, when they do occur, seem to be due most often to lack of hygiene or to the mother being either very young or relatively old.

Four years ago Captain Doury of the Saharan Medical Corps gave me the following concise picture of childbirth as he had observed it among the Tuareg of the Ahaggar. Labor is short and practically painless as a rule, and there is no trouble due to small pelvic openings. Breech presentations are so rare as to be hardly worth mentioning. Premature births, on the other hand, are so common that perhaps as many as 50 per cent of the newborn weigh no more than two to four pounds, but many of these survive, surprisingly enough. Multiple births are very rare indeed. The placenta is usually expelled either immediately after birth or not at all, but since it is retained in roughly three out of ten cases, it often causes very serious trouble. Puerperal fever

249

appears to be very rare and usually not severe, for Doury himself had never seen a case where it was fatal.

Contraceptive practices of a magico-medical nature are indulged in frequently by native women all over the Sahara, but it is extremely doubtful if any of the means commonly employed are ever really effective in spite of the great faith placed in them. The most common treatments of this sort consist of drinking magic potions, wearing special amulets, and secretly reciting cabalistic incantations. But other and more bizarre methods are employed too in some localities as at El Goléa, for example, where women who want to get a rest after repeated pregnancies swallow lead shot that has been dipped in menstrual blood, in the fond belief that each pellet will insure a year's sterility. Voluntary abortion is said to be common on the whole but there is no way of knowing whether in fact it is or not, for practitioners and patients alike maintain the greatest possible secrecy. There can be no doubt that it is often attempted by magico-medical means, but it is more than doubtful that such methods are ever really successful. Moorish women, for instance, have been said to procure abortion by taking massive doses of red pepper, or by fumigating themselves by squatting over hot coals on which resin of *Ferula assafoetida* is being burned; but it is difficult to imagine that procedures of this kind can be effective. Mechanical means may be employed sometimes perhaps, but if they are, nothing seems to be known about them. Infanticide is certainly a common practice, at least among poorer sedentary groups, but it too is shrouded in such an impenetrable cloak of secrecy that no one can hope to arrive at even roughly accurate estimates of frequency.

No reliable figures concerning the birth or death rates of numerically substantial Saharan communities are as yet available, for efforts to establish reasonably accurate counts or even estimates have proved to be all but hopeless. First there is the permanent difficulty of counting nomad noses. And then there is the fact that nomadic and sedentary folk alike are both easygoing and secretive about many aspects of birth and death. According to the official birth records of the Mzab,[2] for instance, there were no stillbirths and no bastards born there during 1955 or 1956, and yet it is simply incredible that this was true. The answer is not far to seek, however, for the body of a stillborn child is looked on as a fearful thing which must be disposed of quickly and in secret, while the newborn infant of an unmarried girl usually disappears in like manner, often enough taking its disgraceful mother with it. Probably not even the Mzabite headmen themselves know just how many cases of either kind occur, but many family scandals—and many a private grudge too—surely lie hidden at the bottoms of local wells.

Another complicating factor in the census problem is that of false birth declarations, usually made for economic reasons of some sort, and here again the Mzab furnishes a neat and clear-cut case in point. Declared births there remained at a remarkably uniform level for a number of years prior to the Second World War. At the outbreak of hostilities in Europe, however, the rate rose abruptly to a new and far higher plateau where it stayed until the war's end, after which it dropped, just as abruptly, to the prewar level once more and has since continued there with its previous uniformity. This curious phenomenon has been explained, doubtless correctly, as due to false birth declarations made for the purpose of obtaining extra allowances of food while rationing was in force. The usual procedure in such cases is for several closely related women, sisters or cousins, to take the newborn baby of one of them and register it one after another, each as if it were her own, thereby securing several false birth certificates in addition to the true one. Reasonably reliable figures for the Mzab, covering the years 1950 to 1953 inclusive, show that at least 15 per cent of Mzabite and 12 per cent of sedentary Arab children of Ghardaia die before the end of the calendar year in which they were born, while 36 per cent and 29 per cent respectively die before the end of their third year. All

---

[2] My data on the Mzab are drawn mainly from copies of original census sheets which were prepared for me through the kindness and under the direction of District Commissioner Charles Kleinknecht and Assistant District Commissioner Jean Moriaz.

that I can say at present about the problem of death rates among children of the Sahara in general is that stillbirth rates and infant mortality seem to be high among sedentary groups, particularly in the northern half of the desert, and relatively low among the southern nomads, although both are doubtless high among the poorer classes everywhere.

The chief obstacles to the study of adult mortality rates in the Sahara are the material difficulty of counting nomads periodically, and the fact that few of the older natives know their exact age. Falling back once more on general impressions, I would say that age at death seems on the whole to be roughly correlated with economic status, but that southern nomads, and possibly those of the far west as well, may perhaps approach the average male age at death of fifty-five or thereabouts that has been claimed for them. Even this figure, however, is very low in comparison with the white American male average of a little over sixty-seven, and the corresponding French average of about sixty-five. Adult mortality rates among sedentary Saharan groups are less difficult to estimate, in theory, than are those of nomads, but what little has been published concerning them fails for one reason or another to inspire confidence as to its accuracy. The situation is complicated too by the occasional appearance of startling and unexpected phenomena. For example, so many Mzabite men go north to make their living that the average number absent from the Mzab can be estimated at somewhere between four and five thousand, and yet Mzabites consider it essential for the post-mortem welfare of their souls that they be buried in their ancestral cemeteries, and they sometimes go to extraordinary lengths to accomplish this. When one of them feels that death is near, he heads for home as fast as he can go, and so it used to be not unusual to see a moribund Mzabite, groggy with drugs that had been pumped into him to keep him going, arrive from some northern city in a taxicab, with two or three loyal friends. But sometimes death strikes too quickly. Even today, when a Mzabite dies far from home, his body may be packed in an old oil drum and hidden away until there is space available for it in a truck load. Then it is taken back secretly

to the Mzab and buried, secretly. All this is done in flagrant vio-
lation of French law, of course, and so the dead involved never
appear as dead in any official records. Their number cannot be
very great, but it is certainly not entirely negligible either.

Public health services in most of the desert still labor under
the serious double handicap of insufficient personnel and inadequate equipment. Even in the French Sahara, where modern
medicine has made impressive progress in recent years, physicians
and infirmaries are still very few and far between. Most of the
doctors in question are young officers of the Army Medical
Corps, whose great enthusiasm and boundless energy and devotion are matched only by the difficulty of the conditions under
which they work; but only important sedentary centers are lucky
enough to have one of these men in residence, and a little infirmary with a few native attendants or, rarely, a European
nurse or two. Since electricity has usually been furnished by small
and antique gasoline generators, as it still is more often than
not, appliances such as fluoroscopes and X-ray equipment were
lacking everywhere until very recently. In addition, most of the
doctors are on the move much of the time, often covering hun-
dreds of miles a week over dusty, spring-breaking trails that
lead to secondary centers, or right across country in search of
nomad camps. It is obvious that under such conditions no one
can make refined diagnoses except in the most clear-cut cases,
and so, even if full records could be kept, they would still be
of very doubtful value for purposes of statistical comparison.
To make matters worse, doctors are faced, although to an ever-
lessening degree, with that general reluctance to consult them
which characterizes most primitive peoples. Saharan natives,
and especially nomads, have been unwilling until very recently
to turn to a European doctor except as a last resort, when they
felt that they no longer had anything to lose, and this is true of
the great majority of them even now. Among most of the Moslem groups women are kept out of the way of male strangers,
and so a doctor can rarely examine any of them except the prostitutes. Thus the disease picture is not only fragmentary but is
distorted as well, by gross sampling errors which have been

unavoidable so far. Thousands of natives fall ill each year and either recover or die without the knowledge of a doctor or of anyone else who might keep medical records of them.

And, finally, it is impossible to evaluate the effects of foreign contact on local health. No one knows and it is now too late to learn exactly what diseases characterized the various peoples of the Sahara before the modern European conquests, nor is it known (with a very few exceptions) which diseases came originally from the north, east, and south, or when. One can make reasoned guesses at the answers to a few of the questions thus posed, but that is all. In fact the term "disease picture" as applied to the Sahara is deceptive in a sense, for it is not yet possible to round out a true picture. At present only a very rough preliminary sketch can be drawn, indicating in a loose and general way what the main outlines of the complete picture may perhaps be like.[3]

Among the afflictions which are most common in the desert, undernourishment, either chronic or seasonal, is characteristic in varying degrees of practically all groups except the middle and upper socio-economic classes of northern and central sedentary centers. Saharan natives rarely die of starvation as such, but whole communities often become so weakened that disease, especially broncho-pulmonary infections, meets with such greatly reduced resistance that illnesses which would be only mild under ordinary circumstances often become fatal. This phenomenon occurs most often in the late winter and early spring, when the supply of food and particularly fresh food is at its lowest and people have been weakened by the cold, by a long period of extreme daily changes in temperature, and by sandstorms. Sedentary Haratin gardeners usually suffer from more or less chronic undernourishment, simply because of poverty, so many of them both look and act prematurely old. Nomads, on the other hand, usually suffer following a more markedly seasonal pattern in which near famine conditions recur with varying severity each year, early in the spring. Malnutrition due to an unbalanced diet

[3] Those who want to go into this question in more detail should consult my *Living Races of the Sahara Desert.*

also does much to weaken nearly all Saharan natives, even the well-to-do. Most sedentary folk naturally eat very little meat, for they very rarely have animals or the means with which to buy and feed them, while nomads seldom eat meat because killing their livestock is tantamount to destroying their main capital investment. Therefore the entire population of the Sahara, with very few exceptions, suffers chronically from some degree of protein deficiency, and, ironically enough, it is the great nomad herdsmen who often suffer most severely. Surrounded by their livestock they are nonetheless condemned to hunger in the midst of plenty.

Visible signs of specific vitamin deficiencies are not seen very often as a rule, although night blindness (*hemeralopia*), caused by a lack of vitamin A, is fairly common among sedentary groups in the northern half of the desert. Scurvy, due to vitamin C deficiency, seems to be practically unknown among southern nomads but is fairly common among northern sedentary groups; and this may well be due to different rates of milk consumption. A more complicated problem is posed by the distribution of rickets, primarily an infantile disease which, like most other manifestations of vitamin deficiency, seems to be much more common in northern sedentary communities than among southern nomadic tribes. But it has also been observed, in the Mzab for instance, that the different frequencies which characterize different ethnic groups within a single community are almost exactly the same for rickets among children and syphilis among their parents; and this makes one wonder if seemingly rachitic conditions among native children in the Sahara may not in fact be due most often to hereditary syphilis. In other words much of what has been referred to in Saharan medical literature as rickets is probably of syphilitic origin.

Weaning usually brings on more or less severe nutritional disturbances among children everywhere in the desert, where infants are usually nursed for anywhere from eighteen months to two years after birth. During this period they are impressively healthy as a rule, but then they are shifted almost overnight to the customary diet of their parents, and their general condition

255

suffers a sudden and spectacular decline so serious that mortality is probably higher at this stage in life than at any other time before or after. Gastro-intestinal disturbances of a more or less violent character are the most common consequences of weaning, while broncho-pneumonic infections often follow as serious if not fatal complications. A curious and pitiful condition which the French call "weaning edema" has been reported frequently as widespread in the Sahara. It usually occurs immediately after weaning, but sometimes begins shortly before in cases where the child has already begun to share its parents' food. The characteristic symptoms are lethargy and general weakness, extensive wasting of the muscles, thirst and sporadic hunger, diarrhea and frequent urination, and swelling which starts in the feet and spreads upwards, sometimes appearing simultaneously in the eyelids also. This rather beriberi-like ailment, which appears to be most common among the sedentary poor and is relatively rare in prosperous nomadic groups, is often fatal, especially in times of famine. French Army doctors have observed that in the Ahaggar post-weaning crises are relatively mild, but tend to drag along with only gradually decreasing severity until puberty, especially among the sedentary Haratin; and they believe that this is due mainly to a lack of sufficient fats and proteins in the diet. They also point out that during the prolonged preadolescent phase of dietary readjustment, the average child is in a fairly constant state of moderate debility, the symptoms of which include emaciation and dryness of the skin, general weakness and diffuse pain, reduced levels of activity and resistance to fatigue, and sometimes defective bone formation, especially in females. Probably at least a third of the Ahaggar Haratin die before reaching the age of ten, directly or indirectly because of malnutrition. Haratin children who survive this crisis usually show a markedly retarded rate of growth, while their elders often look much older than they really are. Children of the nomadic Tuareg, on the other hand, seem to be far less seriously affected, for most of them survive the post-weaning crisis and live on to a relatively ripe old age. It has been suggested that dietary factors may also be responsible for the late onset of puberty in native girls of the Ahaggar, which apparently does not occur as a rule until between the ages of fifteen and seventeen, or even as late as nineteen in some otherwise normal individuals. Curiously enough, children of the nomadic Moors, unlike those of the Tuareg, are said to die like flies because of post-weaning dietary disturbances combined with both rickets and hereditary syphilis.

Rheumatism, particularly in the form of dull and diffuse rheumatic pain, is an extremely common complaint among all segments of the Saharan population, but it seems to be most severe and generalized, as well as least seasonal, among nomads and poor sedentary gardeners. The pains are usually most acute during the daytime, and are concentrated mainly in the joints and in the small of the back. Nearly a century ago Duveyrier remarked that few adults of either sex among the northern Tuareg were free from this affliction, while some became completely crippled, and this observation is just as true today as it was then. The disease, if we can call it that, has usually been explained as due chiefly to the effects of extreme and sudden changes in temperature on people who sleep on the ground and are, for the most part, both inadequately sheltered and but lightly clothed. Undoubtedly malnutrition and venereal disease are also responsible to some extent in many cases.

Diseases of the respiratory system in general, including tuberculosis, are common nearly everywhere, due in the main no doubt to the rigors of the climate. Digestive disturbances are common too, and are often traceable to bad water, a defective diet, or an inordinate consumption of spices and of very strong tea taken boiling hot. Various kinds of worms are common also, as are a number of organisms which cause dysentery. Malaria seems to be endemic at a fairly low level in most sedentary centers of the northern and central zones of the desert. Victims suffer attacks the year around, but there is a definite peak period in early summer, generally in June. And it has been noted also that Negroes and negroid people seem to be more resistant to malaria than white people. The frequencies of most contagious diseases appear to vary in more or less direct relation to the amount of contact that the natives have with people from beyond the limits of the desert. Cancer is probably not particularly uncommon, but it is interesting to note that this disease seems to be very rare indeed or even absent in regions where the water used for drinking has a high magnesium content.

Trachoma has often been called "the scourge of the Sahara," and it well deserves to be, for probably between 70 and 80 per cent of the natives of the desert are or have been infected, and many of them are left partially or completely blind as a result. Frequencies seem to be highest in northern sedentary communities and lowest among southern nomadic groups. Trachoma often irritates the inner surface of the upper eyelid so severely that scar tissue forms there and causes puckering which draws the lashes downward and inward, so that they rub against the eyeball. Continual rubbing then produces whitish patches of translucent or opaque scar tissue on the surface of the eye itself. Saharan natives used to treat this condition by pinching up a fold of skin on the affected eyelid and sticking a thorn or splinter through the fold, thereby causing the formation on the outer surface of the lid of scar tissue whose puckering counteracted the effect of that on the inner surface. I have seen several cases in which this treatment was successful.

Venereal diseases in general are common, but they show a good deal of variation in frequency both regionally and ethnically. Pastoral nomads seem to have the lowest rates on the whole, while caravan men and sedentary folk have the highest. It was also observed however, some thirty years ago, that, whereas the syphilis rate among Mzabite men was well over 50 per cent, the rate among the Jews living in the same community was only half as high, while that of sedentary and nomadic Arabs of the Mzab was 45 per cent. Unfortunately no one has as yet suggested any satisfactory explanation for these curious and striking differences.

Accidents are common in the Sahara and falls are the most frequent type. Nomads, especially old men, fall off their camels or are thrown (particularly during the mating season), while sedentary folk fall out of palm trees or off adobe walls that collapse beneath their weight. Little children often get severely burned or very badly scalded when they toddle over to the fire unobserved to see what is in the pot, and then lose their balance and fall into the coals. Wounds used to be common injuries and still are, though to a less extent than formerly, and they are usually inflicted in one of the following ways. Violent quarrels between family groups or neighboring camp communities are not at all infrequent among nomads, who fight on these occasions with the heavy sticks they always carry, or with knives or stones. The usual results of such encounters are easy to imagine. Sedentary people fight less often and less violently as a rule, and use gardening tools or occasionally knives as weapons. In the urban centers of the northern desert, prostitutes often wear on the right wrist a pair of heavy silver bracelets, each about two inches wide and studded with square pegs roughly a quarter of an inch thick and an inch and a quarter long, and these are used in fighting off unwelcome customers. Many an ardent nomad has lost front teeth or even an eye to these truly formidable weapons.

In the old days, before the suppression of raiding and intertribal warfare, many nomad warriors bore scars of sword or spear or bullet wounds. And every now and then natives also get wounded accidentally. Prior to the recent political upheaval, nearly all communal festivities, and particularly weddings, were celebrated by much firing off of guns and blunderbusses which were often dilapidated heirlooms. These weapons were always stuffed with huge charges of black powder so as to produce as much noise and smoke as possible, and so their barrels burst occasionally, thereby causing a variety of more or less serious injuries of the hands and face. Death from thirst was primarily a risk of raiding, for raiding parties were obliged to travel fast and light, and so carried as little water as possible. Thus, when raiders fleeing from an avenging enemy came to a desert water point and found it either dry or choked with sand, they did not always have enough water left to keep them all going until they could reach another one. And natives still die of thirst in the desert now and then. In 1950, for example, I found a Chaambi, some thirty odd years old, lying at death's door beside the trail.

He had set out all alone, in the full heat of early summer, to walk from Ouargla to El Goléa, over two hundred miles of completely barren desert, some hundred and sixty of which he had covered before his water supply gave out and he collapsed.

There are few ailments in the Sahara that can properly be classed as occupational diseases but there are some. Professional palm cultivators, for instance, often have abscesses and running sores caused by pricks of the sharp tips of green palm fronds. Workers in the salt mines of the south suffer from gross thickening of the skin and corrosive lesions on the lower extremities. The Haratin, particularly those charged with the distribution of water for irrigation, as well as gardeners who work much of the time in wet ground, nearly always show a very marked thickening and cracking of the skin on the feet and ankles. The Negro or heavily negroid laborers who dig and maintain foggaras also suffer from the same complaint, and, in addition, get killed now and then by cave-ins. Professional well diggers suffer from a number of ailments caused by working, with no special equipment, under water, often at considerable depths and for surprisingly long periods. They usually plug their ears and nostrils with tallow, but such precautions are not always fully effective. Apparently, however, they do not suffer from the bends (caisson disease).

Poisonous stings and bites of various kinds of scorpions and horned vipers are common sources of trouble except during cold weather, when the creatures that do the biting and stinging are dormant or extremely sluggish. The stings or bites themselves are very rarely fatal, except in cases of small children or old folks, or people who are very weak or already have heart trouble or some other serious disease. At Taghit, for example, 238 persons reported being stung by scorpions between 1950 and 1955, but of these only one infant, seven months old, died as a result, while in the region of Aoulef, between 1954 and 1958, scorpions stung 353 people without killing any of them. Since the parts most often struck by both scorpions and vipers are the hands and feet, natives often apply tourniquets to keep the poison from spreading through the system, but they are inclined to leave them on much too long thereby provoking gangrene, and so this treatment often does more damage than the poison it is intended to control.

In summing up what is known about nutrition in the desert, it can be said that the diets of Saharan natives are always more or less unbalanced, and usually inadequate in terms of calories according to the theoretical standards of modern medicine. Unbalanced diet, however, is not always quite as serious a problem as it may seem at first glance, for dietary deficiencies usually change somewhat with the seasons so that what is lacking in the springtime, for example, may be made up for in the fall to some extent. Nevertheless there is almost always some disequilibrium present, and almost always some degree of general quantitative deficiency as well, at least at regular seasonal or cyclic intervals. These factors naturally have done much to accelerate the processes of natural selection which seem to have brought out in the peoples of the desert many of their distinctive characteristics.

The generalized disease picture which I have drawn is at best a hazy patchwork sketch. Information on disease in the Sahara is scarce and usually unreliable, simply because it has been practically impossible to come by enough precise data. Most Saharan natives, like many rural Negroes and Indians of the southern United States, take so fatalistic a view of sickness that they look on a hospital or infirmary as a place where one goes only to die. In the words of Larribaud: "In illness the nomad sees something inevitable against which it is futile to fight with merely human weapons." Because of this widely shared attitude, disease in the Sahara escapes even the most assiduous qualified observer far more often than not, and so it is not yet possible to get a broad and detailed view of health conditions as a whole. The French Army Medical Corps, under the leadership of men like the late Dr. Henry Foley and General Paul Passager, has done wonders over the years, but it has never had sufficient funds at its disposal. Now that the oil industry, aided by the French government, has launched a sweeping and well-financed research program under the direction of Dr. Claude Vigan, one can begin to hope for better things to come.

Chapter 10

RETROSPECT AND PROPHECY

I HAVE NOW DEALT with the history of the tribes of the Sahara insofar as it is known. I have described the country in which they live and the problems which must be met in living there, and I have also shown how various native communities developed various ways of life which enabled them to survive and even flourish now and then, each in its chosen habitat. And now the time has come to examine the peoples of the Sahara as an evolving whole.

The dawn of the Christian era marked the beginning of a new chapter in the history of North Africa in general. The Phoenicians had come and gone, but their activities had been limited almost entirely to isolated trading centers scattered along the northern coast of Barbary, and the few who finally remained there doubtless sank, with hardly a ripple, into the great mass of the native Berber population. A handful of Jewish merchant-missionaries may have accompanied the Phoenicians, but if so they seem to have restricted their activities to Barbary, and there can never have been more than a very few of them in any case. Persian administrators and Jewish refugees had penetrated the eastern desert to an unknown extent, but the former left no apparent traces (except perhaps the foggara) and the latter were never more than a very small minority among the population as a whole. The Romans followed, but, even at the height of their power, they never seem to have established themselves anywhere in the Sahara proper except briefly in a few small commercial outposts in the eastern desert. Then came the Vandals, and finally the Byzantines, but neither went even as far into the desert as the Romans had, and neither stayed for long.

The coming of the Romans did, however, bring drastic changes to the desert indirectly, for it caused a series of politico-economic upheavals throughout the north, which, in their turn, set off a whole series of refugee migrations southward and south-westward from Barbary and Cyrenaica. These tribal shiftings involved pagans, Jews, and occasionally Christians, practically all of whom were Berbers, physically Mediterranean in type and speakers of Berber dialects. Once safe in their new desert homes, these peoples formed the communities of which the Zenata and the Saharan Jews are modern representatives. After the collapse of Roman power in North Africa, the Vandals and particularly the Byzantines continued to stir up Barbary, and so periodically stimulated the fluctuating southward flow of Berbers. But at last, as Byzantine power in North Africa faded out, around the end of the sixth century, the southward flight of northern refugees dwindled to an intermittent trickle, and may even have come to a stop altogether for a time.

The Roman occupation of the northern strip of Africa also had another very important and far-reaching though less direct effect. For although the Romans got the bulk of their Negro slaves, ivory, wild animals, and other African luxuries either by sea directly from West Africa, or from the eastern Sudan via the valley of the Nile, they did develop a considerable trans-Saharan trade with the central, and possibly the western, Sudan, by means of caravans which were operated and probably owned as a rule by natives of the desert. This was the beginning of the great caravan trade in slaves, gold, and ivory which was to make the Sahara famous and also infamous throughout the Western world. Although it seems to have had no profound cultural effect on the peoples of the desert, it was the source of a constant trickle of fresh Negro blood which has continued ever since to seep slowly and irregularly into the veins of most of them, both sedentary folk and nomads.

In the second half of the seventh century the Moslem Arab conquest of North Africa began. The first waves consisted mainly of warlike bands and small armies, who had hardly any effect on the native population beyond forcing southward a few more little bands of Berber refugees. With the beginning of the great tribal invasions of the eleventh century, however, the peoples of the desert entered a period of change more drastic than anything they had experienced since prehistoric times. Politico-economic disturbances resulting in almost complete chaos shook Barbary from end to end as the invaders swept westward along the southern slopes of the Atlas mountain ranges, splitting the ancient Berber population into two parts, northern montane and Saharan, which were destined never to be reunited. Nomadic Arab tribes, moving southward and westward across the desert, gradually inundated the whole northern half of the area and most of the far western province which is now the country of the Moors. They introduced and imposed the religion of Islam, and Arabic speech to some extent, among the sedentary peoples of the lands they overran, and they took over control of the northern and extreme western caravan trade routes. The nomadic Berber tribes of the northern desert fled southward before them and sought refuge in the southern half of the Sahara, particularly in and around the central mountain massif. Only in the far west did Arab invaders mix with and convert them more than superficially, in matters of both language and religion. It seems that this whole complex process progressed gradually and so continued until probably about the beginning of the seventeenth century, by which time the basic nature of Saharan tribal groupings had become fairly well stabilized once more, in patterns which still remain essentially unchanged.

One must realize that the various peoples of the desert have never been united, and, moreover, have never even thought of uniting in any common cause, for only by bitter competition have they been able to survive at all. Many of them seem very much alike in many ways, and these similarities are of two different kinds: either they have their roots in a common ancestral culture, neolithic negroid, pre-Islamic Berber or Moslem Arab as the case may be, or they have been imposed in one way or another by the harshness of the environment. On the other hand, the fundamental differences between major groups of basically different origins have always been profound and are unchanging. For example, nomadic speakers of Berber and of Arabic, whose ways of life are so much alike in the material sense, are set poles apart, irreconcilably, by their very different underlying concepts of sovereignty.

The Berber-speaking nomadic tribes of the Sahara think of sovereignty as residing in the collective membership of the community, whose elected chief is simply a chief executive and chief justice. Their practice of choosing him from certain traditionally preferable kinship categories is merely a practical means of limiting the choice to a field in which one can expect to find a suitable candidate most easily and quickly. It has nothing in common with the theory of the "divine right of kings." Among Arabic-speaking nomads, on the other hand, sovereignty is thought to reside in God alone, and He confers it in His mysterious way upon His chosen. The Strong Man who succeeds in imposing absolute authority by force is automatically accepted as God's favorite, while his victim, The Strong Man of yesterday, is spat upon for it is self-evident that he has lost God's favor. A ruling Strong Man's family are all strong too by virtue of his strength, and so succession to the chieftainship is most often strictly hereditary in the male line among Arabs. Individuals vary in strength, however, so that a direct heir is sometimes eliminated by a stronger heir whose claim is less direct, or by some tribesman who has no hereditary claim at all but is stronger than all the natural heirs together. The election or confirmation of a new chief by a tribal council is looked on as hardly more than a convenient means of either executing God's will when He has not expressed it patently, or according it pious recognition when it has been expressed. Thus the Berber and Arab tribes of the Sahara are differentiated basically by the fact that Berber government is essentially republican (as opposed to democratic), with the supreme authority vested in and exercised only by those who are considered the most capable, while Arab government is essentially autocratic, with authority concentrated in the hands of the hereditary head of the family which is most powerful in terms of political prestige, wealth, and warlike prowess—all manifest signs of divine favor. At the level of the individual this basic difference is reflected in the fact that personal rank among Berbers seems to depend primarily on the broad kinship group into which the individual was born, whereas among Arabs it depends to a much greater extent on the qualities and actions of the individual himself and his direct male ancestors. It is obvious that such deeply rooted differences cannot be reconciled in conference, in "a meeting of minds" inspired by "sweet reason." I have already pointed out that succession to chieftainship among the Moors has long been chronically chaotic, and this is so because the Moorish system attempts to combine the conflicting Berber and Arab concepts of sovereignty, which, like oil and water, simply cannot be made to mix. Thus there can be no hope that pan-Saharan unity will ever be achieved otherwise than by some rigid form of Moslem or neo-Moslem Arab dictatorship, or by effective foreign domination, military or economic and paternalistic, or otherwise, as the case may be.

An Arab dictatorship, however, could maintain reasonable stability only by force—it could not afford to be "benevolent"— for, as Carleton Coon has pointed out, the Arabs "have no traditional mechanism for unity, no framework for building up large political structures." The concept of "nationalism" is foreign to Islamic thought, no matter how much Moslem leaders use the term for purposes of propaganda in such places as the United Nations. For, to a Moslem personal loyalty is primarily a family affair, embracing his roughly contemporary male relatives and extending upward and downward to include forebears and descendants. Except in matters of religion, the lateral extension of his loyalty to relatively remote members of his broad community is essentially a practical response to material conditions, which he can turn on and off at will. Even his spirit of religious unity is seldom strong enough to override differences of a more materially cogent nature within the community of Islam as a whole, regardless of the fact that it does tend to and often does draw Moslem communities together in opposition to non-Moslem ones. The story of the Near East during the last few years is, like the history of the Crusades and their immediate aftermath, a striking demonstration of the inability of the Islamic peoples of the Near East, even as a religious whole, to remain united over any considerable period in stable political units, or even alliances, broad enough to encompass more than a single area of common material interests. Almost immediately after the Prophet died, while the echo of his impassioned and repeated calls to union was still ringing in the ears of many men who had themselves heard his voice, the Moslems as a people fell apart, and killed several of their most revered leaders as quickly and brutally as the rulers of Iraq were killed less than two years ago. So was the pattern set at the very dawn of Islam, and so it has continued ever since.

But how about effective European domination of the Sahara? Here again the prospects of lasting peace and prosperity within anything resembling a truly democratic framework are anything but bright; for it seems hardly possible that such domination could be maintained indefinitely otherwise than by force. Even though the natives of the desert have shown themselves recently to be far more readily adaptable to European ways of material life than most people used to suppose possible, they still balk at the line which divides European from Koranic social theory. Again as Coon has pointed out, the Moslem automatically thinks of citizenship in a state as subordinate to religious affiliation. "Even today few Arabs can understand how citizens of different faiths can have equal status in nations" like our own; for such equality is against the teachings of the Koran, against the clearly expressed will of God. "No one could have expected" the Moslems of Lebanon, for example, "to tolerate indefinitely a system which calls for a Christian president." And, since all good Moslems consider themselves God's chosen by definition, the kind of conflict which the terms "colonialism" and "nationalism" (as applied to Moslem Africa) suggest to Western minds, can be seen by them only as a desperate struggle between the forces of the Unbelievers and themselves, the Faithful of Islam. And so they will naturally go on striving, by violence as well as otherwise, for absolute control until they achieve it, unless they are clearly and hopelessly cut off from it by overwhelming force, potential or applied.

What does the future hold then for the tribes of the Sahara? It is hard to say. On the negative side there is no doubt that tribal organizations are breaking down both politically and economically. For, on the one hand, peace in the desert has encouraged sedentary gardeners and artisans to leave the meager but permanent material security of their little settlements, while, on the other, the resulting shrinkage of the agricultural labor pool and agricultural production, added to the decay of caravan trade and raiding, have obliged many of the great desert nomad tribes to change their ways of life and reduce the scale of their operations drastically. Thus both extremes of the native population, the warlike pastoral nomads and the sedentary poor, are being driven towards the intermediate condition of seminomadism and industrial employment. Social structures too are breaking down, partly because of the decay of the old political and economic systems but also because of direct personal contact with Europeans on a rapidly increasing scale and the assimilation of more and more natives into the European socio-economic community.

It seems to me likely that in the future nomadism in the grand manner, already on its way out in most of the Sahara, will fade away with ever-increasing though variable speed in different parts of the area. The lower socio-economic classes will disappear in great part into the ranks of industrial labor and labor engaged in the support of industry, a process which is already well under way in the northwestern quarter of the desert; and the resulting drastic upset of economic balance will finally destroy the existing forms of both social and political organization. Although the social status of the sedentary middle classes will probably remain on the whole much as it is today, their economic outlook is far more favorable, for they have long been engaged in their own programs of commercial development and expansion which can be grafted quickly and naturally onto the newly introduced programs of European industry and commerce. The old nomadic warrior aristocracy is obviously doomed, for desert tribesmen no longer have any need of such a class and its prestige is already growing dim before the dazzling aura of rich newcomers from overseas, oil field crews and uranium prospectors and technicians of all sorts, with their portable air-conditioned villages, their bulldozers and helicopters and other wondrous gadgets and machines, their free and easy manners, and their casual openhandedness. And so, the picture I have drawn of the tribes of the Sahara is in reality a picture of the past, a past which has only just begun to disappear but is disappearing faster every day. And yet, it is only on the basis of a real understanding of this past that anyone can hope to understand, let alone guide, that which is growing out of it.

GLOSSARY

BIBLIOGRAPHY

INDEX

GLOSSARY

A = Arabic; B = Berber; T = Teda; A–F = Arabo-French; S = Sudanese;
Sp = Spanish; TE = Technical English.

abatool (B)	a dish similar to Scottish haggis, made by stuffing the stomach of an animal with its intestines and hot stones
adrar (B)	a mountain, or mountainous massif
ahal (B)	Tuareg nocturnal party, preferably starring a famous female musician
amenokal (B)	paramount chief of a Tuareg confederation
ardeen (B)	small upright Moorish harp, of the zither type
aseeda (T)	the most common cereal dish of the Teda of the Tibesti
assink (B)	a gruel, basic cereal dish of the Tuareg of the Ahaggar
atiafunu (T)	a wild plant whose leaves make a tea-like brew for poor Teda
Azza (T)	a servile class—hunters, artisans, and entertainers—of the Teda
baraka (A)	supernatural power in the sense of "born lucky," more or less emphatically
burnous (A)	a hooded cloak made of wool, or a mixture of wool and camel's hair
Cheraga (A)	(Easterners), the progressive party in most northern Saharan sedentary and many nomadic Arab communities
Chouchan (A)	an eastern Saharan word for Haratin
couscous (B)	a kind of stew, made of grain and vegetables and, occasionally, meat
cram-cram (A)	a prickly weed, whose northernmost extension marks the southern botanical boundary of the Sahara proper
dardai (T)	paramount chief of the Teda of the Tibesti
debi (T?)	see kadmul
djellaba (A)	a loose, short-sleeved, hooded overcoat, worn by Mzabite and sedentary Chaamba men in winter
djemaa (A)	a communal council; also the lay council which performs the executive functions in a Mzabite community. (The term is also used for a mosque as well as for the congregation which meets there to worship; literally it means an assembly.)

djemaa-el-kebar (A)	council of elders
dji (T)	currant-like berries found in the Tibesti
dood (A)	(worms), a local name for *Artemia salina*, a tiny proto-shrimp, the most important economic source of the Dauada
Duti (T)	name given to smiths by Teda of the Tibesti
edjan (B?)	Moorish word for gray, as applied to camels
Enaden (B)	name for smiths among the Tuareg
erg (A)	a waste area of sand dunes
fantasia (A–F)	ceremonial gymkhana
farto (T)	a leather tunic, ancient basic garment of the Tibesti Teda, still worn occasionally by some groups, notably the Azza
floos (A)	vulgar North African word for money, primarily small change; Arabized plural of the Latin *follis*
foggara (A)	a device, consisting of a series of well shafts whose bottoms are connected by a gently sloping tunnel, for drawing water from the top of a sloping water table by means of gravity
gandoura (A)	a voluminous, flowing, sleeveless garment
Gharba (A)	(Westerners), the conservative party in most northern sedentary and many nomadic Arab communities of the Sahara
Ghattasin (A)	the well diggers of Ouargla
guerba (A)	container for water, a goatskin tarred inside
had (A)	a scrubby thorn bush whose southernmost extension marks the southern botanical boundary of the Sahara
haik (A)	a concealing sheet, worn by nearly all northern sedentary and many nomadic Arab women, which completely envelopes the wearer
halga (A)	the theocratic council which performs the legislative and judicial functions in a Mzabite community
Hamria (A)	negroid half-breeds of the Mzab
Haratin (A)	negroid sharecropping serfs of the Sahara
imzad (B)	single-stringed violin-like instrument of the Tuareg
initi (B?)	*see* cram-cram
kaboosh (A)	an edible paste made of cheese, butter, and spices pounded together
kadmul (A?)	a green turban, symbolic of the authority of the Dardai
Kamadja (T?)	the Teda word for Haratin
kessra (A)	coarse, unleavened bread, eaten by northern sedentary and nomadic Arab groups
khaima (A)	tent used by the nomadic Chaamba and Moors, as well as by the nomads of Arabia
khamès (A)	(fifther), Arabic name for a sharecropper, who receives theoretically a fifth of his produce

2 7 4

khol (A)	a greasy black substance applied to the eyelashes by most Saharan women and some men
kif (A)	*Cannabis indicus* or "Indian hemp"—an outlawed narcotic still grown and smoked occasionally
kouriya (S?)	kind of lingua franca, spoken by slaves and their descendants, now nearly extinct
ksar (A)	a fortress or fortified town
kshabia (B)	*see* djellaba
litham (A)	*see* teguelmoust
Maalmin (A)	Saharan Arabic name for smiths, and (more rarely), artisans in general
Majarreros (Sp)	Spanish name for smiths
Marabouts (A–F)	religious and semi-religious individuals and groups not descended from the Prophet Mohammed
mehri (A)	a riding camel
mouzeri (T)	a multibladed throwing knife formerly used by the Teda
Mrabteen (A)	the original Arabic form of Marabouts
quern (TE)	a saddle quern is a flattish stone slab on which grain is ground with another stone, usually shaped like a rolling pin; a rotary quern consists of two flattish circular stones, the upper of which is turned to grind grain placed between them
shebka (A)	a net-like, intricate (dendritic) drainage pattern which dissects some Saharan plains
shegga (A)	indigo-blue cotton cloth of Sudanese manufacture, greatly valued by the Tuareg and Moors
shorba (A)	a highly seasoned soup containing vermicelli and vegetables (usually dried)
Shorfa (A)	men (and families) regarded as holy because supposedly lineal descendants of the Prophet Mohammed
sloughi (A)	greyhound of the southern Sahara, used only for hunting
sof (B–A)	a political party: *see* Cheraga and Gharba
sufi (A)	(woolly), a mystic, member of a religious brotherhood
tahar (A)	(cleanser), man who circumcises Arab nomad boys
teguelmoust (B)	combination turban and face veil, preferably made of shegga, worn by Tuareg men
tendi (B)	(wooden mortar), afternoon parties of young Tuareg
tikomaren (B)	dried cheese, a staple food of the Tuareg of the Ahaggar
tikomarin (B)	*see* tikomaren
toba (B?)	double-headed drum of the Moors
tobol (A)	a drum made of half a gourd covered with skin, the Tuareg symbol of paramount chieftainship
yendjelan (B)	Tuareg word for gray, as applied to camels

GLOSSARY

zaouia (A)	**a** monastic kind of establishment to which Moslems of both sexes can retire from the world
zebu (Hindu)	cattle with a fatty hump, *Bos indicus*
zeriba (A)	cubical (rarely cylindrical) hut made of grass, palm fronds, or brush attached to a framework of sticks

BIBLIOGRAPHY

ABBREVIATIONS OF SERIAL PUBLICATIONS

AAE	Archivo per l'Antropología e la Etnología.
AAnth	American Anthropologist.
AGSO	American Geographical Society. Oriental Explorations and Studies.
AIPA	Archives de l'Institut Pasteur d'Algérie.
AJA	American Journal of Archaeology.
AJPA	American Journal of Physical Anthropology.
Algeria	Algéria.
AmNat	American Naturalist.
AMP	Archives des Maladies Professionnelles.
Anth	L'Anthropologie.
Antiquity	Antiquity.
ASAG	Archives Suisses d'Anthropologie Générale.
ASIF	Mémoires de l'Académie des Sciences de l'Institut de France.
ASPR	Bulletin of the American School of Prehistoric Research.
Atlantic	Atlantic Monthly.
BCEH, AOF	Bulletin du Comité d'Études Historiques et Scientifiques de l'Afrique Occidentale Française.
BIEC	Bulletin de l'Institut d'Études Centrafricaines.
BLS	Bulletin de Liaison Saharienne.
BSAE	Bulletin de la Société Suisse d'Anthropologie et d'Ethnologie.
BSAL	Bulletin de la Société d'Anthropologie de Lyon.
BSAN	Bulletin de la Société d'Histoire Naturelle de l'Afrique du Nord.
BSAP	Bulletin et Mémoires de la Société d'Anthropologie de Paris.
BSG	Bulletin de la Société de Géographie de Paris.
CCF	Cahiers Charles de Foucauld.
CEA	Cuadernos de Estudios Africanos, Madrid.
CPAP–II	Second Pan-African Congress on Prehistory, Algiers.
CPAP–III	Third Pan-African Congress on Prehistory, Livingstone.
CPF–XV	Comptes Rendus de la XVe Session du Congrès Préhistorique de France, Poitiers-Angoulême.
CRAS	Comptes Rendus des Séances de l'Académie des Sciences.
CRSB	Comptes Rendus des Séances de la Société de Biologie.
CSSH	Comparative Studies in Society and History.
Dalg	Documents Algériens.
Eurafrique	Eurafrique.
FOCUS	Focus.

BIBLIOGRAPHY

GLOBE	Globe.
GSA	General Studies in Anthropology.
HAS	Harvard African Studies.
Hesperis	Hespéris.
IFAN	Bulletin de l'Institut Français de l'Afrique Noire.
IHET	Institut de Hautes Études de Tunis, Publications Scientifiques.
ILN	Illustrated London News.
JRAI	Journal of the Royal Anthropological Institute.
JSA	Journal de la Société d'Africanistes.
KUML	KUML.
Libyca	Libyca, série préhistorique.
MAAA	Memoires of the American Anthropological Association.
MAN	MAN.
MEJ	Middle East Journal.
MIFAN	Mémoires de l'Institut Français de l'Afrique Noire.
MW	Muslim World.
NA	Notes Africaines.
PPM	Papers of the Peabody Museum, Harvard University.
RA	Revue anthropologique.
RC	Renseignements Coloniaux (a series of supplements to *L'Afrique Française*).
REP	Revista Española de Pediatría.
RevAnt	Revista de Antropología.
RT	Revue Tunisienne.
SAAB	South African Archaeological Bulletin.
Science	Science.
SMC	Smithsonian Miscellaneous Collections.
Sociometry	Sociometry.
TIBS	Trabajos del Instituto Bernardino de Sahagún.
TIRS	Travaux de l'Institut de Recherches Sahariennes.
ZFAW	Zeitschrift für die Alttestamentliche Wissenschaft.
ZFR	Zeitscrift für Rassenkunde.

BIBLIOGRAPHY

Adams, Robert, *The Narrative of Robert Adams*. London, 1816.

Africanus, Leo (Jean-Léon l'Africain), *Description de l'Afrique*. New ed., translated by A. Épaulard. Paris, 1956.

Alcobé, Santiago, "Grupos Sanguinos en Nómadas del Sahara Occidental." *TIBS*, 1: 23–37 (1945).

——— "The Physical Anthropology of the Western Saharan Nomads." *MAN*, 47: 141–143 (1947).

Alport, E. A., "The Mzab." *JRAI*, 84: 34–44 (1954).

Amat, Charles, "L'Esclavage au Mzab." *BSAP*, 3rd ser., 7: 689–698 (1884).

——— *Le Mzab et les Mzabites*. Paris, 1888.

Anonymous, "Le Mzab." *Dalg*, No. 16 (30 August 1955) and No. 17 (15 and 30 September 1955).

BIBLIOGRAPHY

d'Arbaumont, J., "Organisation Politique au Tibesti." *IFAN*, ser. B, 18: 148–155 (1956).

Arkell, Anthony J., *A History of the Sudan.* London, 1955.

d'Armagnac, *Le Mzab et les Pays Chaamba.* Algiers, 1934.

Augiéras, E. M. and others, *De l'Algérie au Sénégal.* Paris, 1931.

Authier, D., "L'Ethnologie et l'Anthropologie des Toubou du Tibesti Méridional et du Borkou-Ennedi." *Anth*, 30: 577–578 (1920).

Baker, Paul T., "An Experimental Approach to the Effect of Climate on Man." *AJPA*, n.s., 13: 387 (1955).

—— "The Biological Adaptation of Man to Hot Deserts." *AmNat*, 92: 337–357 (1958).

—— "Racial Differences in Heat Tolerance." *AJPA*, n.s., 16: 287–305 (1958).

Balandier, G. and P. Mercier, "Les Outils du Forgeron Maure." NA, No. 33: 8–11 (1947).

Balout, Lionel, *Préhistoire de l'Afrique du Nord.* Paris, 1955.

Barnicot, Nigel A. and others, "Les Groupes Sanguins *ABO, MNS* et *RH* des Touareg de l'Air." *Anth*, 58: 231–240 (1954).

Baroja, Julio C., *see* Caro Baroja, Julio.

Barth, Heinrich, *Travels and Discoveries in Northern and Central Africa.* 2nd ed. London, 1857–58. *Note:* Barth himself wrote a German version of this work which was also published in 1857–58 (at Gotha), and a French translation by Paul Ithier appeared in 1860–61 (at Paris). The texts and footnotes of Barth's English and German versions do not coincide entirely, for a few incidents and ideas set forth in one do not appear in the other. The French edition is an abridged translation of Barth's German text. On the whole the English edition seems the most useful.

Bates, Oric, *The Eastern Libyans.* London, 1914.

el Bekri, *Description de l'Afrique Septentrionale.* Translated by Baron MacGuckin de Slane. Paris, 1859.

Bellair, P., "Le Ramla des Daouada." *TIRS*, 7: 69–85 (1951).

Benhazera, Maurice, *Six Mois chez les Touareg Ahaggar.* Algiers, 1908.

Benoit, Fernand and N. Kossovitch, "Les Groupes Sanguins chez les Berbérophones." *CRSB*, 109: 198 (1932).

Bernard, Augustin, *Le Maroc.* Paris, 1932.

Biasutti, Renato, "I Tebu Secondo Recenti Indagini Italiane." *AAE*, 63: 168–201 (1933).

—— and others, *Le Razze e i Popoli della Terra.* 2nd ed. Vol. 3. Turin, 1955.

Bissuel, H., *Les Touareg de l'Ouest.* Algiers, 1888.

—— *Le Sahara Français.* Algiers, 1891.

Blanguernon, Claude, *Le Hoggar.* n.p. (Paris), 1955.

Bouilliez, M., "Notes sur les Populations Gouranes." *Anth*, 24: 399–418 (1913).

Bovill, E. W., *Caravans of the Old Sahara.* London, 1933.

—— "The Camel and the Garamantes." *Antiquity*, 30: 19–21 (1956).

—— *The Golden Trade of the Moors.* London, 1958.

Briggs, L. Cabot, *The Stone Age Races of Northwest Africa.* Cambridge, Mass., 1955.

—— *The Living Races of the Sahara Desert.* Cambridge, Mass., 1958.

Brogan, Mrs. Olwyn, "The Fortified Farms of Ghirza." *ILN*, 22 January 1955: 138–142.

——— "The Magnificent Tombs Which the 'Home Guards' of Roman Tripolitania Built." *ILN*, 29 January 1955: 182–185.

Brosset, Diégo, "Les Nemadi." *RC*, No. 9: 337–346 (1932). *See also* Diégo, Charles.

Brulard, M., "Le Commerce Caravanier au Fezzân au XIXe Siècle." *BLS*, No. 31: 202–215 (1958).

Buchanan, Angus, *Out of the World, Northern Nigeria*. London, 1921.

Butaye, P., "Le Droit au Commandement chez les Kel Ahaggar." *BLS*, No. 28: 250–256 (1957).

Caillié, René, *Journal d'un Voyage à Temboctou et à Jenné*. Paris, 1830. *Note:* An English translation of this work was published at London in the same year.

Capot-Rey, Robert, *Le Sahara Français*. Paris, 1953.

Caputo, G., "Archeologia." In *Il Sáhara Italiano*, Parte Prima: 301–330. Rome, 1937.

Carl, Louis and Joseph Petit, *La Ville de Sel*. Paris, 1955.

Caro Baroja, Julio, *Estudios Saharianos*. Madrid, 1955.

Carpenter, Bruce R., "Libya: A United Nations Experiment." *FOCUS*, 6: No. 2 (1955).

Carpenter, R., "A Trans-Saharan Caravan Route in Herodotus." *AJA*, 60: 231–242 (1956).

Caskel, Werner, "The Bedouinization of Arabia." *MAAA*, No. 76: 36–46 (1954).

Cauneille, A., "Les Nomades Regueibat." *TIRS*, 6: 83–100 (1950).

——— "Les Hassaouna, Tribu du Fezzân." *BLS*, No. 19: 31–48 (1955).

——— and J. Dubief, "Les Reguibat Legouacem." *IFAN*, ser. B, 17: 528–550 (1955).

Chaintron, J. F., "Aoulef. Problèmes Economiques et Sociaux d'un Oasis à Foggaras." *TIRS*, 16: 101–129 and 17: 127–156 (1958).

Chalmers, J. L. M. and others, "The ABO, MN and Rh Blood Groups of the Basque People." *AJPA*, n.s., 7: 529–544 (1949).

Chantre, Ernest, "Observations Anthropométriques sur Quinze Nomades Sahariens." *BSAL*, 29: 34–40 (1910).

——— "Les Mozabites." *BSAL*, 29: 86–94 (1910).

Chapelle, Jean, *Les Nomades Noirs du Sahara*. Paris, 1958.

Chouraqui, André, *Les Juifs de l'Afrique du Nord*. Paris, 1952.

Cipriani, Lidio, "Abitanti e Caratteri Antropologici." In *Il Sáhara Italiano*, Parte Prima: 355–383. Rome, 1937.

Cline, Walter, "Notes on the People of Siwah and El Garah in the Libyan Desert." *GSA*. No. 4 (1936).

——— "Mining and Metallurgy in Negro Africa." *GSA*, No. 5 (1937).

——— "The Teda of Tibesti, Borku and Kawar in the Eastern Sahara." *GSA*, No. 12 (1950).

Cloudsley-Thompson, J. L. (Editor), *Biology of Deserts*. London, 1954.

Coon, Carleton S., *Tribes of the Rif*. Cambridge, Mass., 1931.

——— "Climate and Race." *Smithsonian Report for 1953*: 277–298 (1954).

——— "Some Problems of Human Variability and Natural Selection in Climate and Culture." *AmNat*, 89: 257–280 (1955).

——— "What Is Race?" *Atlantic*, October 1957: 103–108.

BIBLIOGRAPHY

—— *Caravan.* Revised ed. New York, 1958.

Cornand, G., "Aoulef et le Tidikelt Occidental." *AIPA*, 36: 370–406 (1958).

Courtois, Christian, *Les Vandales et l'Afrique.* Paris, 1955.

Dalloni, Marius, *Mission au Tibesti. ASIF*, 2nd ser., vol. 62 (1936).

Daumas, Eugène, *Le Sahara Algérien.* Paris, 1845.

Denham, Dixon and Hugh Clapperton, *Narrative of Travels and Discoveries in Northern and Central Africa.* London, 1826.

Dermenghem, Emile, "Ghardaia." *Dalg*, No. 11 (1953).

—— "Les Confréries Noires du Mzab." *BLS* No. 15: 18–20 (1953).

Désio, A., "Acque Superficiale e Sotterranee." In *Il Sáhara Italiano,* Parte Prima: 121–138. Rome, 1937.

Diégo, Charles (a pseudonym of General Diégo Brosset), *Sahara.* Casablanca, 1935.

Douls, Camille, "Voyage d'Exploration à Travers le Sahara occidental et le Sud marocain." *BSG*, 9: 473–479 (1888).

Draper, William P., "Remarques Anthropologiques." *In* Augiéras, E. M. and others, *De l'Algérie au Sénégal:* 257–264 (1931).

Dubié, P., "La Vie Matérielle des Maures." *MIFAN*, No. 23: 111–252 (1955).

Dubief, J., "Evaporation et Coefficients Climatiques au Sahara." *TIRS*, 6: 13–44 (1950).

Dupree, Louis, "The Non-Arab Ethnic Groups of Libya." *MEJ*, 12: 33–44 (1958).

—— "The Arabs of Modern Libya." *MW*, 48: 113–124 (1958).

Durand, J. H. and J. Guyot, "L'Irrigation des Cultures dans l'Oued Righ." *TIRS*, 13: 75–130 (1955).

Duveyrier, Henri, *Les Touareg du Nord.* Paris, 1864.

Evans-Pritchard, E. E., *The Sanūsi of Cyrenaica.* Oxford, 1949.

Fàntoli, A., "Clima." In *Il Sáhara Italiano,* Parte Prima: 95–119. Rome, 1937.

Foley, Henry, *Moeurs et Médecine des Touareg de l'Ahaggar.* Algiers, 1930. Also in *AIPA*, 8: fasc. 2.

Forbes, Rosita, *The Secret of the Sahara: Kufra.* London, 1921.

Gabus, Jean, "Contribution à l'Etude des Nemadi." *BSAE* 1951/52: 49–83 (1952).

Gaillard, R. and L. Poutrin, *Etude Anthropologique des Populations des Régions du Tchad et du Kanem.* Paris, 1914.

Galan, P., "Contribution à l'Etude du Problème Alimentaire au Hoggar." *AIPA*, 29: 230–243 (1951).

Garcia, "Moeurs et Coutumes des Tedâ du Tou." *BIEC*, new ser., No. 10: 167–209 (1955).

Gaudio, A. "Apuntes para un Estudio sobre les Aspectos Etnologicos del Sahara Occidental." *CEA*, No. 19: 57–65 (1952).

Gautier, E. F., *Le Sahara.* Paris, 1928.

—— *La Conquête du Sahara.* 5th ed. Paris, 1935.

—— *Le Passé de l'Afrique du Nord.* Paris, 1952.

Gibb, Sir Hamilton H. R., *Ibn Battuta.* London, 1929.

Gibson, Gordon D., "Double Descent and Its Correlates Among the Herero of Ngamiland." *AAnth*, 58: 109–139 (1956).

Glass, Bentley, "On the Evidence of Random Genetic Drift in Human Populations." *AJPA*, n.s., 14: 541–555 (1956).

Goichon, A. M., *La Vie Féminine au Mzab.* Paris, 1927–31.

Greenberg, Joseph H. *Studies in African Linguistic Classification.* New Haven, 1954.

BIBLIOGRAPHY

von Grunebaum, Gustave E., "Islamic Studies and Cultural Research." *MAAA*, No. 76: 1–22 (1954).

—— *Unity and Variety in Muslim Civilization.* Chicago, 1955.

Guasch, J., "El Factor *Rh* en España." *Rep*, 6: 387–390 (1950).

el Hachaichi, Mohammed ben O., *Voyage au Pays des Senoussia.* Translated by V. Serres and Lasram. Paris, 1903.

Heseltine, N., "Toubbou and Gorane." *SAAB*, 14:21–27 (1959).

Holmes, Oliver W., Jr., *The Common Law.* Boston, 1881.

Hornemann, Frederic, *The Journal of Frederic Hornemann's Travels from Cairo to Mourzouk.* London, 1802.

Horrenberger, R., "Recherches sur les Groupes Sanguins dans le Sahara Oranais." *AIPA*, 11: 433–444 (1933).

Hrdlička, Aleš, "The Natives of Kharga Oasis." *SMC*, 59: No. 1 (1912).

Hugot, Henri J., "Une Mission Préhistorique au Mouydir." *TIRS*, 14: 215–217 (1956).

—— "Nouvelle Mission Préhistorique au Mouydir." *TIRS*, 16: 210–211 (1958).

Hunt, Edward E., Jr., "Anthropometry, Genetics and Racial History." *AAnth*, 61: 64–87 (1959).

Ibn Battuta, *see* Gibb, Sir Hamilton A. R.

Julien, Charles A., *Histoire de l'Afrique du Nord.* 2nd ed., revised by Christian Courtois. Paris, 1951.

Keith, Sir Arthur, *A New Theory of Human Evolution.* London, 1948.

Kidder, Homer H. and others, "Contribution à l'Anthropologie des Kabyles." *Anth*, 59: 62–79 (1955).

Kissling, Hans J., "The Sociological and Educational Role of the Dervish Orders in the Ottoman Empire." *MAAA*, No. 76: 23–35 (1954).

Kossovitch, N., "Recherches Séro-Anthropologiques chez Quelques Peuples du Sahara Français." *CRSB*, 116: 759–761 (1934).

—— *Anthropologie et Groupes Sanguins des Populations du Maroc.* Paris, 1935.

—— and F. Benoit, "Contribution à l'Etude Anthropologique et Sérologique (Groupes Sanguins) des Juifs Modernes." *RA*, 42: 99–125 (1932).

Kronenberg, Andreas, *Die Teda von Tibesti.* Horn-Vienna, 1958.

Ladell, W. S. S., "The Influence of Environment in Arid Regions on the Biology of Man." *UNESCO, Arid Zone Research–VIII: Human and Animal Ecology*: 43–99 (1957).

LaForgue, P., "Une Fraction Non-Musulmane en Maurétanie Saharienne: Les Némadi." *BCEH, AOF*, 9: 685–692 (1926). *Note:* Serious doubts have been cast on the reliability of this work, notably by General Brosset, but it is of considerable interest and some value nonetheless.

Larribaud, J., "Tindouf et le Sahara Occidental." *AIPA*, 30: 244–318 (1952).

Leblanc, M. Ely, "Les Touareg." *RA*, 38: 331–357 and 39: 19–44 (1928–29).

—— "Etude Craniométrique et Anatomique de Trois Crânes Touareg du Hoggar." *RA*, 39: 351–363 (1929).

—— *Choses et Gens du Hoggar.* Algiers, 1930.

—— "Anthropométrie et Caractères Morphologiques des Zenata Sahariens." *RA*, 44: 338–349 (1934).

——"Etude Anatomique et Anthropoligique de Squelettes du Hoggar (Mission Reygasse)." *RA*, 45: 197–226 (1935).

BIBLIOGRAPHY

—— "Anthropologie et Ethnologie." *Institut de Recherches Sahariennes de l'Université d'Alger, Mission Scientifique au Fezzan*, I (n.d.—1946).

—— and J. Bergerot, "Nouvelle Contribution à l'Etude de l'Anthropologie Anatomique des Touareg." *RA*, 46: 140–150 (1936).

Leriche, A., "Notes sur les Classes Sociales et sur Quelques Tribus de Mauritanie." *IFAN*, ser. B, 17: 173–203 (1955).

Lhote, Henri, *Comment Campent les Touaregs*. Paris, 1947.

—— *Dans les Campements Touaregs*. Paris, 1952.

—— *Les Touaregs du Hoggar*. 2nd ed. Paris, 1955.

—— *A la Découverte des Fresques du Tassili*. n.p. (Paris), 1958.

Lô, A., "Les Foggaras du Tidikelt." *TIRS*, 10: 139–179 and 11: 49–77 (1953–54).

Lobsiger-Dellenbach, Marguerite, "Contribution à l'Etude Anthropologique de l'Afrique Occidentale Française (Colonie du Niger)." *ASAG*, 16: 1–86 (1951).

Lopashich, A. "A Negro Community in Yugoslavia." *MAN*, 58: 169–173 (1958).

Lotte, "Coutumes des Imraguen." *JSA*, 7: 41–51 (1937).

Lyon, George F., *A Narrative of Travels in North Africa*. London, 1821.

Mandoul, R. and P. Jacquemin, "Etude des Groupes Sanguins au Tassili n'Ajjer." *Institut de Recherches Sahariennes de l'Université d'Alger, Mission Scientifique au Tassili des Ajjer*, I (1953).

Marçais, Georges, *Algérie Médiévale*. Paris, 1957.

Marçais, Philippe, "Notes de Sociologie et de Linguistique sur Beni Abbès." *TIRS*, 13: 151–174 (1955).

Marty, P., "Les Nimadi." *Hesperis*, 11: 119–124 (1930).

Mauny, Raymond, "Autour de la Répartition des Chars Rupestres du Nord-Ouest Africain." *CPAP–II*: 741–746 (1955).

McBurney, C. B. M. and R. W. Hey, *Prehistory and Pleistocene Geology in Cyrenaican Libya*. Cambridge, 1955.

Mechali, D. and others, "Les Groupes Sanguins ABO et Rh des Haratin du Maroc." *BSAP*, 10th ser., 8: 196–204 (1957).

—— "Les Groupes Sanguins ABO et Rh des Juifs du Maroc." *BSAP*, 10th ser., 8: 354–370 (1957).

Meigs, Peveril, "Outlook for Arid North Africa: The Sahara." *FOCUS*, 5: No. 4 (1954).

Mendo, C. R., *see* Robles Mendo, C.

Mercier, Marcel, *La Civilisation Urbaine du Mzab*. Algiers, 1932.

Mercier, P. and G. Balandier, "Emancipation par Rachat des Pêcheurs Imraguen." *NA*, No. 33: 22–23 (1947).

Mignot, A., "La Route Moutonnière Soudano-Algérienne." *AIPA*, 18: 353–357 (1940).

Moller, Herbert, "The Social Causation of the Courtly Love Complex." *CSSH*, 1: 137–163 (1959).

Monod, Théodore, *Méharées*. Paris, 1937.

Morel, H., "Essai sur la Longévité et les Causes de la Mortalité chez les Touareg de l'Ahaggar." *AIPA*, 19: 454–464 (1941).

Mourant, A. E., *The Distribution of the Human Blood Groups*. Oxford, 1954.

Murdock, George P., "Double Descent." *AAnth*, n.s., 42: 555–561 (1940).

Murphy, Robert F. and Leonard Kasdan, "The Structure of Parallel Cousin Marriage." *AAnth*, 61: 17–29 (1959).

BIBLIOGRAPHY

Musil, Alois, "The Manners and Customs of the Rwala Bedouins." *AGSO*, No. 6 (1928).

Neuville, P., "Stratigraphie Néolithique et Gravures Rupestres en Tripolitaine Septentrionale." *Libyca*, 4: 61–123 (1956).

Newman, Russell W., "The Relation of Climate and Body Composition in Young American Males." *AJPA*, n.s., 13: 386 (1955).

Nicolaisen, Johannes, "Slavery Among the Tuareg in the Sahara." *Kuml*, 1957: 107–113.

Noël, P., "Etude Ethnologique et Anthropologique sur les Tédas du Tibesti." *Anth*, 30: 115–135 (1920).

Pascal, J. M., "Essai Médical sur le Mzab." *AIPA*, 12: 83–167 (1934).

Passager, Paul, *Le Service de Santé dans les Territoires du Sud Algérien.* Algiers, 1958.

—— "Metlili des Chaamba." *AIPA*, 36: 508–574 (1958).

—— and R. Dorey, "El Goléa." *AIPA*, 36: 75–152 (1958).

Pauphilet, Didier, "Les Daouada." *IHET*, 1: 115–132 (1953).

Pilters, H., "Ecologie et Ethnologie du Dromadaire dans le Sahara Nord-Occidental." *BLS*, No. 22: 29–35 (1956).

Pond, Alonzo W., *Afoot in the Desert.* Montgomery, 1956.

Pons, A. and P. Quézel, "Premiers Résultats de l'Analyse Palynologique de Quelques Paléosols Sahariens." *CRAS*, 243: 1656–1658 (1956).

Reboul, E., "Le Gourara." *AIPA*, 31: 164–246 (1953).

Régnier, Yves, *Les Petits-fils de Touameur.* Paris, 1939.

Revol, "Etudes sur les Fractions d'Imraguen de la Côte Mauritanienne." *BCEH, AOF*, 20: 179–224 (1937).

Reygasse, Maurice, *Monuments Funéraires Préislamiques de l'Afrique du Nord.* Paris, 1950.

Ricci, E., "Richerche sui Gruppi Sanguini nei Tebu." *RevAnt*, 30: 353–371 (1933–34).

Richardson, James, *Travels in the Great Desert of Sahara.* London, 1848.

Riley, James, *Loss of the American Brig Commerce.* London, 1817.

Robin, Nil J. *Le Mzab.* Algiers, 1884.

Robles Mendo, C., *Antropología de la Mujer Marroquí Musulmana.* Tetuan, 1953.

Rodd, Francis R. (now Lord Rennell), *People of the Veil.* London, 1926.

Sabatini, Arturo, "Anthropologie der Tébu von Kufra." *ZFR*, 3: 253–269 (1936).

es Sa'di, *Tarikh es Soudan.* Translated by O. Houdas. Paris, 1900.

Saïd, Mohammed, "Les Touareg de la Région de Tombouctou." *RT*, 10: 34–49, 116–123 and 209–214 (1903).

Salvy, G. and Barthe, "Les Population Sahariennes: Arabes (ou Arabo-Berbères) et Touareg." *In* Le Sahara Français, *CCF*, 1955: 77–100.

Sauter, Marc R., "Anthropologie de la Population de Genève." *Globe*, 97: 141–170 (1958).

Schmidt-Nielsen, Kurt, "Rapport Préliminaire Concernant la Physiologie du Chameau." *BLS*, No. 22: 16–28 (1956).

Shanklin, William M., "The Anthropology of the Rwala Bedouins." *JRAI*, 65: 375–390 (1935).

Trumelet, C., *Les Français dans le Désert.* Paris, 1863.

BIBLIOGRAPHY

Vieuchange, Michel, *Smara: The Forbidden City*. Translated by F. Allen. London, 1933.

Vigan, Claude, "Médecine du Travail au Sahara." *AMP*, 17: 163–183 (1956).

———— "Considérations sur les Problèmes Humains du Travail au Sahara." *Eurafrique*, n.s., No. 14: 62–68 and No. 15: 76–80 (1958).

Vigourous, M., "L'Emigration Mozabite dans les Villes du Tell Algerien." *TIRS*, 3: 87–102 (1945). *Note:* Due to a misprint the author's initial appeared as "L" in this publication.

———— "Nécropoles Abadhites du Mzab." *Algeria*, n.s., 52: 25–33 and 59 (1957).

de Vos, G. and Horace Miner, "Algerian Culture and Personality in Change." *Sociometry*, 21: 255–268 (1958). *Note:* The authors promise a full book on this subject in the near future.

Weiner, J. S., "Human Adaptability to Hot Conditions of Deserts." *In* Cloudsley-Thompson, 1954: 193–199.

Wheeler, Sir Mortimer, *Rome Beyond the Imperial Frontiers*. New York, 1955.

Wyss-Dunant, E., "Recherches Anthropologiques dans le Tibesti Occidental." *ASAG*, 13: 125–155 (1949).

INDEX

Abadites, 83
Abagazawa, 71
Abalessa, 23, 41
Abd-el-Kader tribe, 195, 196
Aben Ali, 43
Abortion, 249, 250
Abou Abdallah Mohammed ibn Battuta. *See* Ibn Battuta
Abou Bekr ben Omar, 212
Abram, 165
Accidents, 258–259
Adams, Robert, 116–117, 223
Adaptation, thermal, 27–33
Adrar, 74
Adrar-n-Ifoghas, 19, 124
Adultery: among the Tuareg, 129; among the Teda, 175; among the Moors, 220–221
Afghanistan, foggaras in, 12
"African Association," 50
Aghouat, El. *See* Laghouat
Agricultural centers: people of, 66–68; shops, 68
Agriculture. *See* Crops; Garden agriculture
Ahaggar: geography of, 1–3; foggaras in, 12; natron mining, 15; sword-smiths, 44
Ahaggar confederation, 124, 126–128. *See also* Tuareg
Ahals, 130–131, 133
Ain Madhi, 101
Ain Sefra, 4
Air, the, trade route through, 43
Air temperature, 2
Airplane service, 61
Aisha, wife of Mohammed, 79
Ait Lahsen tribe, 213
Ajjer Tuareg confederation, 162
Alcoholic beverages, 243, 244
Almoravides, 41, 81
Alport, E. A., quoted, 83

Amenokal, 127, 135, 136, 137, 141
Americas, discovery of, 46
Ancestors, legendary tribal: Tuareg 150–151, 166; Teda, 177, 187; Moorish, 212, 231–232
Annexe du Hoggar, 125
Antelope, 26
Aoulef, 11, 19
Arab: caravans, 18; horses, 21; hunting, 25–26; invasions, 41, 60, 81, 155, 211, 263–265; nomad groups, 88–89, 190; concept of sovereignty, 265–266. *See also* Chaamba, Berazga
Arm daggers: Tuareg, 149; Teda, 184
Arm rings, Tuareg, 150
Arma, 48
Arrem Baba Saad, 76
Arrem-n-Tlazedit, 84
Art, ancient Saharan, 21, 22, 23, 38–40
Artemia salina, 27, 69–70
Ashanti, 166
Atlas foothills, rainfall in, 7
Atteuf, El, 78–79, 84
Azza class, 186–187; women of, 185

Baker, Paul, 29
Banking facilities, 46
Baraka, 96
Barbary, dual political parties in, 79
Baroja, Julio Caro, 221
Barth, Heinrich, 20, 56–60, 141, 152, 158
Bates, Oric, 128
Battle of Jaibar, 233
Battle of Tit, 203
Bedawins (Bedouins), 118
Bekri, El, 45, 155
Belford, John, 51
Benhazera, Maurice, 152, 160
Beni Isguen, 87

287

Garden agriculture, 71; Tuareg, 135; Teda, 179; Chaamba, 200–201; among the Moors, 226–227
Gastro-intestinal disturbances, 248, 256, 257
Gatroun, 74
Gazelles, 26
Ghadamès, 23, 42, 76
Ghana (original), 42
Ghardaia, 73, 75–76, 84, 87; dissident minorities break away from, 79; Jews of, 80, 90, 91–92; Berbers of, 83; Arab nomad groups in, 88–89; founding of, 191; typical diet of, 239; drinking water, 248; infant mortality in, 251
Ghat, 2, 20
Ghattasin, 95
Ghirza, 40
Gibson, Gordon, 134, 135
Goats, 19–20, 28. See also Livestock
Goboda clan, 187
Goléa, El, 7, 74; cultivated land in, 3; town plan, 75, 76; Chaamba population, 191, 192; palm trees, 201; artesian wells, 248; contraceptive practices at, 250
Goma, 163
Gourara, socio-economic structure of, 103–105
Government, Tuareg, 138–139; Moorish, 217–219. See also Chieftainship; Political organization
Guémama, Amenokal of the Ahaggar, 141
Guerrara, 79
Guns, 184, 259

Haggarenin clan, 162
Hamria, 87–88
Hank cliff, 2
Hannin, 212
Haratin, 71, 72, 179, 219, 226; physical characteristics, 66–67; lowly status of, 67–68, 93, 105; dwellings, 68, 182; and tribute system, 137; Chaamba, 209–210; childbirth among, 249; malnutrition among, 254, 256; and diseases, 260
Harendou, 158
Hassan ibn Mohammed, El, 45
Hassania, 112
Hassaouna tribe, 215

Hatita, 57
Hawata. See Imraguen
Hedgehogs, 25, 237, 239
Henry, Prince, the Navigator, 44
Hérafek. See Hirhafok
Hernias, umbilical, 249
Herodotus, 21, 22, 146, 181
Hillman, William, 51, 52
Hirhafok, pre-Roman trade routes to, 23
Hoggar. See Ahaggar
Holmes, Oliver Wendell, 120
"Holy men," 96; and treatment of slaves, 94–95. See also Marabouts; Shorfa
Hooton, Professor Earnest A., 112n.
Horneman, Frederick, 50–51
Horses, 21; water requirements, 28; Moorish, 223
Household furnishings: Nemadi, 109; Tuareg, 145–146; Teda, 182–183; Chaamba, 206; Moorish, 229
Houses, urban, 75, 76–77
Humidity, relative, 2–3
Hunting, 18, 26; Nemadi methods, 111–112
Huts, Haratin, 68, 182; Teda, 181–182; Chaamba, 206
Hyksos invasion, 22

Ibadites, 83–84
Ibn Battuta, Abou Abdallah Mohammed, 42, 45, 46, 128, 155, 163
Ibn Khaldoun, 45
Ibn Rustem, Abderrahman, 83
Ibotenaten clan, 127
Idjil, salt from, 226
Imenan, 163
Imraguen, 108, 113–116, 219, 247; social organization, 114; described by Robert Adams, 116–117; clothing, 117
In Abbangarit, 180
In Azaoua, 43
In Salah, 74; rainfall, 3; and hairy sheep trade, 19; caloric intake in, 239
Indian hemp, 14
Indigo dye, 156
Infant mortality, 251–252, 256–257
Infanticide, 250
Intellectual exchange, 45
Interbreeding, 102–103; Negroes and, 103, 263; between Chaamba and Tuareg, 210
Iron, 16